D0344646

A Note from the Publisher...

When I first met Clancy Strock over 30 years ago, I remember liking him *immediately*. Maybe it was because we had so much in common.

Both of us grew up on Midwestern farms...both of us majored in journalism at Iowa State University...and we both ended up in Milwaukee.

Clancy was working at an advertising agency, and I was in publishing. Our paths crossed now and again, and I admired the way he wrote from the outset. His was a warm, conversational style spiced with humor.

Eventually, success took Clancy to Kansas City, where he accepted the position of Creative Director for a large ad agency. From there, we lost track of each other as the demand and respect for his unique talent moved him from one city to the next and from one key position to another.

Years passed, and in 1991, I launched a new magazine called *Reminisce* to celebrate "the good old days".

The pages were filled with real memories written by real people, but we needed someone with a special touch to pen a regular column called "I Know...I Was There".

Clancy's heartfelt style made him a perfect candidate, so when I learned he was a journalism professor at the University of Nebraska, I picked up the phone. I was hoping he could find time to contribute to *Reminisce* as well.

Ever since, he's been writing what has become by far the most popular feature in the magazine.

With more than 50 columns to his credit (now presented in this volume), I still enjoy Clancy's special way with words. Like so many readers tell us, it's the first thing I turn to in each issue.

Roy Reiman

I Know...
I Was There

By Clancy Strock

Editor: Bettina Miller
Art Director: Bonnie Ziolecki
Assistant Editors: Mike Beno, Geri Truszynski
Photo Coordinator: Trudi Bellin
Production Assistant: Claudia Wardius
Publisher: Roy Reiman

For additional copies of this book or information
on other books, write: Reminisce Books, P.O. Box 990, Greendale WI 53129
Credit card orders call toll-free 1-800/558-1013

Heartfelt thanks to those who made this book happen: my parents, who filled my entire life with love; my wife, Peg, who is my best friend; Mike Beno, the astute and tactful editor every writer needs and Roy Reiman, who made everything possible.

—*Clancy Strock*

Contents

Contents *(Continued)*

LUCKY PONY. Young Clancy and his sister, Mary (right), agreed their pet should be named "Lindy" in honor of America's newest hero at the time, Charles Lindbergh.

Introduction

By Clancy Strock

PROUD POP. "Here I am with my dad, Oscar Strock. He's perched on the cellar door, showing me off during my first summer."

When I said hello to the world in February of 1924, my mother and I enjoyed the maternity ward's hospitality for *10 days*. The bill was $88.

The recollections that follow are mostly about the middle 50 years of this century...the era in which that $88 bill for 10 days in the hospital evolved to the current rate of $650 for three *hours* in the emergency room!

Of course, I wasn't around for the first 25 years of the 1900s—and I'll confess to being bewildered and bemused by the last 25.

My generation has made its journey through the twentieth century in a nerve-jangling mixture of deep fears and high hopes. What a roller-coaster ride it's been!

The first conscious memories I have are of the Depression years. In an odd way, growing up in those desperate times was actually a lucky break, because all of the years that followed have been "better" years. Unlike today, there was no place to go but up.

The '30s also taught me the comforting truth that deep down, most people are brave and caring. When the street beggar asked, "Brother, can you spare a dime?", we could, and did.

Each of us possesses surprising strengths which fortunately we seldom need to tap...but it's good to know they're there. When push comes to shove, we will set aside our selfish ways and give our last crust of bread to someone who has none.

It's difficult to be permanently cynical about the American spirit after witnessing so much generosity and love in my life. My adult children read about the '30s and wonder aloud if their generation could tough it out if similar times return. I assure "yes".

Granted, the greedy were still among us in the Depression years, and plenty were committed to acquiring wealth at the expense of the common working man.

The '30s saw long, bloody strikes in the coal fields and factories as workers united to get a fair day's pay.

There were picket lines, sit-ins and soup kitchens for the determined men who hadn't seen a paycheck in months, but persisted in demanding a fair shake.

Things were desperate on farms, too, which at the time was where 20% of our population still lived. The Dust Bowl and insect plagues destroyed crops and animals alike. Desperate Okies headed for California in the vain hope of a better life. Midwestern farmers went bankrupt and moved into the cities.

Still, my memories of those years are more about love

and goodness than desperation and disaster. And about Franklin D. Roosevelt's "New Deal", which, despite the skeptics, really did begin to turn things around.

To begin with, several hundred thousand men entered the Civilian Conservation Corps. And a new farm program gave the government dictatorial powers over our food supply, from farm to kitchen, attempting to at least get farm prices back to World War I levels.

The NRA (National Recovery Act) urged employers not to work their help more than 8 hours a day or pay less than 40 cents an hour. Employers who joined in this voluntary measure proudly flew the NRA "Blue Eagle" in their front windows.

An idea called "work relief" gave vouchers for food and rent, but the recipients were expected to pay back the value of the vouchers by laboring on public projects.

The Works Progress Administration put 4,000,000 people to work at everything from building bridges to acting and writing. Many of today's post offices date back to those years and are still brightened inside with murals painted by WPA artists.

Slowly but surely, things got better. Then, just as we had solid reason for optimism, the war cauldron began bubbling again. I recall newsboys crying out early in the morning that Germany had invaded Poland. *Now what?*

Dad, a veteran of World War I, wondered how it could happen so soon after he'd helped fight "the war to end all wars".

The U.S. became a reluctant partner in a most unwelcome conflict. Our high school debate team argued whether or not the U.S. should officially become isolationist and let the Europeans and Asians settle their own squabbles their own way. "No more American boys for foreign wars" was the angry rally cry.

We weren't at war yet, but young men were drafted into military service. The popular song of the day was *Good-bye dear, I'll be back in a year.* Fat chance.

National anxiety took over us once again. Then came the Sunday afternoon everyone my age can well remember...when a symphony concert on the radio was interrupted with the bad news Pearl Harbor had been bombed. Most of us weren't even positive where Pearl Harbor *was,* much less why Japan had attacked it.

MILITARY LIFE had its occasional bright sides, including this chance to sit on the sea wall in Galveston, Texas and smell saltwater for the first time.

I was 17 at the time and had no doubts of what the future held for me. Sixty days later when I turned 18, I hitchhiked to Des Moines, Iowa to join the Army Air Corps. The enlistment center was thronged with others just like me.

Once again, the war years brought Americans together as a selfless team. Rosie the Riveter may not have known it at the time, but she established forever that women could competently handle any job, including the traditional men-only occupations. Rosie broke the trail for generations of women to follow.

But it was a time of deep grief, too, as more and more windows displayed the gold stars that meant a son had been sacrificed to the cause of liberty. They were the best and bravest of our youth. You can't help but wonder now how many might have been destined to find the cure for cancer, write great literature or invent things we still haven't dreamt of.

A gentle, caring, devout couple who had rented me a room when I first went to college lost both sons in just ten days...one a pilot in Europe, the other an infantryman in the South Pacific. Neither parent ever recovered from the tragedy. There were thousands of other families just like them.

Finally, several months after VJ Day, I stepped off the troop train that brought me home and discovered a world of enthusiasm and optimism. Anything was possible! You could learn a trade or even get a college education, thanks to help from the G.I. Bill of Rights.

The economy had lots of catching up to do, and jobs were plentiful. When the boss gave us our first good raise, we began shopping for the first home of our own...a place where we would raise our family. Just $14,000 would buy a brand new 3-bedroom house with attached one-car garage, and the interest on the mortgage wasn't more than 4 percent.

Upward, upward we flew. Better jobs, more pay, bigger homes... and *two* cars in the garage.

There was no limit. Hey, a man finally scaled Mount Everest! Another broke the "impossible" 4-minute mile barrier. The first commercial jet planes sped us coast-to-coast in a few hours. "Plastic money" called a Diner's Club Card made its debut. And a young man named Elvis Presley introduced a whole new sound to the music scene.

Then all too soon, the rug was jerked out from under

us yet another time. The Korean War brought the old worries back. Who would serve this time? How many would return? And was our own country really being secretly destroyed from within by Communists, as Joe McCarthy claimed?

Worse yet, were we about to be incinerated by atomic bombs? Our children went through survival drills at school and came home terrified. Should we build that bomb shelter in the backyard? And if we did, what would be left when we finally emerged from our hole in the ground?

For that matter, A-bombs and Communists were of less immediate concern than the raging polio epidemic. There were 58,000 cases reported in 1952 alone, taking more than 3,000 lives. No one was safe.

Meanwhile, Orval Faubus stood in a Little Rock schoolhouse door, defying the mandate for racial integration springing from a controversial Supreme Court decision. And a courageous black lady named Rosa Parks did the unthinkable when she refused to sit in the back of a Montgomery, Alabama bus. In the aftermath of that crisis, Martin Luther King, Jr., was thrown into a Montgomery jail.

Looking back, the Fifties stands out as the decade that jerked our emotions around more than any other in this century. It was a baffling brew of Joe McCarthy, the new suburbia, interstate highways, Disneyland, "I Like Ike", Alger Hiss, the Iron Curtain, tail-finned autos and opportunities everywhere.

And remember all those post-World War II babies we worked so hard to raise and give a better life than we had known? They turned into teenagers during the '60s and loudly rejected all those solid, middle-class values we parents had grown up with. They demonstrated, rioted, tried to outdo each other in scruffiness, openly used drugs, closed down universities and just generally raised hell.

I look back on the '60s and marvel that I somehow survived trying to be a parent. By comparison, World War II was a snap.

Today those rebellious, worrisome adolescents tote around laptop computers, carry telephones in their pockets, mow their suburban lawns, coach Little League baseball and run American businesses.

Joy to gloom, high hopes turning overnight into unshakable dread...that's the story of the middle half of this century in a nutshell.

But though Americans were often quarrelsome and cantankerous and confused, there was a fundamental goodness that surfaced whenever times were tough.

We didn't prey upon each other—we helped each other. We didn't fear strangers—we welcomed them. We shared our bounty with others not because it meant a tax deduction, but because it was the right thing to do. We didn't just preach the Golden Rule. We tried to live it.

And the beggar could, indeed, aspire to be a king. Dreams did come true if you were willing to work hard enough. How lucky to have been born into the land of endless opportunity!

The stories that follow are my memories of those years and the people who made my world such a joyous place. I hope they also remind my grandchildren of how things *can* be and, perhaps, inspire them to lead their generation into the next century with hope and faith in the future.

I know it's possible....

I was there.

♪ounds and Scents
⌒ Trigger Memories ⌒

Gail Denham

For much of her childhood, my wife, Peg, lived on the shore of Lake Michigan near Sturgeon Bay, Wisconsin.

Only a few dozen yards from her door stood a lighthouse operated by the Coast Guard. It was equipped with a foghorn that boomed out its warning on nights when the weather was bad. That foghorn was as much a part of Peg's childhood as are traffic noises to folks who grew up in the city.

Now, many years later, whenever we're staying somewhere near the water and a foghorn is sounded, Peg says it instantly triggers a vivid image in her mind: She's a little girl again, securely snuggled under the covers as a winter storm sends roaring breakers onto the nearby shoreline.

It's truly magic the way a sound or a scent can transport you back to another time. For example, whenever I hear *Finlandia,* it's the 1930s again: I'm sitting in music appreciation class at Central School in my hometown of Sterling, Illinois. That's where the teacher, Ruth Caughy, opened up the world of good music to me, explaining how music could tell a story and create pictures in the listener's mind. What a gift she gave me!

But the piece of music that can put tears in my eyes is *The Stars and Stripes Forever.* I'll bet this song strikes many of you the same way, because it's capable of creating a hundred images.

It makes me recall glorious band concerts in the park, Fourth of July fireworks, Saturday morning parades at military bases and high school band concerts in a gymnasium full of beaming parents. Those were proud times...family times...joyous times. Thank you,

14

John Philip Sousa. What a gift you gave your country!

I'm positive you know what I mean about the power of sounds and scents to trigger wonderful mind pictures, because *Reminisce* readers send us so many stories describing things that take them back in time.

They recall how a summer shower evokes the music of rain on the tin roof of a humble home where they grew up. Suddenly, they're 8 years old again!

The sound of a calliope at the carnival conjures up pictures of a much earlier time, when a child was perched on Dad's strong shoulders as the Sells-Floto Circus paraded down Main Street with colorful wagons pulled by giant Belgian horses.

A fleeting scent may bring memories of the sweeping compound used to clean the school corridors. And who can hold a newborn grandchild, freshly bathed and powdered, without a surge of sweet memories of the days when we gingerly held our own firstborn in our arms?

The rich fragrance of lilacs never fails to bring me an especially happy memory from high school days. Mom and Dad decided I could have an after-the-spring-prom party in our home—the first party I ever "hosted" on my own.

It was a blissfully balmy night, warm enough to have the windows open. We rented a record player, borrowed a stack of 78 rpm's from friends, rolled back the living room rug and danced to Harry James, Tommy Dorsey and Glenn Miller.

There was a long hedge of lilacs near the house, and they were in full bloom. That evening, a light south breeze carried their sweet scent into the house as we danced and enjoyed Mom's homemade punch and cookies. I can't remember a happier night during my high school years.

On the other hand, when I drive down a country road in the summer and smell new-mown hay, a different sort of mind picture comes to the screen in my head.

I'm back in the searing, parched summers of the '30s, helping Dad put up hay. We were still farming with horses in those days, and haying was hot, dirty, punishing work. The only time I felt good about it was when the job was finished and I could plunge my head into the tub of cool water on a bench under the grape arbor.

A neighbor's dog barking at night transports me back to that same time. I'm in my tiny bedroom, head next to the window, hoping for a faint breeze to relieve the heat of a July night.

Off in the distance, the dog on a neighboring farm tries a few tentative barks. Then one on another farm answers. Soon all the dogs within a mile are exchanging their stories about the day's events...or whatever it is that dogs talk about late at night.

Another fragrance that brings strong memories is that of new leather. Today I can open a box of new shoes and find myself back at Graebner's Shoe Store, with its two long walls lined with shelves, floor to ceiling, holding hundreds of shoe boxes.

It's once again the day when Dad broke the budget to buy me a pair of *$5 shoes* for my high school graduation. Dad said I'd need a pair of good shoes for my college years. They were brown Florsheims, and I felt special every time I wore them.

Peg says that stepping inside a candle shop at the mall never fails to put her back in the choir loft at St. Joseph's Church in Sturgeon Bay. It's the aroma of incense in the air that does it.

Sometimes scents or sounds maddeningly set off an elusive memory that lasts only a second or two...not long enough to give me a mind picture, but just long enough for me to realize that it's associated with something good. So good, in fact, that I struggle hard to recapture it.

But then the scent or sound is gone, and I can only hope that someday I'll encounter it again—for longer than a moment or two.

Occasionally these memory triggers seem to work in reverse. The other night, a TV documentary on World War II showed a 105mm artillery battery in action. For an instant, I could smell gunpowder and feel the punishing pressure shock of those big guns.

I was back at Fort Sill, Oklahoma, where life on the firing range centered around The Blockhouse on Signal Mountain. Every former artillery man knows exactly what I'm talking about.

More memories from the World War II years came to me during our last move. I discovered a dusty cardboard box marked "Odds and Ends". How informative! It hadn't been opened in years, and I decided it was time to see what treasures and trash might be inside.

As I feared, there was a lot more trash than treasure. But one item I found was the old billfold I'd carried while in the service. Why

I'd hung on to this is a complete mystery.

I pulled it open with the faint hope there might be money inside…but I discovered a *memory* instead. What hit my nose was the smell of mildew and mold and decaying things unique to the tropics.

In an instant, I saw a long row of canvas tents on a slender arm of dry ground, surrounded by swamp and jungle on the island of Leyte in the Philippines. That "transient camp" was where I spent my first few days in a foreign land.

The smell was…well, it sure wasn't northern Illinois. But to think that memory was trapped like a magic genie inside a 50-year-old billfold!

If I had to pick the scents that never fail to conjure up beautiful mind pictures, the choice would be easy. Let my nose catch a whiff of freshly brewed coffee or sizzling bacon and eggs, and I'm back in northern Wisconsin, where we did a lot of family camping when the kids were young: I'm in a stand of tall fragrant pines framing a mirror-surfaced lake. A blue jay squawks his good morning, and my sleepy kids come tumbling out of their sleeping bags to stand by the campfire, where the coffeepot perks.

Coffee, bacon, eggs and a pine tree scent in crisp morning air— there's nothing better!

Speaking of blue jays, their shrill call can set off another treasured memory—of annual summer visits with my grandparents, who lived in the quiet little town of Dixon, Illinois.

On lazy summer afternoons, there wasn't much to disturb the tranquillity except the angry scolding of blue jays in the elm trees lining the street. For some reason, we didn't have blue jays on the farm, so their call was a novelty and is forever linked to rocking on the front porch with Grampa Stevens as he shared his memories with me.

Whether it's pungent sauerkraut in the crock or the eerie call of a screech owl, the aroma of homemade bread baking or the nicker of a horse, the "new" smell of denim britches or the cacophony of a high school band tuning up—those special scents and sounds are a remarkable free ticket to our past.

$\mathcal{W}$hatever Happened to Sunday Drives?

Here it is, a warm, sunny Sunday. Church services are over and the brunch dishes are cleaned up…now what?

Let's check the TV listings in the paper—there's a baseball game on one channel and a pro golf tournament on another.

The local movie houses are offering a wide choice of films, but none holds much appeal. There's a book I haven't finished, but it's not due back at the library for another week.

What to do, what to do? Years ago, families never faced such indecision on Sundays. The unanimous choice was always the same: *Let's go for a drive!*

For my family, Sunday just wasn't Sunday without a long meandering drive to nowhere in particular. The main idea was to get out of the house and see what was going on in the world. "Where shall we go?" Dad would ask. We'd all chip in with ideas—the airport…Castle Rock Park…Aunt Martha's house…wherever.

Living on a farm as we did, our summer drives always began with Dad checking out the neighbors' crops. Who had the tallest corn? Had the drought burned up their pastures as much as it had ours? Were the oats far enough along for the threshing ring to swing into action?

Many a Saturday morning, Dad sent me out with a scythe to cut down the weeds along our roadside fence. He figured it would make *his* corn look taller to the neighbors who'd be taking *their* Sunday drives!

Sometimes we'd set out for a nearby town to "drop in" on friends or relatives if they happened to be home and not taking their own Sunday drive.

If we did catch them at home, we'd be warmly welcomed. Little Jimmy would be sent scooting to the neighborhood grocery for a few pints of ice cream (there were no refrigerators with freezer compartments back then), while the hostess made iced tea or lemonade.

The kids from both families would scurry upstairs, where the girls would talk about new doll clothes and the boys would inspect a balsa wood model airplane that was currently under construction or haggle over baseball card swaps.

Meanwhile, the adults sat in the living room or out on the porch talking about weather, politics, local events and when—if ever—the Depression would end.

One Sunday each month, we visited my dad's Uncle Otto and Aunt Mary. When we arrived at the older couple's home, my sister, Mary, and I would be shooed into the front parlor, where we were allowed to inspect Uncle Otto's remarkable collection of coins from all over the world.

When we became bored with that, we'd open the latest copy of *National Geographic* and catch up on tiger hunting in India and boomerang throwing in Australia.

That got boring, too…but what came next was worse. Mary and I felt like convicts doing time on death row, knowing that when the adults had finished swapping family gossip, they'd expect a "concert".

Mary would get out her violin, and I'd uncase my cornet. Even in the best of hands, violins and cornets are not ideal instruments for duets. Somehow we labored through a hymn or two and perhaps *Whispering Hope* or *The End of a Perfect Day.* We were awful.

My favorite Sunday drives were in summer when Mom packed a picnic lunch. There were lots of nice parks within 40 miles of home, many of them alongside the Rock River.

We'd settle down in a peaceful spot and feast on cold fried chicken, potato salad, coleslaw, fresh rolls, pickles and olives, washed down with lemonade from the big green thermos jug. A thick chunk of chocolate cake topped things off.

Then we'd just sit on the grass under a big old elm tree and watch boats scoot up and down the river past fishermen who never seemed to catch a single fish.

Another favorite destination was White Pines State Park. A swift shallow stream wound through the park, and the main road crossed that stream four times.

There was a narrow footbridge across each ford. Cars plunged through the hub-deep water, while whooping kids on the bridge enjoyed being drenched with a refreshing spray of the cool, clear water.

That park was heavily wooded with a magnificent stand of towering trees. Trails padded with brown pine needles meandered through them, uphill and then down into dark glens heavy with ferns. No man-made cathedral I've ever seen comes close to the beauty of that forest.

At least once each summer, we'd take a Sunday drive to a nearby gristmill. It was owned by an ancient gentleman who claimed the Indian chief Black Hawk used to make regular visits to have corn ground for his band of warriors. Looking back, I think it's unlikely the old fellow ever actually met Black Hawk, but his stories were spellbinding.

The real purpose of our visit was to gather watercress that grew near the mill, where springs bubbled up out of limestone rock. The watercress was crunchy-crisp and sweet as candy. Trust me, it was worth the long journey.

That summer outing was followed by another family event in autumn. Dad knew a fine woods where hickory and walnut trees dropped an abundant crop. Gunnysacks in hand, we gathered our winter nut supply as squirrels protested from the branches.

Another good day-trip was to the northwestern corner of Illinois, magnificent rolling country you'd never expect to find in our pancake-flat state. We'd walk around Galena, where Ulysses Grant lived for many years. Then we'd stand on the banks of the Mississippi and try to envision how things looked back when the steamboats brought great log rafts downriver from Minnesota and Wisconsin.

Not too far away was the state's vest-pocket version of the Grand Canyon, the Apple River Canyon. Trails went down into the deep gorges, where your shouts were rewarded with echoes that bounced around like a Ping-Pong ball.

As fine as my memories of Sunday drives remain, I do recall

some downsides. Roads weren't terribly good back then, and tires were prone to blowouts.

Dad carried a patching kit and pump so he could repair a flat tire on the spot. While he was sweating and grumbling, Mom sat in the car fanning herself and we kids explored the roadside ditches, practiced our cow-calling skills or petted a curious horse that came up to the fence.

After World War II, when I had a family of my own, a favorite Sunday diversion was a drive to model homes that were on display. It wasn't that we were in the market for a new house...it was just fun to see how "the other half" lived. Some of those homes even had *two* bathrooms! I've since learned that real estate agents everywhere call folks like us "Sunday gawkers".

A perpetual Sunday drive request from our kids was for a trip on "the roller-coaster road". That was a hilly blacktop stretch a few miles outside of town that featured a long series of abrupt ups and downs.

Traveling briskly along this road, everyone in the car came close to weightlessness as we topped each hill and was then mashed into their seat at the next dip. *WHEEE! OOOOF! WHEEE!* It wasn't exactly NASA training for life in outer space, but it came close enough.

And speaking of flight, it was always fun to drive to the nearest airport, park near a runway and watch airplanes take off and land. Where had they been? Where were they going? That's a Sunday diversion some families still enjoy.

No matter where you lived, there were plenty of interesting things to do on Sunday drives. You could take another look at homes where your ancestors once lived...check the progress on the new barn a neighbor was building to replace the one that burned down last summer...visit "shirttail" relatives...or take in a nearby town's Watermelon Festival or Sauerkraut Day or Fourth of July parade.

Wherever you ended up, it was good to get out of the house and see what was going on in the world.

What to do, what to do? What could be better than another Sunday drive? I know...I was there.

$\mathcal{D}$oes Anyone 'Save Up' Anymore?

H. Armstrong Roberts

The other day, a friend pulled me up short with this observation: "It seems like ours is the last generation to have used the now-extinct phrase, *I'm saving up for...*"

Know what? I think he's right.

I'm not saying that everyone today is living beyond their income. Most folks just seem to be living *ahead* of their income. These are the days of instant gratification. See it now, buy it now. Why wait? Just whip out the credit card and it's yours.

Most of my grandchildren aren't quite old enough for a credit card of their own, so they've turned Mom and Dad into their personal VISA resource. "Puhl-ee-z, Dad," they whine. "I'll pay you back." Yeah, sure.

The idea of saving up for the latest "Hootie and the Blowfish" CD is an absurdity in their young eyes. Just whine long enough and Dad will pull out his credit card. Buy now...Dad pays later.

Yet it doesn't seem so long ago when everyone seemed to be

saving up for something—a new car, a sofa, a Red Ryder BB gun, a Sunday-go-to-meeting suit…just about anything that cost more than a few dollars.

It wasn't that people couldn't get credit, it was more a matter of caution. If you lived through the Depression, you learned that it wasn't wise to owe anything to anyone, so you saved until you could pay cash.

As best I can recall, my introduction to saving up for something involved collecting the seals from cans of Ovaltine. When I had the necessary number, I could send them off (along with 25¢) and receive a genuine Little Orphan Annie decoder badge.

It was a matter of considerable urgency, since without it I was unable to decipher the secret messages broadcast at the end of each radio program. These were clearly messages of vast importance, and I needed to know!

To make matters worse, my pal "Stoney" already had the decoder but wouldn't tell me what was going on. My other problem was that Dad refused to buy Ovaltine, calling it a frivolous luxury at a time when we were buying day-old bread to stretch the food budget.

I finally poured out my woes to a sympathetic aunt, who began buying Ovaltine so I could have my precious seals. This was the good news. The bad news was that every time I visited the dear lady, she insisted I drink several glasses of the stuff.

I've never admitted it until now, but Dad was right—Ovaltine was not essential to life on this planet. I didn't even like the taste.

Well, you know how the story ends. After 6 weeks, during which I checked the mailbox 42 times, I got the decoder…only to discover that the secret messages were certainly nothing the FBI needed to know about.

Nevertheless, it was the start of a career devoted to saving up for…I saved up for every Tom Mix trinket the Ralston Purina people promoted. I saved up (a long, long time) for a bicycle. I saved up for college and, later, an engagement ring. Still later, it was for a business suit I needed when I got my first real job.

Meanwhile, everyone else I knew was saving up for something, too. An uncle hoarded Popsicle sticks, which were used in his model-making hobby. He patrolled Lawrence Park every Sunday evening after the weekend crowds had gone home, head bent low as he scanned the ground for the gooey little pieces of wood.

I know…it sounds terrible. But what he created with those little sticks eventually turned into a lucrative business for a man who could find no employment in the '30s.

Mom, like most women, saved fabric scraps and popped them into her scrap bag. She later turned the odds and ends into doll clothes and even quilts.

Nor did she ever throw away a button. When a garment was thoroughly worn out, she snipped off the buttons and tossed them into her special box. When I lost a button from a shirt or jacket, she could always find a proper match. (Nowadays, my daughter, Terry, fondly remembers the hours she spent playing with those buttons during annual summer visits to her grandparents' home.)

Somewhere back then, General Mills came up with perhaps the most popular saving plan ever. All of its products began carrying coupons that could be redeemed for silverware. Soon women everywhere were saving the coupons and begging neighbors and friends for any they didn't plan to use themselves.

Churches and PTAs got into the act, too. When an entire congregation saved the coupons, it wasn't long before their church kitchen had enough sets of silver to handle a big banquet in style.

Just now I checked a box of Bisquick in the pantry, and sure enough, the coupons live on. The program today has been expanded, offering "kitchenware and accessories". Imagine that! Maybe there *are* still people out there who are "saving up for".

My wife, Peg, also saved up for a bicycle as a kid, but hers was a more complicated situation. She and her sister Pat shared one clunker of a bike between them, leading to the sort of sisterly strife you'd expect.

Clearly they needed another bicycle, and summer brought the solution. Her family lived amidst the cherry orchard region of Wisconsin, and those growers needed pickers.

The work turned out to be grueling and the pay minimal. Soon their dad took pity on the youngsters and pitched in until the money needed was in hand. From then on, the girls rode the new bike on alternating days. Half a new bike was better than none at all. Work for it, save for it.

Peg also remembers baby-sitting full days for a nearby family. Her duties included fixing meals, doing dishes and keeping the house clean—and she was not working for generous wages.

She scrupulously saved every penny. Her dream was to go to summer camp, and the only way she could hope to do so was by earning the money. She set her goal, went to camp and savored every moment to the fullest because she'd worked so hard to earn it.

Most of us remember the days of "trading stamps" issued by Gold Bond, Eagle, King Korn, S&H and others, then given out by grocers and most department stores with every purchase.

The stamps had to be glued into books, which usually meant an evening every month or so when the entire family sat around the kitchen table, licking stamps by the hundreds.

Several books full could be redeemed for all sorts of merchandise...small kitchen appliances, sporting goods, swing sets, radios, TVs—you name it.

Saving up 10,000 stamps seemed like a daunting task, but there was a Mixmaster at the end of the rainbow, so you patiently filled up stamp books until you reached your goal.

Best of all, it seemed like you were getting something for free. At least it wasn't money that came out of the household budget. Of course, the stuff wasn't really free. Your friendly grocer had to pay for the stamps and simply raised his prices to cover the cost. So, you'd paid for the Mixmaster on the installment plan without knowing it.

Eventually some stores discontinued the stamps and cut their prices accordingly. Soon the competition had to follow suit, and trading stamps vanished from most places.

There's a humorous footnote to my trading stamp memories. When I was living in Minneapolis many years ago, a friend from Chicago was passing through on business, so we agreed to meet on a street corner downtown at 5 p.m.

At the appointed hour, he came toward me, nearly doubled over with laughter. On his way to meet me, he had passed a place where King Korn trading stamps could be exchanged for merchandise. The big sign on the street said King Korn Redemption Center. "Until I got there and saw what it was," he laughed, "I figured it was some sort of offbeat religious outfit!"

No, there aren't many people who are "saving up for" these days. Instant gratification is what everyone wants, and that's too bad, because there's a whole lot of truth in the old saying that "anticipation is usually better than realization".

I vividly recall the weeks of feverish expectation while I waited for that Orphan Annie decoder badge. I'd have to dub those the "days of sweet agony".

When that badge finally arrived, it wasn't anything like I'd

SOCKING IT AWAY. When the day of a big purchase arrived, out came the basket of coins and the sockful of cash. Like the couple above, some saved up their money at home.

imagined, and my disenchantment was complete after a few evenings of decoding those inane secret messages. In a week or two, the decoder badge was in my dresser drawer, unloved and unused. The real thrill had been in the anticipation, which started with saving up the Ovaltine seals.

But to be fair about it, Peg's week at summer camp was even better than her most optimistic dreams during those long weeks of baby-sitting. She enjoyed both the sweet agony of anticipation and the happy fulfillment.

Licking thousands of trading stamps coated with an evil-tasting glue was scarcely a delight, but it paid off in little luxuries that cash-strapped families otherwise could not have afforded.

Yes, "saving up for" has its own special, priceless rewards.

Thank Goodness for Modern-Day Marvels

Ewing Galloway

A while back, one of our younger readers wrote a letter and took me to task for so often making unfavorable comparisons between how things are today and how they used to be.

He suggested I was one of those grumpy old men who simply couldn't cope with the '90s...and reminded me that lots of things weren't so hot back when I grew up.

I'll defer to my wife, Peg, on how big a grouch I've become, but the young man did have a good point—we live in a magical

A FROST-FREE FRIDGE got a warm reception from buyers—especially those who could recall the days when icebox drip pans would flood the kitchen floor.

time, and most of us enjoy luxuries today beyond the dreams of even the wealthiest, most powerful people in any other era.

I wrote the young man back and thanked him, adding that he had inspired me to write a "let's count our blessings" piece for *Reminisce*. And here it is.

First off, let's consider a few simple luxuries, like the pleasure of waking in the morning to the smell of freshly brewed coffee —while still snug in bed. (A reliable timer faithfully turns on my coffeepot at precisely the time I designate the night before.) Sure beats getting up on a chilly morning and stoking the cookstove to get things perking!

We also used that old cookstove to make toast to go with our coffee, but today the automatic toaster does that—and even asks how brown I'd like it.

Another morning task gladly forgone is having to heat a pan of hot water on the stove top to get a comfortable shave. You'll never hear me complain about having hot water at a turn of the bathroom tap.

And speaking of bathrooms, I won't even bother to get into a discussion of that little house out back with last year's Sears and Roebuck catalog hanging from a nail. But isn't it nice to enjoy a shower bath? Sure beats heating pails of water and hauling them upstairs to the bathtub on Saturday night.

Every summer, no matter where I've lived, I again wonder how in the world we ever got along without air-conditioning—especially during the searing summers of the Dirty Thirties.

In those scorching Dust Bowl years, Mom routinely "closed up the house" shortly after dawn, shutting windows and drawing the shades to capture whatever cool air had seeped inside overnight and to keep out the new day's blazing sun.

A valiant little oscillating fan from General Electric sat on the floor all afternoon, whoofing a faint breeze around the living room. It didn't help much, though, even if we stripped to our BVDs.

Something else we take for granted in summer is the modern refrigerator and freezer. Say what you will about the childhood joys of chasing the ice wagon and snitching slivers of ice to crunch, I'd never trade my electric fridge for an old-fashioned icebox.

For starters, my modern model doesn't have a drip pan that fills up and floods the kitchen floor if I forget to empty it. What's more, refrigerators and freezers have eliminated the need to tackle the sweltering, tedious summer job of canning.

How nice it is to bring fresh-picked green beans in from the garden and have them in the freezer an hour later! What a pleasure in January to pull out a package of your own frozen green and red peppers for a pot of chili, as well as peaches that taste almost fresh-picked for dessert.

Recently I went back to visit my boyhood home in northern Illinois and once again traveled the familiar 12 miles of the old Lincoln Highway between Sterling and Dixon.

This narrow two-lane road that twists and turns like a lost snake was once part of the principal route between the East and West Coasts. Back then it was jammed with trucks and buses and tourists and traveling salesmen. We considered it a miracle to average 45 miles per hour.

Gas stations were few and far between, and the only "oases" were shady elm trees alongside farm fields. There were even places in Nebraska where you had to stop to open and close gates as you crossed rangeland!

Long stretches of this major highway were unpaved and near-impassable in wet weather. Foolhardy travelers had to hope that a friendly farmer would hitch up a team of horses to drag their car out of the mire.

Lengthy trips usually called for a couple of spare tires lashed to the roof or back bumper, because you could count on a blowout every 100 miles or so. A tire-patching kit, pump, a few extra fan belts and a basic set of tools were standard equipment.

In summer, bugs were the bane of long-distance drivers. Remember how your windshield became plastered with smashed insects—especially at night? Sometimes you could no longer see the road.

I worked a whole summer at a filling station on the Lincoln Highway. A major chore during those days before self-service was washing windshields. In fact, it was a big reason tourists and truckers stopped in at night—they didn't need much gas, but they sure needed a clean windshield.

Thanks to modern pest control and a more streamlined design to windshields, we now only get a few splatters while speeding down the interstate, nothing like those buggy old days.

Another thing that bugged me back in the good old summertime was pushing an Eclipse mower across our too-large yard. It seems my childhood was spent chasing that mower around the house.

Every spring, Dad took it to a man in town who made a nice living sharpening lawn mower blades. Even so, the Eclipse was a cranky brute that demanded constant tinkering as summer wore on and the blades wore down.

Power mowers are a big improvement, as are snowblowers if you live in northern areas. Nothing's more daunting than waking up to a 10-inch overnight deposit of wet snow when your only ally's a scoop shovel.

Indoors, the lot of the homemaker has improved immeasurably. For instance, young mothers aren't faced with the prospect of washing a million diapers, running them through the clothes wringer and two tubs of rinse water, then hanging them out on the wash line.

And let's not forget the full day spent at the ironing board working through several baskets of kids' clothes, Dad's dress shirts, pillowcases and sheets, blouses and housedresses. Give thanks for fabric softeners and no-iron clothing.

Things are a lot easier for women in the workplace, too. I'm sure there isn't a working woman in the world today who'd want to go back in time a few decades.

It must have been so frustrating to correct a typing error when the boss had asked for five carbons of a document. Remember cutting stencils for mimeograph machines…and transcribing dictation from those old Dictaphones with carbon cylinders? Tillie the Toiler did not have it easy.

Those were the days when the winter air was black with soot from burning soft coal. It settled on rooftops, fouling rainwater in cisterns, made little drifts on windowsills and inevitably seeped into the house. It clung to laundry hung outside.

Far down my list of favorite ways to spend a morning is a trip to the dentist. But how things have improved since the days of the foot-powered drill! Best of all is the fact that youngsters today are growing up cavity-free, thanks to fluoride and more attention to dental hygiene. Someday they'll ask, "Hey, Grampa, what's a cavity?"

Last, but far from least, is the fact that we no longer must sit helplessly by the bedside while a loved one loses a battle against pneumonia, scarlet fever or diphtheria. The abiding terror of polio is just a bad memory, and appendicitis isn't a death sentence anymore.

The list could go on and on. All of us privileged to have been around for most of this century have seen (and benefited from) more improvements in life than any people in all of known history. At least when it comes to material stuff.

But there are still a good many niceties from the past I can't and don't want to forget. The lack of simple civility heads the list. I very much would like to bring back the days when most people were polite to one another and were more tolerant of each other's idiosyncrasies.

Life is rich and rewarding today, better in dozens of ways than when I was young. But I don't want to forget all the things in the past that brought me joy…the "good old times" that *Reminisce* is all about. And I'm sorry for those who never had a chance to experience them.

$\mathscr{W}$ork-Savers Eased
$\approx$ Household Toil $\approx$

Photos: J.C. Allen and Son

Nothing smells better than freshly laundered sheets that have been sun-dried on a breezy day. Of course, few people hang their sheets on the line anymore…and no matter what the ads say, fabric softener does *not* smell like sunshine and fresh air.

Sun-dried sheets are something we traded in exchange for progress. As nice as it would be to sleep on such sheets every night, I doubt many housewives would give up the household work-savers that have improved their lives in this century.

"Man's work is from sun to sun, but woman's work is never done," went the old adage. How true!

On the northern-Illinois farm where I grew up, Monday was always washday. It started bright and early with kettles of water steaming on the stove and bars of P&G or Fels Naptha whittled into soap chips. Extra-dirty clothes were given a preliminary treatment on the scrub board.

A bit of bluing was added to the final rinse water in the hope that the whites would be whiter than those on the neighbor's clothesline. Their washing machine sat outside near the windmill. It was powered by a one-cylinder gasoline engine that sputtered along with an erratic *pop, pop-pop-pop, pop.* Our washing machine was in the basement.

As the day progressed, Mom hauled each load—washed, rinsed and wrung—upstairs and out back to the clothesline. The clothes were pinned to the line, and a small pole was used to prop up the sagging rope.

But the job wasn't quite done, because small disasters were commonplace. The clothesline sometimes broke…or a wind shift might bring a cloud of soot from nearby rooftops or dust from plowed fields. Often a wandering cloud dumped an unexpected extra rinse on clothes that were nearly dry. Occasionally a passing bird left a calling card.

In winter, clothes were hung out even in zero-degree weather and allowed to "freeze dry". Something else froze, too—folks' fingers. Looking back, I figure Monday got its bad reputation because of laundry. Even so, I still miss those fresh-smelling clothes and sheets.

Tuesday was no treat, either—it was ironing day. I vividly remember my 5-foot-2 Grandmother Stevens toiling in her kitchen, pressing a mountain of clothes with flatirons lifted hot off the top of her cookstove.

Is there a woman over the age of 50 who doesn't remember ironing stacks of diapers, frilly little-girl dresses, tiny corduroy overalls, a bunch of men's shirts and handkerchiefs and a whole lot of other stuff? Electric irons made the task considerably more convenient but no less time-consuming.

My funniest memory of ironing day involves the electric cord dangling beneath Mom's ironing board. Once when our house cat was in his "I'm-the-Mightiest-Tiger-in-the-Jungle" mood, he pounced on that cord and sank his teeth into it.

The cat instantly went airborne, tail as rigid as a bandleader's baton with every hair on his body sticking straight out. He recovered—but never again went into the kitchen when he saw that the ironing board was set up.

When "wash-and-wear" clothes finally came along, veteran housewives across the country were happy to fold up their ironing boards and unplug their irons for the last time. And things improved in other areas, too.

Back in Grandma's day, even people of modest means often had a "girl" who lived with the family or came every day to help with the cleaning and cooking. After World War II, that sort of help became unaffordable. Food companies responded by producing products that cut down on preparation time.

A revolutionary invention called Bisquick let housewives make dandy baking powder biscuits with minimum time and effort. From there, it was a short jump to cake mixes.

They were not an instant success, however. Older women in particular shied away, preferring their own "from-scratch" recipes. Others viewed "box cakes" as a form of cheating the family.

I recall Mom being wary of the new mixes except for the angel food variety. Her record with angel food cakes was dismal—they came out of the oven smaller than when they went in, looking like solid little cake-tires.

She'd always blame such failures on us kids, claiming they fell because we slammed doors or jumped on the floor at critical times. But for some reason, angel food cakes from a box seemed impervious to leaping children and slammed doors. Betty Crocker put Mom back into the angel food cake business.

Then along came frozen vegetables...and freedom from the arduous "canning season".

In late summer, we'd all be pressed into service picking heaping pails of crisp string beans from the garden...or sitting on the back stoop shelling peas and husking bushels of sweet corn. While Mom plucked plump red tomatoes from the vines, I climbed up into the cherry tree to harvest the fruit at its very best.

There were mason jars to be scalded, big kettles of water to heat and paraffin to melt for sealing jars filled with jelly. The whole family sweltered together, working as an assembly line in an overheated kitchen cooled only by an electric fan in the window over the kitchen sink.

When canning season was over, shelf after shelf in the pantry was filled with vegetables, fruit, jelly, apple butter and pickles that would carry the family through the long winter ahead.

Nowadays, you just open the freezer case at the supermarket and stock up. I don't miss the hubbub and toil of canning, but I do miss the satisfaction I felt opening a jar of sweet-smelling strawberry preserves made from berries picked with my own hands.

My daughter-in-law still puts up dill pickles and shares some every year. They're a vivid reminder that nothing from the supermarket comes close to homemade. When I open a jar, the pungent aroma instantly creates a mind picture of the pickle crock my mother used.

The endless drudgery of homemaking has eased in other areas, too. Vacuum cleaners came along to replace the old Bissell. Central heating and furnace filters eliminated the soot and ashes that regularly messed up the house. And now you can hire people to shampoo the carpets and even your favorite easy chair.

I do contend that one time-saver—the automatic dishwasher—is a mixed blessing. There was something to be said for the togetherness of kids washing and drying dishes after meals. It wasn't a lot of fun, but it made them realize a home isn't a luxury hotel for small people—it's a place where everyone pitches in.

Certainly a lot of what it takes to be a mother and homemaker has changed, but "Woman's work is never done" is as true today as it was half a century ago. It's just taken a different form.

Two-career families are almost the rule these days. My daughters and daughters-in-law all have full-time jobs plus all the responsibilities that go with being a mother, wife and homemaker.

There are still clothes to mend, bedrooms that need new wallpaper, menus to plan, petunias to plant and family matters to discuss with the husband.

These women would be bored to death shaving a bar of P&G soap into chips every Monday morning before carrying buckets of hot water down to a washing machine in a dark, musty basement. Being freed from the old-time grind of homemaking has been good for them and the whole family.

Nevertheless, I sometimes wish my grandchildren could know what it's like to snuggle down into fresh-off-the-line sheets that smell like summer sunshine. There's nothing better.

$\mathscr{S}$taying Warm Was A Winter Challenge

Ewing Galloway

If you live in the northern half of this country, there comes the day when you step outside and a voice inside your head warns, "Uh, oh, winter is coming."

Perhaps it is a sharp new edge in the breeze, or it may be that the sky suddenly has taken on the look of old pewter, punctuated with skeins of geese heading south. You notice that the dog is sporting a thicker coat of hair and the robins have vanished.

Yes, winter is on its way—but not to worry. These days it's more of an inconvenience than a major problem. We're able to step out of a toasty house into a cozy attached garage—and get into a car with a heater that actually works. Then we can drive to a nice enclosed mall to shop in comfort amidst fountains and flowers.

But it wasn't all that long ago when staying warm in winter took considerable effort and ingenuity.

The big old cast-iron kitchen stove was every family's gathering place. Nothing thawed out frosted toes faster than propping up your feet on the open oven door of a Kalamazoo or Round Oak range ornamented with its white porcelain trim.

Most winter days, a big kettle of Mom's homemade vegetable soup simmered on the back of the stove. Its rich blend of aromas made the kitchen seem that much more welcoming.

The kitchen stove had another important job, too. When the outside temperature plummeted and snow filled the air, Mom hung washday clothes on a folding wooden drying rack that took up most of the kitchen. The stove dried them in a hurry.

Central heat was an unknown luxury until early in this century. Even the wealthy relied on fireplaces throughout the house until Benjamin Franklin invented his pot-bellied heating stove.

Later, homes turned to an improvement called a "base burner"— a jukebox-sized cast iron monster dolled up with nickel-plated trim. Sears' top-of-the-line Acme Sunburst model went for $23.95 during the '20s. The company claimed the stove, plus 3 tons of coal, could keep a large house warm all winter, with "no cold corners."

Heating stoves usually resided in the most-used room of the house. As the cold crept through uninsulated walls, everyone moved their chairs closer to the heat, regardless of what the advertising said about no cold corners. A piece of mica in the stove's door let you watch the crackling flames, and somehow that made you feel even warmer.

Then along came the Estate Heatrola, which could be installed near an outside wall. Ads boasted that the Heatrola would turn your home into a popular gathering place and improve your social life throughout the winter.

Although our farmhouse was built in 1920, it was equipped with central heating channeled through the house to hot water radiators. In the early morning when Dad stoked up the furnace, the radiators gave off friendly clinks and clanks that told you warmth was on the way.

We could usually afford to start out the heating season with a load of coal but eventually needed to economize by burning corncobs.

Every autumn after the corn was shelled, we filled a small building near the house with several wagonloads of cobs. My after-school chore each day was to tote bushel baskets full of cobs down to the furnace in the basement.

When corn dropped to 10 cents a bushel and became cheaper than coal, pound for pound, many farmers discovered that whole ears of corn worked just fine in the furnace. Plenty went up in smoke during those years.

Whether we were heating with coal or cobs, there was a lot of skill required to tending the furnace in really frigid weather. Dad stayed up late, carefully "banking" the fire and closing down the dampers so it would burn slowly through the night. Then he got up early to start it roaring again.

A major heating advance was the Iron Fireman, a contraption that automatically moved coal from the coal bin to the furnace. It saved endless trips to tend the furnace and even let you wake up to a warm house.

Still, there was more to keeping a house snug than a good heater or furnace. Dad remembered how his family put a layer of fresh straw under the rugs for insulation—and stacked bales of straw or hay around the foundation of the house. (They also put out lots of mouse traps.)

Until we could afford storm windows, we covered our north- and west-facing windows with wax-impregnated cloth cut from a long roll and tacked up outside with strips of lath. It was far from transparent but did let some light in—and kept those winter gales from whistling through the windows.

But you couldn't stay indoors from November to April. Eventually you had to go outside and brave the elements, so "long johns" were an absolute necessity. A bachelor neighbor once told Dad that he took only two baths a year—once before donning his winter underwear and then again when he took it off in the spring. Mom said that explained a lot about why he didn't have a wife.

Little kids were bundled up in layer after layer of clothes—long johns, heavy trousers, flannel shirts, thick woolen sweaters, long woolen stockings, snow pants and a quilted jacket, topped off with

BUNDLING UP against driving snow was no bundle of joy. Modern fibers keep today's jackets waterproof, warm and lightweight, but back then, wool coats just got wetter and heavier.

mittens, stocking caps and bulky woolen scarves that covered faces up to the eyeballs. (And I almost forgot to mention the 4-buckle galoshes.)

Children of overly protective mothers were so heavily dressed that their arms stuck straight out as they waddled along, fearful of falling down because they could never get up without help from a playmate.

Because cars had no heaters, trips of any distance were a challenge. Ancient buffalo robes or heavy woolen lap robes proved a big help for passengers, but left the poor driver shivering.

Dad had a collection of granite slabs from the local monument maker's scrap pile. He had started using them as foot-warmers back in his horse and buggy days, and they served just as well when cars became common.

Dad heated the slabs on top of the furnace, wrapped them in burlap and put them on the floorboards of our car. They kept our feet warm during the entire 40-mile trip to Rockford, which was the farthest we ever dared to venture in winter.

Windows frosted over fast when a car was full of passengers. One popular remedy was to mount a 4-inch fan with rubber blades on the dashboard. It moved enough air to keep a peephole open on the windshield in front of the driver. When even that didn't work, Dad used a single-edged razor blade to scrape off the frost.

As best I can recall, the first car heater debuted sometime in the '30s and tapped into the gas line for its fuel. It usually worked just fine, but filled the car with faint gasoline fumes. Eventually Detroit made heaters a standard part of every car, and winter driving became fun.

No prudent driver left home without a set of chains, a scoop shovel and a sack of sand. Confronted with a husky drift across the road, you first charged it repeatedly, trying to bull your way through. If that failed, it was time to put on chains and get out the shovel.

Many farmers drove Dodge cars in those days. They had a lot of power, and the framework was higher off the ground than most. This gave it a decided edge plowing through deep snow on country roads.

A winter storm legend in our family concerned my coming into the world. The February night before I was born, a serious blizzard blocked our only road into town and the hospital. Fortunately, Dad got on the party line and recruited most of the neighbors to keep the road shoveled clear during the night.

No matter how bad the weather, farmers still had animals that needed tending. Our dairy barn was a snug oasis during blizzards, warm and full of pungent animal and hay aromas that perhaps only a farmer can savor.

You instantly sensed the welcome from animals excited at the prospect of being fed and watered when you stepped inside. Horses nickered and nuzzled your shoulder as you walked past their stalls. The cows struggled to get up, and the usual cluster of cats ran to huddle around your feet, knowing there would soon be pans of warm milk fresh from the cow to lap up.

Winter was a formidable, punishing presence back then, and it was you against Old Man Winter. Victories were hard-won, but all the sweeter because of it.

Jobs of the Past Aren't Forgotten

GOOD-BYE, CENTRAL. Technology replaced the friendly worker known as "Central", but those who recall this helpful voice keep only fond memories of those ol' party line days.

The summer I turned sixteen, Ted Johnson hired me to work in his filling station. I'm not sure he ever knew my name, other than "Hey, kid", but to this day, I still live by "Ted's rules".

Every square inch of Mr. Johnson's filling station was so spotless that a fussy brain surgeon would have been comfortable performing the most delicate operation—even in the grease pit.

This was astonishing, considering that filling stations are by nature grungy places. But not his. When you made a mess, you cleaned it up. Instantly. When you used a tool, it went back to its special place on the tool rack. *Right now.*

Not that the man was a fanatic about cleanliness—quite the contrary. He claimed to be a lazy man at heart, but he knew that by keeping things orderly as you went along, you never had to face the day when it would take hours to tidy up. And, if you put things back where they belonged, you never wasted any time hunting around for them.

SERVING CUSTOMERS at the grocery store taught teenage boys a lesson in manners—and they knew to show up for the job neatly dressed and groomed.

Ted's rules worked, which is why I still follow them today, even though I only had that job for three months. Like Mr. Johnson, I'm too lazy to be disorganized.

As I tell my kids, I never had a job that didn't teach me something important. Of course, many of those jobs don't even exist today...for kids *or* adults.

Full-service filling stations, for instance, vanished long ago. There are no uniformed lads who sprint to your car, pump gas, check tire pressure, fill your radiator, check the oil and wash all the windows.

Now you pump your own gas and slip a credit card into the slot on the pump while someone in a locked, bulletproof glass cage warily watches. Poor soul, he's being cheated out of learning "Ted's rules".

Nor are there Western Union messenger boys, grocery delivery kids, elevator operators or theater ushers anymore.

Over recent years, in the process of putting together the monthly "Old Party Line" feature in *Reminisce*, I've had a chance to talk to dozens of interesting men and women who in their youth held some of those now-extinct jobs.

At the end of our chats, I always ask what—if anything—they learned from their work. Without fail, they reply, "I learned to be dependable" or "It taught me to get along with other people" or "I learned to be a good worker."

Indeed. My neighbor over the back fence is supervisor for a dozen or more privately operated prisons here in Florida. They're unique in that every inmate must work. In one prison they make high-quality office furniture. The profits then go into a victim-restitution fund.

"The two biggest problems we have with these people," he tells, "is teaching them to come to work on time and get along with fellow workers." Still, he's proud to note that the "graduates" of these prisons have the lowest rate of return to jail in the state. Coincidence? I doubt it.

I'll confess, though, that I'm hard-pressed to come up with anything I learned from another extinct job, that of pin-setter in a bowling alley. It was one of many spare-time stints (all at 25 cents an hour) that helped pay my way through college.

Pin-setting quickly gave you empathy for those ancient galley slaves, who labored at their oars to the beat of a drum as the overseer's whip cracked overhead.

A pin boy's life was just as

UNIFORMED carhops hold a revered space in nostalgia for friendly and efficient service.

hopeless. As fast as you could get the pins back on the hardwood, someone knocked them down again. Plus, your well-being was in peril with every shot, as pins flew into the pit. My shins *still* bear the scars.

So what did I learn? Maybe that it was more urgent to get an education than I had originally thought!

When you think about it, lots of jobs that gave employment to both kids and adults are with us no longer. Milkmen. Ice men. Friendly operators we knew as "Central". The ladies who pounded the piano at the music store, demonstrating the latest sheet music hits. Firemen on the old coal-burning locomotives.

Or how about clerks in men's hat stores? When is the last time you bumped into a gentleman sporting a derby?

HATS OFF to the genteel clerk in the haberdashery who took the time and interest to help customers select the perfect hat.

For a few years, I bought mine at a Milwaukee haberdashery with the euphonic name of Pantke-Harpke. But you didn't just walk in and buy a hat. No, indeed. First you were studied and queried by an impeccably dressed clerk. It was essential that your hat fit your personality and station in life. Arriving at the absolutely correct style was nothing to be taken lightly.

Nor did you just plunk down your money and walk out with the final selection. Not without first receiving a tactful lecture on the proper care of your new purchase. It was as though Messrs. Pantke and Harpke were entrusting you with a beloved child of their own.

Those were the post-World War II days, however, and returning servicemen were thoroughly sick and tired of any kind of head gear. Wear a hat? I think not!

My Aunt Hazel worked as a designer in a millinery store. She was so talented that fashionable ladies traveled long distances to have hats custom-designed by her. They even brought along the garment the hat was to be worn with so the style and colors would be a perfect complement.

But then the carefree, bare-headed trend was adopted by ladies, too. (Aunt Hazel was lucky. She was ready to retire anyway.) Today we see our Presidents and First Ladies hatless wherever they go. And I think they look just fine.

All those jobs…gone, gone, gone. The rag man and the door-to-door scissors sharpener. The soda jerk and drive-in car hops on roller skates. And motion picture projectionists. (I know…theaters still have projection booths, but now it's mostly a matter of turning on the machine and letting it run.)

When I worked as a projectionist, full-length movies arrived on several reels, with the previews, MovieTone News and cartoons on a separate one. Two projection machines were necessary so that we could switch from one to the other as little cue spots appeared in the upper right-hand corner of the screen.

My immortal moment of shame was during a showing of *Phantom of the Opera.* The point of high drama was when the Phantom, high up in the opera house, sawed through an enormous chandelier meant to squash an unsuspecting soul on the floor far below.

The last scene on that reel—just before switching machines—was a close-up of the chandelier as it was severed from its chain.

GONE ARE THE CLERKS who helped gentlemen choose the perfect wood-handled umbrella or walking stick.

The first scene on the next reel was a shot from the floor, following the chandelier as it sickeningly dropped down, down, down. The theater audience was breathless with tension. Then came my cue spot signaling to switch machines. *Ooops.*

What burst upon the screen was lively *dah-dee-dah-dah* music and the opening of a Loony Tunes cartoon.

There was a dead, shocked silence in the theater below. Then an angry roar as 400 pairs of eyeballs swiveled around to peer back where I cowered in the booth. Lesson learned: Take nothing for granted. Never assume. Check and check again.

One man I talked with on "The Old Party Line" told about his adventures selling flavors and extracts door-to-door in the remote hills of the Missouri Ozarks during the '30s. Farms were a mile or more apart, so it took a lot of trudging down dirt roads to make a dozen calls a day. Not that it was a fertile sales territory, either. Most people he called on were flat broke.

When he finally gave up, he had only a few dollars to show for many months of tramping around the hills. But on one house call, he met the woman he eventually married, so it was all worthwhile. And in later years, he made a handsome living selling lake property and real estate in northern Minnesota.

The point is, he learned about *people* on that first job. It didn't pay much then, but it returned dividends several decades later.

I'm sure you can think back to a crazy variety of jobs you took to feed the wolf slavering at your door. And I expect you didn't enjoy some of them any more than I did. They sure weren't what you had in mind for a satisfying lifetime career.

Probably years later, you were startled to discover that some of those jobs taught you lessons that will last a lifetime. Just as "Ted's rules" did for me.

$\mathcal{H}$ooray! I'm Sick!

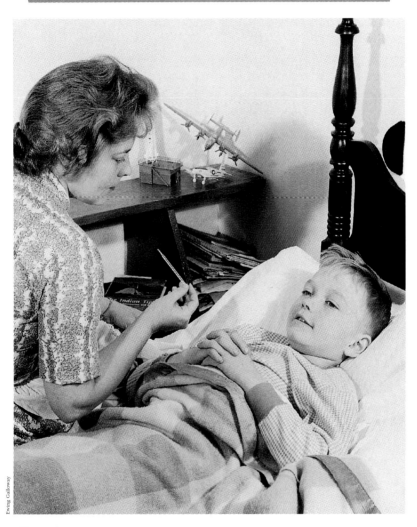

Ewing Galloway

Despite all the advances in medical science, lots of people still get sick around February and March. It just seems inevitable during that time of year. These days, I worry about every sniffle and sneeze …but back in my childhood, the possibility of becoming sick was a beacon of hope on the bleak post-winter horizon.

After all, being sick meant I got to stay home from school! And if luck was with me, my illness hit just a day or two before some long-postponed piece of homework was due.

Not that I could successfully *fake* being sick. I just wasn't that accomplished as an actor, and Mom was much too good at spotting fake maladies. (She'd been a teacher and heard every excuse ever cooked up by malingering students.)

Most years, though, I was "lucky". Measles, mumps, chicken pox or one of the other childhood diseases usually managed to strike around March. I could also count on at least one serious cold that qualified for a few days at home.

"Dr. Mom" had a thermometer fixation. At my first signs of illness, she would bring out the thermometer and thereafter stick it in my mouth on an hourly basis.

Looking back, that simply may have been a good way to shut off my whining for a while. (I've since learned that it doesn't really take 10 minutes for a thermometer to give an accurate reading.)

Mom's treatment of choice for colds and such was Vicks Vapo-Rub, smeared liberally over the chest. Had those little blue jars come in an institutional size, I'm sure she would have purchased them by the case. While Dad kept the farm running with baling wire, Mom kept the family healthy with Vicks.

Other moms had their own remedies. A garlic bud on a string

DR. MOM'S best remedies weren't the preferred curative of kids when it came to castor oil and smelly salves... but a bowl of homemade chicken soup really made the grade when staying home sick from school.

tied around the neck was popular in some homes…hot lemonade was also thought to have curative powers, and hot mustard poultices spread over the chest were used a lot, too.

For some kids, head and chest colds meant spending time under a big bath towel, leaning over a hissing contraption that blew medicated steam into the air.

We now know that a cold takes 7 days to cure if you treat it and a week if you don't. But most moms of that era hadn't yet learned this.

My mom also had total faith in cod-liver oil, both as a treatment and a preventative. I was not fond of cod-liver oil, even the "improved" (but still vile-tasting) mint-flavored version.

In fact, I was so *un*-fond of it that Dad had to forcibly administer the tablespoonful dosage every day. I put up a valiant fight but always lost, whimpering and gagging.

More serious ailments sometimes required a visit from Dr. Mc-Candless, the gentle man who ushered me into the world. Although we lived on a farm some distance from town, he routinely made house calls in his Model A Ford.

He'd climb the stairs to my bedroom, sit on my bed, ask how I felt, listen to my chest through his stethoscope, peer into my mouth and ears and give me a small piece of candy. Then he'd leave the room for a conference with Mom.

Even though he didn't *do* anything, I always felt considerably better after a visit from Dr. McCandless. There were many times in

Steve Wanke/F Stock

49

those pre-health insurance years when Dad covered Doc's fee with 4 dozen eggs or a couple of dressed chickens.

As much as I relished missing school, there were some drawbacks besides Vicks and cod-liver oil to be considered. Food, for one thing.

In our house, sick people didn't get much to eat. Mom invented "hospital food" long before hospitals came up with their universally detested diet of dry toast, thin soup and plain gelatin.

She not only believed in starving a cold but also starved fevers, measles and sprained ankles. After 3 or 4 days of that, returning to school seemed like a good idea.

My wife, Peg, on the other hand, recalls treatment that was much easier to stomach. Her mother, Eleanor, marshaled a whole arsenal of "comfort foods" like cream of tomato soup, toasted cheese sandwiches or hot oatmeal laced with plenty of sugar. She also served her "patients" hearty casseroles loaded with potatoes and vegetables.

Even today, Peg turns to those old-time dishes when she's feeling a bit under the weather. We both also remember milk toast—a bowl of warm milk with a piece of toast floating in the middle like a jellied raft.

It may sound bland, but when you had a sore throat and a runny nose or a bad case of mumps, milk toast wasn't all that bad.

Boredom was another problem for sick kids. Television hadn't even been dreamed of, let alone the Nintendo games that keep my grandchildren amused for hours when they're feeling poorly.

There was also the now-discredited belief that kids with measles had to spend their time in a darkened room to prevent damage to their eyes. If anything could focus your mind on the miserable itching that went with measles and chicken pox, it was lying in the dark with absolutely nothing to do!

Sometimes, in desperation, I'd turn on my bedside radio and sample the soap operas that Mom and my grandmother endlessly discussed. I didn't have a lot of empathy for Larry and Mary Noble's *Backstage Wife* tribulations, nor was there much about *Guiding Light* that interested a little kid. The noon market reports on WLS weren't terribly entertaining, either.

There was one daytime show, however, that unfailingly brightened the day—*Vic and Sade* was a winner no matter what your age.

The folks who lived in "the little house halfway up the next block" were always good for a chuckle. And afterward, along toward suppertime, came the "kid soap operas"—*Tom Mix, Jack Armstrong, Buck Rogers* and *Little Orphan Annie.*

The best cure for boredom (unless you had measles) was reading. Not only did a good book make you forget your illness, but it also whisked you far away from Depression and Dust Bowl miseries.

I could join Tom Swift and his pals as they ventured into an eerie cave in Guatemala...or hide in the apple barrel with Jim Hawkins as he listened to Long John Silver plot how to grab the riches on Treasure Island.

Perhaps I might join Captain Nemo far under the sea in his incredible submarine...or marvel at the ingenuity of the marooned Swiss Family Robinson.

Even so, solitary confinement was no fun. And after a day or two, my plaintive whining from the upstairs bedroom began to fall on deaf ears. Mom would then sternly inform me that she had better things to do than run up and down stairs all day.

One year, my sister, Mary, managed to one-up me in the health department. It was decided that her tonsils and adenoids had to be removed. No one in the family had been in a hospital since I was born, so Mary suddenly became the family celebrity.

Visiting her on the night after her surgery, we walked into the hospital room to find a bedside lamp shooting sparks and the lamp shade in flames. We later wondered what would have happened had we not walked in at that moment. It made great conversation for months.

Not only did Mary get a lot of attention and sympathy when she came home, but she also got all the ice cream she wanted. I sat in my room and sulked. Why didn't anything *really bad* ever happen to me? Why was she the lucky one?

As I grew older, Mom started playing hardball when I used sniffles as an excuse for missing school. She went to my teachers and brought home stacks of work for me so I wouldn't "fall behind". That crafty move did more to improve my health than all the Vicks and cod-liver oil in the state of Illinois.

The Family Doctor Once Handled It All

Old Doc McCandless was the only doctor I had until I went into the military in 1942. He brought me into the world and later sat at my bedside when I was sick.

He would have been perfectly competent enough to set a broken leg, too, had I ever snapped one. He was our family doctor—the only one we needed in rural northern Illinois.

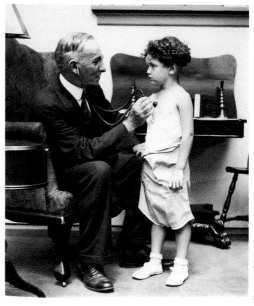

H. Armstrong Roberts

It was common in those days for doctors to be "physician/surgeons". That meant they spent their mornings in the operating room and afternoons and evenings seeing patients—in the office or in the home—until far into the night. It was a grueling life.

I don't recall when the first "specialist" hit our town, but it caused quite a stir. He called himself an eye-ear-nose-and-throat doctor. Imagine that—a doctor who concerned himself only with illnesses above the shoulders!

As time went by, even that split up. Soon we had ear-nose-and-throat doctors. Others specialized in eyes.

I was thinking about that the other day while waiting in the office of a retinal specialist. He's not an eye specialist, mind you—he's an expert in just *part* of the eye. I was tempted to ask him if he concentrated, perhaps, only on left eyes. But I decided to mind my manners.

The town in which I live today has a 50-acre piece of ground populated with stylish little brick buildings, each containing doctors who are specialists. There's a building full of orthopedic doctors, another with arthritis specialists, another with cardiovascular experts, another with dermatologists and another with kidney specialists.

Doc McCandless would be astonished. But though he may have been a generalist with only limited knowledge in many areas of medicine, he did know something very important. He knew his patients.

Chances are he'd delivered them as babies, helped them grow up healthy and cared for them as adults. He had established a lifetime relationship. They didn't need to fill out a three-page questionnaire when they came into his office and update it on future visits.

Doc didn't need to consult your file to remember that you had a mild problem with high blood pressure, either, or remind you that your parents were both diabetic and you should be alert for any symptoms.

Because he knew his patients, Doc was also aware that not all of them could afford to pay him promptly. During the Depression, he carried patients on his books for years without complaint. A lot of those bills were never collected.

A friend whose father was a doctor in those days said her dad's accounts showed $60,000 in uncollected bills when he passed away. That was an enormous amount in those times.

Speaking of carrying, I'd sure like to know what Dr. McCandless carried in his scuffed black bag besides a thermometer and a stethoscope. It wasn't packed with miracle drugs, because none existed then.

Many diseases then were so feared that their victims were kept isolated under quarantine. Remember that dreaded word?

Without effective medicines, the only defense against epidemics was to put the entire family under the equivalent of house arrest when a kid came down with something.

The local health officer came to your home and tacked up a bright red sign on the door: "QUARANTINE! WHOOPING COUGH."

No one could come in or go out. A delivery boy left groceries on the front porch and scooted back to safety.

Being in quarantine sure brought the family closer together, but not very happily. For a kid, it was especially trying—there was no television for entertainment, so you read books, played games and mostly moped around. To add to the misery, your teacher dropped off school assignments so you wouldn't fall behind your classmates.

The first ray of hope came in 1928 when penicillin was discovered. Finally, men like Dr. McCandless had an effective weapon against infections.

The most devastating disease was polio. It killed, crippled and put people in iron lungs for endless years. It was a fearsome plague for which there was no defense. Parents everywhere lived in mortal fear every time a child came home with a fever.

Then, in 1954, Jonas Salk began successfully vaccinating children against polio. It was as though a great black cloud of fear had been lifted from every home in America.

There was a lot of tuberculosis around in the early days, too. If the family could afford it, the patient was sent to a dry climate in the mountains of North Carolina or the desert in Arizona.

But the chances of recovering were between slim and none no matter where you went or what kind of care you got.

Advances in medicine during the last 40 years have been breathtaking. Whereas Dr. McCandless had to diagnose by experience and instinct, today's doctors let machines do much of the diagnosing. "Wait until the lab reports come back, and I'll tell you what's wrong with you," says the doctor.

Until recently, doctors often had to do "exploratory surgery" to find out what was happening inside. Nowadays there are machines that buzz and click and clunk and purr as they inspect your innards from outside your body.

They're wonderful gadgets. But spend half an hour with one of them, and the bill will be close to what Dr. McCandless earned in an entire year. An MRI machine doesn't make house calls, either.

And here's another thing. With all the advances in medicines and machines and space-age technology we've seen today, we still don't have a hospital gown that's comfortable, simple to fasten and lets you walk down the corridor without worrying about what's on display to those who are behind you.

Speaking of hospitals, as far as I know, three of my four grandparents never spent a day in one. Were they of sturdier stuff? Was it because fast foods and frozen dinners hadn't been invented? Or were they just lucky?

My Aunt Grace, who became a nurse in the early '30s, says that sick people were mostly cared for at home. You didn't go to a hospital unless you needed surgery, had been in a bad accident or were having a baby.

Given the state of the medical arts in those times, hospital care couldn't do much for lots of people. Patients stayed home, and the family looked after them or hired a "practical nurse" who came in for 12 hours a day to provide more skilled care.

Those nurses really cared about every patient. They worried about them, tried to comfort and encourage the frantic families and felt heavy responsibility as a critical part of the patient-care team. Truth to tell, they were the "doctor" when the doctor couldn't be there. And they did a good job.

Lots of us remember people like Dr. McCandless and Aunt Grace. We remember the feeling of security when we were being cared for by someone who was a longtime acquaintance.

Which, I guess, explains my unease when a doctor I've never met comes into the examining room, quickly shakes my hand without making eye contact and asks, "What seems to be the matter today?" while thumbing through the questionnaire I filled out an hour ago.

What's the moral to all this? I guess it's another case of accepting trade-offs. You gain something here and lose something there. I felt really good when the doctor who specializes only in retinas assured me everything was okay. If anyone should know for sure, it's him.

But at the same time, I miss chatting with a friendly, concerned man who heard me cry as a newborn and has listened to all my complaints ever since.

Progress is wonderful. But a wise woman once put it in perspective. "Progress," she said, "is trying to make things as good as they used to be."

I'll go along with that. I know...I was there.

*S*chool Shopping Was A Downtown Adventure

Archive Photos/Lambert

Archive Photos/Lambert

NEW CLOTHES took legwork. You could usually count on an entire day traipsing from store to store in order to hunt down the elements of a complete back-to-school wardrobe.

Time passes at a strange pace when you're young...how well I remember. The days, weeks and months between September (when school resumed) and June (when it ended) seemed to drag on for several lifetimes.

Summer vacation, on the other hand, whizzed by at supersonic speed. It began on that wonderful last day of school. Wow! "School's out, school's out—the teacher let the fools out!"

At Lincoln School in Sterling, Illinois, that glorious day was celebrated in the park across the street. There were sack races, three-legged races, wheelbarrow relay races and lots of others, all with prizes for the winners.

One year there was a Maypole dance, which the boys unanimously agreed was really dumb and only for sissies. I don't recall ever having it again.

Galvanized horse tanks were full of ice and soda pop, and

there was free ice cream for everyone. The usually stern teachers were also in good spirits—probably as giddy with relief as we were.

Three golden, glorious months of total irresponsibility stretched ahead. There were trees to climb, creeks to swim, frogs to catch, and dark woodlands to explore. There was baseball to be played, even books to read "just for fun" on the front porch. And no alarm clock demanding that I rise and shine.

Alas, at about the time I was settled into this comfortable life of leisure, Mother spoke those dreaded words: "It's almost time to go downtown and buy your school things."

My world crashed. Reality hit. Another endless year of school was just around the corner. Where had the summer gone?

That was the bad news, but there *was* a bright side. I could look forward to new clothes, new books, and maybe even a new lunch box. It was a bit like Christmas, except you had a chance to pick out your own presents.

Many of my friends' parents insisted that you couldn't beat the stuff in the Sears & Roebuck catalog for sturdy clothes that would last all year. But Dad had a strong feeling about patronizing local merchants.

For clothing, there were just three choices in Sterling. Well, actually only two for us because one of them catered to the gentry and was far too expensive for our budget.

The store Mom and Dad favored was one with the memorable slogan, "Classy Togs for Dad and Lad". Honest! It offered a good selection at affordable prices. Counters were piled high with woolly-smelling pullover sweaters, corduroy trousers, boxes of shirts, long-john underwear and much more. Long racks were filled with heavy mackinaw jackets to fend off the nastiest howling blizzard.

Clothes back then were a lot different from those we find today in the big discount stores. Manufacturers actually made stuff a kid couldn't wear out in 60 days! In fact, most kids' garments were so sturdy that they became part of the family, passed down from sibling to sibling with only an occasional patching and mending.

When it came to choosing clothes, I had the color sense of an addled parrot. I was strangely attracted to combinations such as green shirts and maroon britches, possibly topped off with an argyle sweater.

Mom, meanwhile, didn't have much sympathy or time for what was trendy among boys my age. The result was a tug-of-war between my whines of "they'll laugh me out of school if I wear that" and Mom's adamant stand: "I won't send a child of mine out in public wearing such a getup!"

Mom always won. Fortunately.

Next stop was the shoe store just down the street. Dad was the family authority on this subject, although I'm not sure why. Maybe it was because he was good at repairing the leather harness for our work horses.

Whatever the reason, he was in charge when we stepped inside the shoe store. It was a long, narrow place with floor-to-ceiling shelves of boxed shoes as far as you could see. Chairs placed back-to-back ran down the middle, except for a special shrine in the center where the X-ray machine stood proudly.

Like the clothing of the day, shoes were plain and durable. They were 100% leather and sewn together, rather than glued or stapled. A really good pair cost $3. (The most expensive were the Florsheims favored by bankers and lawyers, which ran as high as $5!)

After measuring my feet, the clerk prowled along the shelves, pulling out a half dozen boxes. Dad immediately checked the prices on the cartons, disqualifying two or three even before they were opened. I'd try on the others and finally make my choice.

Then came the exciting part—a walk to the spooky X-ray machine. Peering through a little porthole, I could actually see the bones in my feet. Dad would look, too.

"Stop wiggling your toes," he'd command as he confirmed the proper fit. Dad always insisted on shoes that were a little too large, saying I would grow into them.

When paying for the shoes, the clerk usually threw in a spare set of laces and sometimes a can of shoe polish.

As we walked out the door, Dad delivered his standard speech. "Those are good shoes. They cost a lot of money, and they'll last a long time if you take care of them." The implied threat was clear: If the shoes didn't last a long time, the fault was solely mine.

Our final stop was the store where schoolbooks, notebooks, pencils and erasers were sold. Mom had a list of required textbooks, sent out early from school. First we looked for used books in decent condition, usually with success if we got there early enough.

The real prizes were books previously owned by girls, because they took good care of them. Boys viewed textbooks as enemies, weapons or tools…and it showed. They also had a tendency to leave them out in the rain. Girls often underlined important things in their books (which often was helpful) and drew hearts with initials inside (which was annoying).

My special focus was in choosing a new three-ring notebook. I was sure in my heart that the right notebook would magically transform me into a scholar. Or at least a respectable student.

What I wanted was a sturdy, serious-looking notebook. Covers with cartoons or animals or clever sayings were definitely out. The notebook of my dreams would also have divider pages with tabs, so I could designate a well-organized section for each class. A pocket inside for a ruler and pencils was also important.

I began to think of the elusive "perfect notebook" much as King Arthur viewed Excalibur. It would make me invincible in the classroom. Frustrated parents would point me out to their own children and say, "Why can't you be like him? He's so organized!"

I never did find the magic notebook, by the way. Fortunately, science eventually understood my plight and invented the home computer. It's the answer—as long as the power doesn't go out.

At last the exhilarating day downtown was over, and I was properly equipped for another endless school year. Driving home, Dad would grumble about how much prices had gone up and where would it ever end. Imagine, $1.50 for a shirt…$1.50!

He then delivered part two of the lecture about how he had shelled out a lot of money to buy good-quality stuff and it would last a long time if I only learned to take care of it.

I heard that speech dozens of times. It must have sunk in, because today I still wear a dandy-looking pair of shoes I purchased 25 years ago. You were right, Dad—stuff does last a long time if you take care of it. Even longer than the eternity in which a school year seemed to stretch out for a 10-year-old.

The Old Schoolhouse
Is Just a Memory

H. Armstrong Roberts

It couldn't be!

That was my first startled reaction when I went back to my old hometown and discovered they'd torn down the schoolhouse I'd attended through sixth grade.

Lincoln School had a square block all to itself in our small town of Sterling, Illinois.

It was a rectangular two-story brick building with a cupola that housed an enormous school bell. Now, in its place stood a sprawling one-story modern school building.

I guess the old schoolhouse had to go—it was showing its age even when I was there in the early '30s. And I'm sure the fire insurance company didn't approve of the two wide wooden staircases and the polished hardwood floors. The heating system was antiquated, and the classrooms on the northern end were invariably gloomy on cloudy winter days.

Still, I can't help but feel sorry that the old building is gone. For better or worse, it was the place where thousands of kids got their first glimpse of what education was all about. Who could count the memories stored in the classrooms, corridors and bricks of old Lincoln School?

Those of us who weren't "halter-broke" vividly remember the

long, long trip up the staircase to the principal's office. No condemned criminal ever dreaded the 100 steps to the electric chair more than we dreaded a confrontation with the principal.

I expect he was a nice man at heart, but he dealt with our childish crimes in a stern and unyielding manner.

He also must have been a master of child psychology, because he always saw to it that our terror was heightened by a long wait in the outer office before being ushered into his presence. Our anticipation of what dire things might happen to us soared with each passing minute.

I still remember one visit following a playground snowball fight, something that was strictly forbidden. One kid—I no longer recall who—tossed the first snowball, and the battle was on...but with an inventive new twist.

There were dozens of ancient oak trees on the school grounds that produced bushels of acorns. My friends and I reckoned that a mere snowball could be turned into a lethal weapon by packing it with acorns.

We were proud of our new technological advance in playground warfare, but one of our victims turned us in. That meant trudging

Harold M. Lambert

PAYING GLORY TO "OLD GLORY". Saying the daily Pledge of Allegiance was a fond ritual for students and helped instill respect and pride for our country and fellow citizens.

THE PASS COMPLETE! Students under constant surveillance of Teacher the Terrible learned the fine art to exchanging notes on the sly—or else paid the consequences.

up the long flight of stairs to the principal, who did not applaud our ingenuity.

Teachers, besides, could be fearsome authority figures. I particularly recall the humorless lady who taught my second-grade class. She had no illusions of being a surrogate mom—she was Marshall Earp and Judge Roy Bean in her classroom.

Equally intimidating was my fourth-grade teacher. When scoldings didn't work, she banished troublemakers to the cloakroom, an unheated place festooned with wet coats hanging from iron hooks and four-buckle galoshes covered with melting snow on the floor. There was no ventilation, and the place smelled like a wet goat. It was not a good spot to spend your afternoon.

If solitary confinement in the cloakroom didn't work, the teacher was capable of meting out physical punishment. I'll never forget the day she wrestled one large, obstreperous lad to the floor and whaled away with her ruler on his backside.

I can't recall whether or not it tamed him, but it had a permanent calming effect on all the rest of us!

As we advanced through the grades, the desks grew larger. They were the traditional ones with ornate wrought-iron frames, a fold-down wooden seat, an inkwell and a desktop that lifted up for access to a space where you could store your books.

The desks were graduated in size, from smallish ones in the front to larger ones in the rear. If you were a little kid, you were destined to spend your school years immediately under the nose of every teacher, which meant you couldn't pass notes or whisper very often.

The old desks were a regular archive of school history, as those who passed through carved their initials and a record of their infatuations ("JL+PS") in the desktops.

The best part about Lincoln School was the playground, replete with swings, teeter-totters and "giant strides" there under the great sprawling oaks.

There also were two baseball diamonds. Home plate was marked with a wooden slab, but the other bases were wherever the basemen happened to be standing.

Everyone who wanted to play was given a chance. The two captains (the two best players by common agreement) took turns choosing players.

One captain tossed a bat into the air. The other captain grabbed it by the barrel. Then they alternated hands as they worked their way to the top. Whoever got "eagle claws" (the final grip at the top) got first choice. The worst player was chosen last and had to play right field. I played right field a lot.

There were two or three places in the school yard where you could play marbles, a diversion frowned upon if you were caught playing "for keeps". (We all did; we just didn't admit it.)

The rest of the school yard was grass where you could sprawl in the shade and visit with friends. I feel sorry for kids these days who go to schools with asphalt playgrounds. They have all the attractiveness of a mall parking lot.

While the teachers were pretty much a solemn lot, the elderly janitor was every kid's best friend. He liked kids and made no bones about it.

His special favorites were allowed to help him ring the school bell, tugging on a thick old rope that hung down from the cupola. "First bell" signaled that it was time to scurry inside the school. "Second bell", 5 minutes later, meant if you weren't sitting at your desk, you were in immediate peril of being tardy.

The only ones given special dispensation to be late were the crossing guards. Being selected as a crossing guard was the ultimate honor—you received an official-looking Sam Browne belt and got to boss around motorists and your peers. Those of us who were not chosen sneered at the guards, calling them toadies and teachers' pets…but secretly, we envied them.

On the second floor of Lincoln School were two classrooms with a fold-up divider wall. This made it possible to convert the two rooms into a makeshift auditorium for PTA meetings and school programs.

This auditorium was also the site of my first public appearance, stumbling through *The March of the Wooden Soldiers* on a seriously out-of-tune piano. It was my introduction to mindless, knee-rattling, wet-palmed stage fright—a solid clue that I was not cut out for the life of an entertainer.

I suppose that Lincoln School eventually needed to be torn down. I'm sure it was time to replace it. But they couldn't tear down the memories.

That old school taught us our "Three Rs", the Palmer Method of Penmanship, the Pledge of Allegiance, reverence for our country, a respect for authority and the rudiments of becoming decent citizens.

It taught us that life outside the home nest was not necessarily going to be easy, but it sure was going to be exciting. Thousands of us owe a lot to old Lincoln School.

LOOKING BACK on younger days when dreams still seemed possible, the lessons learned in and out of the classroom would serve us a lifetime.

64

Where Have All Our Heroes Gone?

Have you noticed how we seem to be seriously short of heroes these days?

I don't mean those "manufactured" heroes who are built up by a lot of media hype and then knocked down a year or so later.

And I'm not speaking of big-time sports figures, whose "heroism" is measured not so much

TEACHER GETS AN "A". Reunited with high school instructor David Stryker (left), Clancy got to thank a hero for steering him to a lifelong writing career.

by their deeds as by the size of their paychecks.

The heroes I'm talking about are the ones who quietly touched and even changed our lives by the examples they set. They were real people you knew. They didn't charge 8-year-old kids $10 for an autograph or demand special treatment in restaurants; rather, they did things that stayed in your memory forever.

Okay, maybe "hero" is too strong a word. So let's settle for something milder and call them *the people we looked up to.*

For example, I remember when the local policeman was someone you looked up to—literally. At least, he *seemed* taller than anyone else in town, and he knelt down to eye level when he talked to little kids. He was friendly and knew everyone by name.

Still, this nice officer wasn't anyone to take lightly. You knew he was tougher and braver than any bad guy who tried to disturb the peace. He had a lot of power, but didn't throw it around. For sure, you wanted him on your side. These days, not enough people look up to or respect police officers.

Then there was the family doctor, who worked 20-hour days 7 days a week. He made house calls without complaint and carried his black bag wherever he went.

You felt better the minute he walked into your room and sat beside you on the edge of your bed. He didn't need to read your file, either, because he'd known you since the day he brought you into the world.

Most doctors in those days weren't well rewarded for their skills, and many bills went unpaid for years. But, then, they had gone into medicine to *heal* people—not to make a lot of money.

We looked up to the local newspaper editor, too whether we agreed with him or not. He could make things happen in the community and was the local authority on world affairs, the economy and whether or not merchants would be hurt if the town fathers installed parking meters on Main Street.

Whatever cause you might be promoting, it was prudent and useful to first get the blessing and backing of your newspaper editor. With him behind you, almost anything was possible.

Veterans of the Spanish-American War and World War I were heroes, too. Some hobbled along on crutches or peg legs, while others were still wracked with coughing from exposure to poison gas in the trenches of France.

These men continued to serve by marching in Fourth of July and

HEROES OF THE PAST. Faded cursive on the reverse side of this 1922 photograph notes that veterans of "all wars" marched in this patriotic Memorial Day parade scene.

Brown Brothers

Armistice Day parades, proudly wearing their scars and medals. We honored and looked up to them because they'd gone far from home to fight when their country needed them.

Black Jack Pershing, the man who led the American Expeditionary Force in "the war to end all wars", was a jumbo-sized hero, as were Dwight Eisenhower and George Patton. Unfortunately, generals stopped being heroes to many people around the time of the war in Vietnam.

We also looked up to governors and congressmen. Yes, some of them were proven to be scoundrels. But, we didn't automatically assume they were crooks just because they were in politics.

Unless they really disappointed us, we were respectful of elected officials. They were the best we could find to represent and lead us, and they always showed up to give a rousing speech from the platform in the park on the Fourth of July. They also seemed to genuinely care about the people they represented. People were to be served, not manipulated.

I doubt any U.S. president ever will be looked up to in the way Franklin Roosevelt was. Of course, none before or since walked into a bigger mess. He quickly surrounded himself with others we respected, and together they took swift action.

Through the desperate days of the Depression and then the biggest military conflict in the history of the world, FDR towered as our one best hope of salvation. His fatherly fireside chats gave us courage, even though the pantry was bare.

Not everyone liked him, that's for sure. My grandfather Stevens regarded him as the Devil incarnate. But even Grampa had to admit that a lot of things were in a bad way and "that man in the White House" *was* trying to save the country. Grampa just didn't agree with the way FDR was going about things.

Every four years when I watch the two major parties scrambling to find someone—*anyone*—electable, I have to admit that political heroes are in scant supply now, even though we need them more than ever.

The *true* unsung heroes and heroines, though, were those weary people sitting across the supper table. Our parents.

My Dad certainly was someone I looked up to. He was stronger than I was, knew all sorts of things I didn't know and could fix anything from a piece of machinery to a bird with a broken wing.

Somehow, he kept his sense of humor, no matter how desperate life was for us.

He always seemed to make the right decision, too, even when it meant I had to go fetch the dreaded razor strop.

Dad and I didn't spend "quality time" with each other, because no one had coined that goofy term yet. We didn't go to ball games together, and we didn't go fishing until he was 70 and I had kids of my own. He wasn't my buddy, and he wasn't my pal. He was my *dad*, and I looked up to him.

Grampa Stevens was another hero of mine. He began working at 13 and later studied hard to become a telegrapher for the railroad. He could recite long passages from Dickens and Thackeray, even though his education had stopped in the sixth grade. He knew the batting average of every single player for the Chicago Cubs and White Sox and what the next pitch should be when you had a three-and-two count on Mel Ott.

On fine summer days, we'd take a walk down to Fulf's drugstore in Dixon. He would pull out his leather coin purse and give me a dime for an ice cream cone and a small bag of lemon drops.

Then we'd find a park bench beside the river and he started reminiscing about his life. He even remembered the day a horseman had galloped by, shouting the news that Lee surrendered at Appomattox!

Another family member I looked up to was my Uncle Earle. He had been to far-off, exotic places such as San Antonio, Texas. He had eaten in Chicago restaurants. He also played good jazz piano and went to college.

To me, he was a nice blend of Fred Astaire and Cary Grant—nattily dressed, always freshly barbered, slightly ironic in his view of the world and exactly what I aspired to be some day in the distant future.

Finally, any talk of heroes simply must include schoolteachers. Early on, I dimly sensed that they held all the keys to what I wanted out of life.

One, a freshly minted Northwestern graduate, in fact *did* put me on the path to an immensely happy life. It happened the day he called me aside and asked what I intended to do after leaving high school.

When I told him I had no ideas or plans, he suggested I

FINDING A HERO in good ol' yester-year didn't seem to be such a tall order like it is these days.

should consider becoming a writer. A writer! What a ridiculous idea. But he worked with me, encouraged me and even talked the local newspaper into giving me a part-time job after school and then a full-time summer job as a cub reporter.

He changed my life forever, and by a strange quirk of fate, David Stryker and I now live in the same town. He says he's pleased with the way I turned out. Thank you, David.

People often tell me about their own personal heroes—mothers, grandmothers, aunts and uncles, pastors, neighbors, teachers and countless others who took the time to care about another human. We remember them with gratitude and a great deal of affection.

Just knowing these special people made you a better person for life. Sometimes they set examples that still guide you today. Some taught you about honesty and about honor.

Others taught you to believe in yourself no matter how badly the cards were stacked against you. Some taught you about compassion and charity. They showed you the Golden Rule does work if you just give it a chance.

Were they just people you looked up to, or were they *heroes?* I don't know—but we could use a fresh supply any day now.

$\mathscr{A}$ Good Old Fair Was Midway to Heaven

Let me confess: I never met a fair I didn't like. Big state fairs, little county fairs, vast expositions—I love 'em all!

Unfortunately, a good old-fashioned fair is getting harder and harder to find. Too many have become urbanized, with the focus on stock car races and big-name celebrities. There aren't many calves in the 4-H barn these days, and there seem to be far too many people hawking magical kitchen utensils.

Many of the big state fairs are held in larger cities like St. Paul, Milwaukee and Columbus. They're teeming with city folks who wouldn't know a Hampshire hog from a Duroc and have come mostly to mob the midway, anyhow.

The fairs I remember were considerably different. They were a celebration of excellence in personal skills such as homemaking and farming...a place to show off your best and applaud your neighbors' best.

Most of all, fairs were family events, intended to amuse, amaze, entertain and thrill Mom, Dad, Sis and Sonny.

To *really* enjoy a fair in the good old days, you had to be there when the gates opened and stay until the harvest moon came up over the grandstand infield. Fairs were always a dawn-to-dark event—things really changed by the hour, and you sure didn't want to miss any of it.

For example, any fairgoer worth his or her salt would insist on arriving early to watch the fair "wake up". If you didn't, you'd miss the aromas of bacon and coffee coming from the tents where food was served...and the sight of animals being exercised, shampooed, curried and pampered like Hollywood celebrities.

To you or me as spectators, it may have been just another morning at the county fair. But to the people grooming those animals, it was like the dawn of Super Bowl Sunday.

Nowadays, some of my favorite show barns—like the Poultry Exhibit building—seem to be missing from most fairs. How I re-member the rows and rows of wire cages filled with Leghorns and Rhode Island Reds and Buff Orpingtons and Barred Rocks... plus some of the darnedest feathered creatures you ever saw.

Some sported a rainbow of colors. Some were the size of pi-geons, while others were big enough to fill the whole cage. They had exotic names and ancestries going back to far-off Ori-ental or European countries.

These days there aren't many good goat exhibits, either. (The last one I saw was at the Missouri State Fair near Sedalia.) Time was when you needed to really be interested in goats to enter a goat barn on a hot August day...but I always found it was worth the sacrifice.

Of course, you could say the same thing for the swine barns, but there was something magical about the way a pig could be turned into Cinderella by a good showman.

Give them a good sudsy bath, dust a little baby talc on the places that were supposed to be white and use a little stove polish on the parts that were supposed to be black, and presto—the pride of the sty!

Just a few steps away was the judging pavilion. If you were in luck, they'd be judging one of the junior classes for FFA or 4-H youngsters.

71

Never mind the livestock—the real show was on the faces of the kids. They were proud, scared, hopeful and nervous all at the same time as they jockeyed to catch the judge's eye at the magic moment when their animal was posed just right.

Months and months of attention, training and grooming had gone into that one moment. There was an awful lot riding on it.

I vividly remember the year I took a Poland China pig to our county fair. In my eyes, she was the fairest porker in the land. I had midwifed her into the world, kept her in a snug box behind the kitchen cookstove that cold March night and tried to teach her a few social graces as she grew.

At the fair, I slept on a bale of straw beside her pen, gave her the complete beauty treatment in the morning and, with pounding heart, took her into the show ring.

Alas, she was spurned by the judges. My heart was broken, and perhaps hers was, too. But we got over it.

Win or lose, lunchtime was always a fair highlight. I don't know about you, but I never had a sit-down meal at a fair in my life. And hang the cholesterol—that was the day to go for corn dogs and funnel cakes and every other greasy goody you could find at the food wagons.

There were plenty of sweets, too. The summer I discovered Drumsticks ice cream cones, I spent $1.10 on them in a single day…at 10¢ apiece.

While my sister and I savored the flavors of fair food, Mom and Dad usually headed for the exhibit buildings, where rows of gleaming mason jars, meticulously packed with perfect

string beans and tomatoes, were on display. Elsewhere there were cakes and pies and jams and jellies, zealously guarded by the ladies who had produced them. A blue ribbon at the county fair—or, better yet, the state fair—meant neighborhood bragging rights for years.

Later, Dad would mosey over to the agricultural exhibit building to size up the 10-ear samples of field corn and entries in the wheat, oats and soybean competitions. Every year he vowed to enter some samples of his own, but he never got around to it.

Meanwhile, my sister and I rode the tilt-o-whirl and the Ferris wheel and the bumper cars, working our way up to the really scary stuff.

In between rides, we'd watch lanky farm boys trying to knock over milk bottles with baseballs, hoping to win a panda bear and impress their girlfriends.

We'd also stand and listen to the pitchman outside the sideshow tent. His entreaties were awfully repetitive, but every so often he'd bring out a few examples of the "freakish" wonders to be revealed inside—strange specimens such as the bearded lady, the alligator man or the "world's tallest midget".

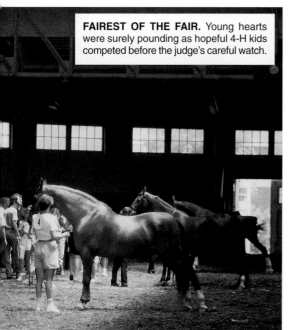

FAIREST OF THE FAIR. Young hearts were surely pounding as hopeful 4-H kids competed before the judge's careful watch.

I desperately wanted to go in...but not badly enough to face my dad's wrath if he found out what I'd wasted my money on.

Over in the grandstand area, the harness races were in progress. Nowadays, it's more likely stock cars or monster tractor pulls.

I know—time marches on...but I still prefer the harness races.

Finally, when the sun set, a whole new fair began to dazzle our eyes as strings of colored lights turned the grounds into a sort of Times Square on the prairie. That's when we all got together and headed for the grandstand show.

One year, Mom and Dad let me bring a buddy along. The show was entertaining enough, but my pal regularly went off into gales of hysterical laughter.

"What's so funny?" Dad asked him.

"Just watch," my friend

BEST OF FIELD. City folks might not see a kernel of importance when it came to awarding ribbons for field corn, but the farmers were all ears.

said. "There's a man at the side of the stage who keeps holding up a big sign that says APPLESAUCE."

Well, my friend was close—but what the sign really said was APPLAUSE. For the rest of the night, it was my dad who guffawed whenever that sign went up!

Finally, after the grandstand show was over, instead of fighting traffic in the parking lot, we'd take one last stroll through the animal barns. The lights were low. A few exhibitors were sitting on bales of straw, trading tales in soft voices. Others were unrolling their sleeping bags.

All the glitter and gabble and garishness of the nighttime fair seemed a thousand miles away...and so did the drought and 10¢-per-bushel corn, a mounting load of debt and lots of other worrisome things we faced during the Depression.

Fairs were magic, and many of them still are today. Maybe it's because fairs attract real people—the ones who smile, are quick to shake hands and look proud of their children. They don't think the county fair is corny at all. And neither do I. 🚕

Doesn't Anyone Write Anymore?

Gail Denham

The day after Christmas (when the holiday excitement had calmed down a bit) was always a hallowed time. That's when I could take serious inventory of my loot and begin to enjoy it.

Best of all, there was an entire, lovely, empty week ahead before school resumed.

Still, an ominous cloud hung over my world. The problem was that thank-you notes *had* to be written for every single gift from the aunts, uncles and grandparents.

Mom was relentless about this and only allowed a 7-day grace period, not subject to negotiation. If you hadn't written your notes by the end of that week, the unacknowledged gift disappeared into her closet. So, I wrote thank-you notes.

I devoutly hope no one ever saved them, because they were

pitiful. And I hope none of the relatives compared my notes, because they were basically a form letter.

"THANK YOU VERY MUCH FOR THE NICE (NAME OF GIFT). IT IS EXACTLY WHAT I WANTED. LAST NIGHT WE WENT TO SEE A MOVIE WITH NELSON EDDY AND JEANETTE MACDON-ALD. HE WAS A CANADIAN MOUNTIE AND RODE A BLACK HORSE. IT WAS SWELL. I HOPE YOU ARE WELL. I AM, TOO.

You see, the message wasn't really important. What mattered was the fact that you had written and sent a card. Mom was firm in her belief that writing thank-you notes was a crucial part of good manners.

Nowadays, such graciousness has pretty much vanished, along with nearly all other forms of letter writing. Instead, we pick up the phone.

On Christmas day, the calls go back and forth between our family. The grandchildren line up at the other end to say their thank-you's while Mother stands nearby to prompt them. "Hello, Grandpa. Thank you for the...uh...(*"Sweater!"* Mom hisses.)...uh, *sweater.* It's really neat."

Well, you can't fault them for not recalling your gift. After all, they've just finished opening dozens of them. Since time began, the old saying is reversed with kids: It's the *gift* and not the thought that counts.

We truly do enjoy hearing their voices, but those scrawled, smudged, laboriously printed little notes are precious, too.

One of my kids asked if I had a fax machine here at home. When I told her I had no need for one, she said the grandchildren would love to fax letters to my computer. Ah, the times, they are a-changing.

Call me an old crock if you will, but I believe thank-you notes are a part of good manners. A large chunk of the world, however, appears to be too busy for the social niceties.

There's been a lot of hand-wringing lately about how kids, and even adults, can't read or write. Only if you've been teaching recently (as I have) can you fully grasp how bad the problem is. People who have just a vague acquaintance with spelling and grammar are walking off the platform with university diplomas!

Someone said that reading is the act of thinking. So is writing, only more so. I think that part of our current illiteracy mess has come about because we've stopped being letter writers. It's just too easy to pick up the phone.

Long ago, letters were a kind of glue that helped hold families together. For example, Mom had an uncle who, as a young man, moved away from Illinois to settle in a mythic place called California. He didn't really "leave" the family, though, because he was a prolific writer of letters.

Several times a year, Mom's tribe would be enlightened by his eloquent tales of life in the Golden West. His letters were so vivid that none of us felt an urgent need to visit the state. We knew everything we needed to know about it.

Those were the days when lots of people had special stationery and envelopes. Children were given paper with cute little kittens or puppies frolicking at the top. Teenage girls seemed to prefer violets or lilacs overprinted on pink paper.

Successful men went for engraved, watermarked bond paper that had a businesslike crispness. Proper women proclaimed their high station in life with embossed, monogrammed stationery. You revealed a lot about yourself by the stationery you used.

Besides writing letters, people used ornate note cards. Some were minor works of art with embossing and lace edges. After a party or dinner at someone's home, etiquette demanded that you send a card with a short handwritten note of thanks.

Today we pick up the phone the next day and say thanks for a wonderful time, and can I please have your recipe for that marvelous butterscotch-lamb soufflé?

You should see the letters and stories sent to *Reminisce* by our readers. The first thing you notice is that they come from people who *like* to write. They grew up in a time when spelling and grammar counted.

One letter almost made me jump out of my skin. The penmanship looked exactly like my mother's! Was this a note from the grave?

No, but it was from a lady of Mom's generation—back when elegant penmanship was one mark of a well-brought-up lady. Now there's another lost art!

Speaking of Mom, she kept every single letter I ever sent her. They filled a big box with "Coe, Gaulrapp Turkey Farms" printed on the side. (I hope there was no connection in her mind between turkeys and my letters.)

In recent months I finally knuckled down and went through those hundreds of letters. They're a whole record of my life. (Or, at least my biased and self-important version of it, from the time I was 14.)

The first letter was from Kansas City, where I was taking part in a national event for high school students. I'd never ventured more than 50 miles from home, and it was my first long stay in a big city, more or less on my own.

The overall tone can best be described as "gee whiz!" But I was prudent enough to *not* report sailing paper airplanes and dropping water bombs from the sixth floor of the old Robert E. Lee Hotel.

Then there are the letters from college and of my adventures in the military and letters covering all the years that followed—until I, too, settled for using the telephone.

Enjoyable as telephone chats are, you can't wrap them in ribbon, put them in a turkey farm box and save them to re-read decades later.

People communicate on a whole different level in letters than they do face-to-face or on the telephone. We tend to write about the stuff that *really* matters.

Ewing Galloway

WHAT TO SAY? Sometimes it took all the concentration a kid could muster to figure how best to thank Auntie for that swell sweater!

I learned that when I came across some of Dad's letters that Mom saved. There were only a few of them, because Mom and Dad weren't apart all that much in their 50-plus years of marriage.

Dad was never a demonstrative man, so it simply didn't occur to me that he and Mom were actually *in love.*

His letters stunned me. I discovered a part of the man that I had never even known. Even in his 60s, he wrote whimsical, affectionate, boyish love letters to my mother.

It brought home the simple

truth that letters, to many of us, are a way around our shyness or inability to express our feelings face-to-face.

I find it excruciatingly difficult to sit across the dining room table and tell a son or daughter how much I admire them as adults. I have much less trouble doing it in a letter, although I don't do it nearly often enough.

Are we faced with future generations who have no appreciation for the joy of writing and receiving letters, whether they are happy, sad or funny? Is the Future World to be nothing but faxes and e-mail?

Well, maybe there's hope.

I have a 20-something grandson who writes long, witty, slightly goofy letters that always brighten my day. He tries hard to be blasé and sophisticated, but he still gives me a glimpse of the world as seen through young eyes not beclouded by cynicism and bitterness.

When his sister finished college, she, too, turned into a letter writer. Hers are so newsy and candid that we feel like we are sharing her tumultuous life.

Another grandson is just starting high school. On the phone, he's mostly a "yes" and "no" sort of guy, but his letters unmask him as a thinker with a sly wit.

I'll bet there are lots more like them out there. It's possible they don't write because they're waiting for a letter from us. Think about it.

Mom had the right idea, or the "write" idea, if you can stand the pun. She made sure my sister and I learned to enjoy writing letters, even if it did take some gentle "blackmail" in the beginning.

PLEASANT SURPRISE. Being on the receiving end of nice, newsy letters is the best—but you won't get 'em if you don't write 'em!

Chores and Odd Jobs Once Kept Kids *Busy*

Harold M. Lambert

The other day, my 12-year-old grandson and I were visiting on the telephone when he hit me up for $300. "Would this be considered a loan?" I asked. No, indeed. An outright gift.

Whoa! How did he come to confuse me with a government agency? What was going on here?

Well, he said he needed the money for a snowboard, whatever that is, and earnestly explained that this was not a *really good* snowboard—but, he could manage with something inferior. For now, anyhow.

I then gently inquired about the state of his finances. He was broke, he admitted, and saw no prospects of things improving.

I explained that I was in similar shape (as far as not seeing much hope of things improving). Couldn't he perhaps do a few odd chores around the house that would bring in the needed cash? Well, no. He was too busy with other things to do chores. Besides, he needed the snowboard *now*!

THE TASK AT HAND was never too tough for young tykes to handle. Kids then were *used* to doing chores.

My, how times have changed. When I was growing up, you did chores every day and didn't expect to get paid for them. Chores were also the ransom Mom and Dad extracted if I wanted a piece of freedom.

Go fishing down at the creek? Yes, but only after you mow the lawn. Play baseball with the guys at Lincoln Park? Certainly, when you're done washing the storm windows—the same ones you'll help put up tomorrow.

Still, my sister and I didn't regard this as particularly cruel and unusual punishment. It's just the way things ran back then.

In her case, the price of freedom might entail folding laundry or peeling a big pot of potatoes because company was coming or tearing up bread for turkey stuffing.

Or, we both might be sent to the garden to pick peas and then shuck them while sitting out on the back porch steps. I can't think of any important lessons I learned from shucking peas, but I learned that everything you want seems to carry a price.

For farm kids, there wasn't much time for anything *but* chores. There were chores you did before going to school and chores waiting when you came home. There were empty milk cans to lug in from the road and corn to shell with a hand-sheller in the corn crib—which you then had to feed to the chickens. There were eggs to gather and milk to carry to the calves and hay to

IN A LATHER. Girls didn't "bubble over" at the prospect of doing dishes, but that was the price you paid before going outside to play afterwards.

throw down from the mow for the milk cows.

During the Depression, kids were expected to go out and find after-school work or weekend jobs, and the reason was simple: The family needed money!

One popular kid job was selling *Colliers, The Saturday Evening Post,* and *Ladies' Home Companion* magazines door-to-door.

You not only earned a couple of cents per sale, but you also accumulated "Brownie" and "Greenie" points that could be cashed in for a flashlight—or a bicycle, if you sold about a carload of magazines.

In those tough times, not many people could spare even a nickel, so you had to do an awful lot of knocking.

One of my pals came up with an unbeatable, if shady, system. He would hide his supply of magazines under a bush and leave just one copy in his magazine sack.

Then he'd pull his jacket collar up around his neck, put a pitiful look on his face and rap on a door. If the lady of the house declined to buy, the little crook would begin to sniffle.

"Ma'am, this is the last magazine I have left, and my dad won't let me come home until I sell them all. I'm afraid I'll miss supper again tonight."

Who could resist him? After making the sale, he'd trot back to his secret cache, slip one more magazine into his sack and move on to the next house. He was the champion salesman for Curtis Publishing Company in our town and probably became a howling success in the business world.

Other boys got jobs delivering Western Union messages. The company even furnished a bicycle and an official-looking cap. You could also deliver groceries, set pins at the bowling alley, shine shoes or hawk newspapers on busy street corners.

No matter what, you took your week's earnings home to your

mother. If things weren't too tough, she might even give you back a quarter to fritter away on personal luxuries.

One job I would have done without pay was ushering at either of our two local movie houses. Ushers got to wear snappy maroon uniforms with gold trim, carry flashlights and see the movies for free. They had the authority to *shush* rowdies in the audience and even expel them if they wouldn't mind their ways.

Some of those part-time jobs led to permanent careers. An acquaintance in Milwaukee, Wisconsin tells about the day he turned 16. His dad bought him his first pair of long trousers and gave him a dime for streetcar fare. "Go find a job, Louie," he said. "You're a man now."

Downtown, he spotted a sign that read "Office Boy Wanted". He ripped it off the glass, walked up a flight of stairs and asked to see the man in charge.

Louie strode into the man's office and tossed the sign on his desk. "You don't need this anymore," he said. "I'm ready to go to work."

He got the job...and 55 years later retired as secretary/treasurer of the company. That sort of thing really happened in those days. Horatio Alger stories could come true.

For other boys, pumping gas was good part-time work, except when you had to patch flat tires. That was the era of inner tubes, and by the time you worked the tire off the rim, found the hole, repaired it with a Shaler Hot Patch, tested it in a tank of water, then put things back together, you could work up a pretty good sweat.

The born risk-takers sought caddie jobs at the local country club. It was a dicey business because what you earned was strictly up to the golfer. The tightwads tipped 50 cents, but the big spenders might give their caddie $3—or even more if they'd just won an important match.

Girls were expected to get out and

DELIVERING for Western Union was a popular kid's job—and you even got to wear a swell uniform.

find jobs, too. Some worked as waitresses or car hops at the drive-in. My wife clerked in the local bakery and baby-sat. (In those times the baby-sitter was expected to fix meals for the kids, wash dirty dishes and even do some housecleaning.)

When she was a little older, Peg worked in a butcher shop, serving customers during the day and cleaning out the meat cases after closing time. Woe to the butcher today who tries to tell her that a hunk of sirloin is a T-bone.

Other young women clerked at F.W. Woolworth or Kresge's. Some went into the orchards to pick cherries or peaches. In big cities, they might have done seamstress work in the sweatshops.

Oftentimes, kids needed a special work permit to get a job, especially if they were under 16. It wasn't all that rare to lie about your age, and everyone more or less winked at the age requirement because they understood how desperate families were.

Oddly enough, when you look back over all those odd jobs and chores we did back then, you suddenly realize that most of the jobs don't exist anymore.

The grocery doesn't deliver. Western Union has no uniformed lads speeding to your home. Gas stations are self-service. Kenmore or General Electric wash the dishes and do the laundry. Pinsetters were replaced by automatic contraptions years ago, and only a few upper-crust country clubs still have caddies.

We're not far from the day when our newspaper will be "delivered" overnight to our computer screen, so we won't need newspaper carriers. The movie theater shows seven films at once but gets along with one ticket-seller and one usher.

Maybe that's why kids watch so much television and play those mind-numbing video games. Perhaps there aren't as many ways to earn a buck, even when you *are* willing.

Too bad. I certainly did my share of griping about chores and odd jobs, but I also know that every single one taught me stuff that was useful the rest of my life.

I learned the importance of delivering at least a dollar's worth of work for a dollar of pay. I learned to show up on time and get along with people, and I learned to be nice to cranky customers, regardless of how unreasonable they were. I'm still not sure, though, that I learned much from shucking peas.

Puppy Love Was Tender and Tense

Archive Photos/H. Lambert

One of the rewards of writing my recollections for *Reminisce* magazine is that I'll often hear from people I lost touch with decades ago—former friends from the old hometown, college pals, ex-neighbors and nice people I once worked with.

I even received a letter from a lady who said my mother was her first schoolteacher in the one-room country schoolhouse north of Sterling, Illinois!

It was also a happy surprise when one of my grade school classmates dropped me a letter. She wrote about the time that I had presented her with a Hershey bar after she'd been away for the funeral of a beloved relative. I guess we were in the fifth grade at the time.

Now, thinking back, a 12-year-old boy had to be *seriously* in love to give a girl his Hershey bar...and I was. She never knew it, though. I was far too shy to do anything but worship her from afar, select her valentine with special care—and sacrifice a Hershey bar on the altar of devotion.

I even left the Congregational church and joined youth groups at the Lutheran church to which she and her family belonged. But I never could build up the courage to ask her for a date or even tell her I liked her. She was a city mouse and I was but a stammering country mouse. Had she turned me down, my entire life would have been ruined. That's puppy love for you.

Kids today still have crushes, but all the rules have changed. In my day, for example, girls *never* called boys on the telephone.

PUPPY LOVE was better if left a secret, but it was OK to send that really cute boy or girl an extra-nice Valentine.

Instead, they waited (and waited) for the boy of their dreams to phone them. Now my grandsons are hounded with giggly calls from young ladies at all hours. They *pretend* to be annoyed.

The only chance we had to display our interest in someone was when we kids swapped valentines at school, dumping them into a big cardboard box the teacher provided. The popular kids got lots of cards, while the social outcasts received but a few.

My big moment of crisis was at the stationery store. I'd search and search for the perfect valentine card to send to the object of my affection. It proved to be a tricky piece of diplomacy. I wanted her to know I thought she was special, but I had to steer clear of the ones that were too gushy. I probably even signed it "from you-know-who".

After finding just the right card, I'd helter-skelter scoop up another dozen for other classmates without paying much attention to what they said.

After Valentine's Day, the next big sweethearts' occasion was May Day. Dad always used to say that the sap flowed in the spring —in young boys as well as in trees and shrubs. I was just as sappy as the next guy.

Remember May baskets? Mom would save those cylindrical cardboard Quaker Oats containers which, cut in half, made two nice "baskets".

A TUNNEL FOR TWO was the perfect place for couples to relish in a romantic moment.

My sister and I covered ours with crepe paper, attached a pipe-cleaner handle, then filled each basket with popcorn and jelly beans.

As with the valentines, there was always one basket intended for that special person in my heart. I'd add a few more crepe paper ruffles to it, plus an extra dozen jelly beans and a sprig of forsythia to make it more fetching.

When we finished and our 30-odd May baskets sat displayed on the dining room table, it was easy to pick out the ones I had made. They looked like they'd been left out in the rain and then stomped on by a horse. The crepe paper was rumpled and stained with gooey smears of flour-and-water paste, and the handles were twisted and bent, as though afflicted with an advanced case of arthritis.

Meanwhile, my sister's baskets were perfect and looked like... well, like they had been crafted by a *girl*.

On the big day at just about sunset, Mom or Dad would drive us from house to house, the back seat full of May baskets. We'd scamper up to the front porch, deposit our gift near the door, ring the bell and then flee like burglars back to the car.

As we drove away, we'd peer through the back window, hoping to see the object of our affection step outside to pick up our love offering.

And so we went, winding our way up and down the neighborhood streets. (Do you suppose the guy who started United Parcel Service got his idea delivering May baskets?)

Another more permanent way of showing one's affection was to carve hearts and initials on trees.

The truly daring scaled the town water tower and painted the news for everyone in the community to see. Nowadays, of course, the kids use overpasses. I recently saw one overpass spray-job that said "Nancy Loves Jim". Then someone had painted beneath it, "No She Don't!" (Take that, Jim!)

Once word got around that you were "sweet" on someone, however, you risked the shame of having classmates chalk "Wally Loves Wilma" on every sidewalk around school. Then all you could do was pray for rain.

Years ago, childhood romances simmered with the same intensity they do now. Puppy love dates back to when Caveman Og whacked Cavegirl Ogette with a tree branch to show how much he cared.

But kids of my era were on a much shorter leash than now, with strict parent-imposed curfews, fewer cars and neighbors who weren't above peering through the lace curtains to check on your comings and goings.

Fathers came equipped with a secret stopwatch in their head that clicked on the instant you brought their daughters home from a date. When your fond farewells on the front porch lasted too long, the porch light suddenly blazed overhead and her dad scowled through the little glass window in the front door.

Of course, kids always try to stretch curfews to the limit, and then a little beyond. Our family lived on a gravel road in the country, so nighttime traffic was rare. The headlights of cars coming north from Sterling shone right in my parents' bedroom window.

All too aware of this, I took special precautions on nights when I returned home after the dreaded curfew. I'd speed up our '39 Plymouth, flick off the headlights, shift to neutral, turn off the motor and attempt to coast all the way to the garage.

It was tricky business, considering that I had to negotiate a left turn into our lane without throwing gravel or running up on the lawn. But, practice makes perfect and I became a regular Stealth bomber!

I had also charted which steps squeaked and carefully stepped over them as I climbed upstairs in my stocking feet. Somehow, though, Dad always knew to the minute when I had arrived home.

Small towns like ours provided their own unique obstacles to romance. There was always the issue of who *you* liked versus who your mother *thought* you ought to like. Rarely was there a match, because puppy love is blissfully, stubbornly resistant to family feuds or friendships. Remember Romeo and Juliet?

My parents were determined to promote a romance between me and the daughter of their friends in a nearby town. So intent on matchmaking were they, that Dad shelled out a shockingly large amount of money so I could take the young lady to see *Gone with the Wind* and treat her to a soda afterwards.

Well, remember what Rhett Butler says to Scarlett O'Hara at the end of the movie? I think that's how we felt about each other, too. It was our one-and-only date.

Still, the slower pace of romance had lasting dividends. We know a neighbor couple who originally became attracted to each other when they were 8 years old, but didn't marry until they were in their 20s. Now after three wars, three children and two grandchildren, they obviously are still very fond of each other.

My own parents "courted" for many years, but they didn't marry until both were well into their 20s and Dad could move his bride into a brand-new farmhouse.

Puppy love is a wonderful, sleep-robbing, all-consuming, heart-pounding and totally irrational part of growing up. Looking back, I wouldn't have missed it for anything. What sweet agony it was!

Still, I would *never* want to go through it again. After all, it cost me a Hershey bar.

SAPPY YOUNG BLADES who felt "serious" about their affection often carved out a sweetheart's initials in the bark of an old tree trunk.

*H*ow Homes Have Improved ...Or Have They?

The greatest home decorator in history is retired now, and I really miss him.

"Jack" worked the night shift for free and produced dazzling artistic masterpieces to delight us on chilly mornings when we arose.

I'll bet you remember him, too—he was Jack Frost. From late fall through early spring, he created fantasy forests and landscape scenes on every windowpane. They were one-of-a-

SPACIOUS old homes with those big, inviting front porches really don't leave much room for improvement.

kind works of art, best admired as the first rays of the morning sun illuminated the intricate icy patterns.

We'd hurry to gaze at Jack's work because it lasted only until the radiators under the windows heated up and the freshly stoked furnace took the chill out of the house.

Jack Frost's "retirement" coincided with some big changes in homes that came after World War II, particularly the use of storm windows and thermal glass. A recent drive past the farmhouse in northern Illinois where I grew up during the '20s and '30s reminded me of vast differences in what we've come to expect as proper housing.

I have nothing but wonderful memories of that house…but I must admit things have improved a lot.

Back in the days of coal-fired furnaces, folks "banked" the fire on cold nights. That meant heaping in about as much fuel as the furnace would hold and trying to adjust the damper to keep a slow fire going all night.

By morning, the temperature in the house had dropped to somewhere between brisk and brr-rrr-rrr! We'd grab our clothes and scurry to the kitchen, where Mom was making breakfast and the cast-iron cookstove was pumping out some warmth.

Heat didn't remain very long in our house. Like most that were built years ago, it wasn't insulated. The few homes that were had layers of newspaper inside the walls, which you may have discovered if you've ever tried to remodel an old home.

For several years, our "storm windows" were pieces of semi-transparent waxed cloth that we tacked on the outside in November. The material let in a decent amount of light but didn't permit a view of the outdoors. It was like living in an igloo, but it did stop wind and even snow from coming through the poor-fitting window units. (Waking up with a snowdrift on the windowsill beside your bed does not bode well for the day ahead!)

Our view of the great outdoors became a whole lot clearer when Dad did away with the waxed cloth and took the big step of fitting all our windows with storms and screens. That was the good news.

The bad news was that we became married to the semiannual ritual of taking down the storms and putting up screens, then vice versa. Half a day was spent either washing the storm windows or repairing and repainting the screens.

During one of those sessions, my sister's husband-to-be was trying to make a good impression by helping Dad, but he lost his balance coming down the ladder and stepped through a stack of eight screens. Every one ended up with a hole just about big enough for an adult eagle to fly through without mussing his feathers.

My sister did marry the guy, but Dad never got over being nervous when he was around.

Eventually, Dad also replaced our coal stove with a new oil-fired furnace, which kept the house warmer through the night but meant

I could no longer "slide down my cellar door" (as the old song goes).

The switch to oil and gas furnaces made coal chutes and coal bins unnecessary...and also chased away the man who delivered coal, often tediously lugging bushel baskets of the stuff from the street to our coal chute.

During the Depression, when we couldn't afford coal, our farmhouse fuel was corn cobs. They gave off an intense heat but didn't last as long as coal. On below-zero evenings, Dad had to stay up until midnight feeding the furnace. By 6 a.m., the fire had been out for hours and the house was as cold as a meat locker.

Chilly as those early-day homes could be, at least they were quiet. That was because they were built with genuine plastered walls. Remember? Such walls were prone to crack, but they more than made up for that by providing a lot of soundproofing between rooms. (Today's plasterboard walls are so thin that you can hear a mouse twitch his ears two rooms away.)

The homes most of us grew up in had only one bathroom. Maybe the Vanderbilts had 20 bathrooms, but the rest of us got along with one and were grateful it was *inside* the house and not 100 feet out back in the orchard.

In cold climates, one of the more essential bathroom fixtures was the electric or kerosene heater which was turned on just before you hopped into the tub.

I really miss those heaters that made the bathroom so toasty warm. Ours had a copper reflector with a little wire-wrapped ceramic cone in the center. It glowed a cheery cherry-red while toasting your backside as you toweled off.

As nice as indoor plumbing was, though, that single bathroom became the source of more family friction than any other room in the house, especially if the family was large. I have a theory that the first generation of air traffic controllers probably grew up in families with seven kids and a single bathroom. You can just imagine the bickering:

"Mom, she's been in there for 20 minutes and I'll never get to school!"

"Mom, I've got to *go-o-o-o*, right now!"

"Jimmy, get out of that bathroom this instant or the whole family is going to be late for church!"

After growing up in a home like that, keeping 22 assorted aircraft from colliding would be a cinch!

Another household feature seldom seen these days is the milk chute. Gone, too, are the friendly milkmen who used them. Having a reliable milkman was a big improvement over having your own cow. He took away the empty bottles and left newly filled ones, along with containers of cottage cheese, cream and eggs. Show me a cow that could do that!

In the good old days, lots of homes had a "summer kitchen" too, a holdover from Colonial times when indoor cooking was done in the fireplace. Our summer kitchen was in an enclosed back porch where the icebox also stood.

During warm-weather months, Mom cooked out there on a cantankerous, smelly kerosene stove that would erupt like a volcano whenever a pot boiled over. But it sure beat firing up the massive kitchen stove when the thermometer hovered around 100°.

Big eat-in kitchens were the rule then, too. The dining room was used for Sunday dinners and whenever company came, but otherwise it was just a room you walked through on your way to the kitchen.

After World War II, when homes were shrunk to save money, builders began promoting "corridor" kitchens—really a hallway with kitchen cabinets and appliances on both sides. No longer was the kitchen a main hub where the family gathered for three meals a day. Nor was it where homework was done, bills were paid and "family court" convened when necessary.

These days, big kitchens are making a comeback. Perhaps there's hope for the American family yet.

My Grandfather Stevens' home was like many built in the late 1800s, boasting both a "front parlor" and a living room the family used every day.

Front parlors were generally reserved for ceremonial occasions such as pastoral visits, family Christmas gatherings, wedding receptions and wakes. Families who had an upright piano usually kept it here along with their heirloom furniture and bric-a-brac.

All other days of the year, the front parlor was strictly off-limits. Its shades were drawn (so the sun wouldn't ruin the upholstery and curtains) and the sliding pocket door was pulled shut.

In our home, we didn't enjoy the luxury of a parlor, but we did have what was called "the den". It was "den-ier" than most I've seen—barely big enough for two hibernating bears.

Tiny as it was, our den held a daybed, a couple of upholstered "easy chairs", a tiny rolltop desk, Mom's always-busy Singer sewing machine and the tulip-horn radio with its dozens of dials and switches.

The four of us in our family gathered there most evenings. It was also the warmest room in the house, so that's where we headed to thaw out after working or playing outdoors in cold winter weather.

During the summer, our family gathering place was the front porch. It was blissful to sprawl on the "glider" which hung by chains from the ceiling. Gently swaying from side to side, I turned the pages of a favorite book, engrossed in the adventures of Robin Hood and the evil Sheriff of Nottingham.

In the evening, we'd sip freshly squeezed lemonade and enjoy the quiet of the country while fireflies lit up the wheat field and the Milky Way illuminated the clear night sky.

Sure enough, though, some good ideas come back. Now homes have a living room and a family room. The living room is kept neat and tidy for entertaining guests, and the family room is where families *really* live.

There's no question—homes are more livable now, what with central heat, air-conditioning, hot water from the tap and all the rest. But I miss Jack Frost and his ever-new morning art exhibit. I know…I was there.

Don Condon

BEFORE central heat arrived, you worked up your own heat keeping the woodpile stocked and hauling logs to the stove.

$\mathscr{M}$akin' Do' Was
A Way of Life

A COMFORTABLE SIGHT. It was common to see Mother seated at her old treadle sewing machine—often staying up late to finish projects. She could turn feed sacks into high fashion, and any of the leftover scraps were saved for patches or used in quilts.

The other day I noticed a penny on the asphalt of the supermarket parking lot. An old, old reflex made me pick it up, even though my rational mind said there's not a lot you can do with one cent these days.

I can still remember a time in my life when a penny was worth a whole lot more than it is today—you could buy a piece of candy with it, or a penny postcard at the post office.

Back in those days, "found money"—even a penny—was a real stroke of luck. Most times, anyway. Our town harbored an eccentric gentleman who, unobserved, would hide pennies, nickels and even dimes on top of door frames and high window ledges where they couldn't be spotted.

Days later, he'd stand on the sidewalk outside the bank, nonchalantly reach up and run his hand along the window ledge, then let out a happy yell. "Look what I found up there—a nickel!"

Pretty soon everyone in town was checking places where only pigeons roosted, hoping to find hidden treasure. The old man would just watch it all and cackle happily.

Such treasure hunts were part of "makin' do" back in the '30s. Hardly anyone had money to spare, so we did all sorts of things to stretch what little we did have.

My folks were great at makin' do. They were recycling stuff long before it became the environmental crusade it is today.

Take waxed paper, for example. Bread came wrapped in a double layer of good, sturdy waxed paper. The inner wrap was pure white, while the outer wrap was imprinted with the product name, weight and so forth.

When the bread was used up, Mom carefully pulled the wrapper apart, pressed out the creases and stored it to use for our lunch-box sandwiches. One loaf of bread yielded enough waxed paper for four sandwiches.

I expect electricity was a lot cheaper back then, but Dad was still intent on using as little as possible. It was a major offense to walk out of a room and leave a light burning. The first infraction earned you a standard lecture—the famous "Do you think I'm made of money?" speech. The second offense rated a swat on the behind.

Dad also saved wire as hay bales were opened to feed the cattle. He was the Michelangelo of baling wire—there was nothing on the farm he couldn't repair with a length of it. Looking back, I sometimes think our entire farm was held together with used baling wire.

Like everyone else in those times, we did our own shoe repairs. Good all-leather shoes lasted a long time, but eventually holes showed up in the soles, and heels were worn down paper-thin.

CURING sausage was another cure for lean times when folks knew how to stretch out a dollar—and like most anything made at home, it tasted a lot better than store-bought.

If the weather wasn't too sloppy, cardboard insoles worked fine for a few days. Some of the longest-lasting cardboard came from the very box the shoes were sold in.

More permanent repairs could be made with rubber soles and heels purchased from Woolworth's. They were smeared with glue and stuck to the bottoms of your shoes.

Sometimes the glue lost its grip along the front of both shoes, leaving me to walk down the school corridor with my soles making a loud *flap, flap, flap.* One pal said it looked like I had two hungry alligators fastened to my feet.

While dads generally did shoe repairs, most mothers were excellent seamstresses, capable of producing entire wardrobes for their daughters. Cloth from feed sacks was popular, as many readers of *Reminisce* have recalled. It started out stiff and scratchy, but a few washings turned it into comfortable, serviceable clothing.

Every woman had a "rag bag" and a button box, too. The rag bag was handy for emergency patches, and after a few years, it also provided enough makings for beautiful quilts, some of which remain family heirlooms today.

I'm sure many women of my generation can look at those old family quilts and spot small colorful patches of what was left over from an Easter dress they'd worn, a school skirt or mother's favorite apron.

Speaking of patches, does anyone under 60 mend things anymore? Or darn socks? Maybe that's why our grandchildren wear those raggedy blue jeans with gaping holes in the knees—no one in the house knows how to sew on patches!

For years, Mom also made slipcovers for our worn, lumpy sofa. But then Dad decided that upholstering wasn't exactly a high art, so he took to reupholstering our chairs.

His first couple of attempts were short of perfection, but eventually he became an expert at both upholstering and refinishing furniture.

Lots of people even learned to dry-clean their own clothes in the '30s. The only problems were that clothes smelled like naphtha for weeks and the dry cleaning fluid had an ugly habit of exploding while you worked with it.

Most folks made their own soap chips from a big bar of P&G or Fels-Naptha with a paring knife. In 15 minutes or so, you had a bowlful of soap chips ready to dump into the Maytag wringer washer.

Makin' do also meant having a huge garden. Even those who lived in city apartments turned plenty of vacant lots into community gardens during the Depression.

A good garden could feed you in summer and carry the family through much of the winter. You planted enough of everything so there would be an abundance for canning string beans, lima beans, corn, tomatoes, beets, peas, strawberries and raspberries.

Backyard fruit trees provided cherries, apples, peaches, pears and plums, and the grape arbor produced grapes for jelly and grape juice.

Gardens became a big family project. Dad did the spading when the kids were little, but after that, it was up to the kids to rake the soil smooth, plant the seeds, hoe the weeds and pick the crops.

Canning was a summer-long job, with lots of jars to sterilize in a hot July kitchen, beans to snap, peas to shell, carrots and beets to prepare and corn to shuck. But when the work was over, the entire family could admire the shelves of colorful jars, knowing that every person had contributed to the bounty.

Home-canned foods tasted a lot better than what comes from the supermarket today, too—ask anyone from my generation. I'm positive that pies made with our own cherries were far better than any cherry pie I've sampled since…and no commercial product could ever match Mom's strawberry preserves or come close to her canned whole tomatoes.

Looking back on those days, I realize we were being "ecological" without knowing it. We never threw anything away without first considering whether it could be used again. Not much was wasted.

And no one had to preach about doing the right thing for the environment back then—we did it as a matter of sheer necessity. I know…I was there.

A.M. Wettach

LONG ROWS in the garden meant long, hot days toiling in the soil, but a stocked pantry assured families there would be plenty to eat when the days got shorter and colder.

Family Possessions Anchor Us in Time

Grampa Stevens, a tall man with a generous mustache, came to breakfast every morning wearing a three-piece suit, complete with a white shirt and bow tie.

He wasn't dressed up because he was going anywhere important—this was his everyday dress (unless he planned to work out back in his sizable garden).

Grampa spent a lot of time in his high-backed wooden rocker near the front window, where he could watch the world go by, work crossword puzzles and listen to Chicago Cubs and White Sox baseball games on the radio.

A man of strong opinions and unpredictable mood swings, he detested "that idiot in the White House" (FDR), invoked total household silence during *Amos 'n' Andy* broadcasts and would stalk out of the house if he lost at pinochle.

On the other hand, he was always most patient and loving toward his grandchildren.

As was common in those days, Gramma referred to him as "Mr. Stevens" outside the house and "Fred" when the family was around. She doled out to him an allowance of 25¢ a week, which he spent on pipe tobacco, matches and sometimes a nickel bag of lemon drops for me.

I remember his vest was speckled with holes caused by burning embers of Prince Albert that dropped from his pipe. And on the smoking stand next to his chair was a small ceramic container which held the kitchen matches he frequently needed to relight the pipe when it went out during one of his lengthy tirades. In fact, it seemed to me that Grampa didn't smoke tobacco, he "smoked matches".

As you can see in the photos (right), the match holder shows two faces of a mustached man—one a jolly laughing face, the other dour and scowling.

Whenever I sat down to talk with Grampa, I always checked to see which face was pointed in my direction. In my childish mind, it seemed a barometer to the mood he was in at the moment. To me, that match holder *was* Grampa Stevens.

All my memories of the man are wrapped up in that small piece of ceramic, which is now in a glass case here in my den. A picture of Grampa hangs nearby.

Grampa Stevens died in 1942 on my 18th birthday, but that half smiling/half scowling match holder has kept him very much alive in my memories for more than 50 years.

I'll bet every person reading this has similar keepsakes displayed at home. Perhaps it's some jewelry...or a quilt...a piece of furniture...or a bean pot passed along from generation to generation. We cherish these things, I think, because they're anchors to our past.

My wife, Peg, has an ornate porcelain teapot that she particularly prizes. It's the one she used as a small child to prepare tea when her mother was ill in bed.

That teapot probably wouldn't fetch $5 from an antique collector, but it's priceless to Peg. It brings back mind-pictures of a pigtailed little person proud to be taking care of her mother, instead of the other way around.

It's almost magic the way these inanimate objects contain so many rich and important memories. One look at them instantly brings back warm images of people we loved and fun times we enjoyed back in the good old days.

Maybe that's how the legends about the genie in the bottle got started...except the wishes that these relics grant us are memories we never want to lose.

In our entry hall at home, there's a little wooden table with a marble top. Just right for holding a bouquet of flowers, it stands beneath a mirror that visiting ladies can use to be sure their hairdos are properly in place.

When you look closely at this stand, you can clearly see it didn't come from an expensive furniture store. There are obvious imperfections in the ornamental carving done on the black walnut.

It's a well-traveled little table, made by some unknown craftsman, probably in Hagerstown, Maryland. In 1860, it came down the Ohio River on a flatboat, part of the household goods belonging to Jacob and Margaret Kornhaus. They lived in Indiana and then Illinois.

Later, the table was passed along to their daughter, Amanda, whom I came to know as Grandmother Strock. The table sat for years in her "front parlor", where special guests were entertained.

Then it went to my parents, where it stood in their living room near the front door. Eventually I ended up with it and carried it along as we moved to Missouri, New Jersey and Nebraska. Here in northern Florida, it's still doing its job of welcoming guests.

I wish I could sit down and have a chat with that little table. What family stories it could tell!

Almost without fail when I'm visiting someone's home, they'll proudly call my attention to their own special treasures like that table.

"Let me show you the belt buckle and buttons from Great-Grandfather's Civil War uniform...step into the bedroom and see the little bedside lamp that once belonged to my beloved grandmother...look at this McGuffey Reader that Grandpa used in the one-room country school he attended."

To unsentimental people, such stuff is quickly dismissed as trash. All it does is get in the way of the pristine decor worked out by some pricey interior designer.

I'll admit that sometimes the line between trash and treasure is quite fine. After all, you can step into any antique store and find aisle after aisle of the same stuff all of us have saved.

Take old license plates. Many restaurants wanting to create a nostalgic atmosphere have walls covered with them, along with butter churns and cherry-pitters and other artifacts of days gone by. But their license plates didn't come off the blue 1939 Plymouth that was the first car I ever drove.

Their vintage tags bring back no memories of trips to the roller rink in nearby Dixon or of double-dating for the senior prom or of the tongue-lashing I got from Dad when I imprudently mentioned that the family car ran nicely at 70 mph. (Gosh, I thought he'd be thrilled!)

No, it's not the object, it's the memories that are somehow locked inside.

You can pick up ancient gold pocket watches in most antique shops or flea markets these days. Some of them still keep accurate time. But I know neither of my sons would prize them the way they do the one that Mom gave Dad when they were married, or the one that once belonged to their great-grandfather, Samuel Strock.

Many *Reminisce* readers have gotten into the wonderful hobby of tracing their ancestral roots. Genealogy is fascinating, even when you stumble across the occasional family black sheep. It's good to know where we came from and how we became who we are.

Ceramic match holders, gold watches, quilts and old license plates are a form of genealogy, too. They're history you can hold in your hands or put inside a glass display case. They're special safe deposit boxes filled with memories.

A while back, Peg and I moved into a smaller home, so we decided to have a garage sale. It was high time to get rid of a lot of stuff we'd lugged around during many moves, but now the moment of truth was at hand: What was treasure and what was trash?

Did I really *need* to keep 50-some years of license plates? Of course not. Well...except for one or two from the old Plymouth and another from the 1930 Willys that had preceded it.

And then there were those old wedding gifts that had never been used—and never would be. They had collected no patina of memories, so they went on the sales table.

It turned out to be fairly easy sorting trash from treasure. However, I confess to putting up a spirited defense on behalf of a truly ugly ceramic cockatoo flower holder.

I have no clue about its history, except that Mom always kept it on the little marble-top hall table that traveled down the Ohio River.

HEIRLOOM books, furniture, bric-a-brac and hand-made quilts prove to be favorite family mementoes.

Maybe Dad won it at a carnival when they were dating. Or possibly it was a wedding present. Wherever it came from isn't important. To me, it's an anchor to my past and the home I grew up in.

It just didn't seem right to get rid of it, even though we've never found a use for the gaudy thing. Peg graciously agreed to spare it on the condition that it never leave the bookcase here in the den...unless we ever have another garage sale.

Trash or treasure? I've discovered the distinction is clear. If there's a good memory hidden inside, it's treasure.

How else could I see, again and again, Grampa Stevens scratch a kitchen match, rekindle his pipe, contentedly puff out a cloud of blue smoke and hastily brush glowing crumbs of tobacco off his pockmarked vest?

I know, I was there...and every day I look at these treasures, I'm there again.

Family Heirlooms Help Recall Our Past

MEMORIES HANDED DOWN. When Mom passes along her antique china or silver to a son or daughter, she's really giving vivid "reminders" of many special family meals.

Like many people our age, Peg and I have to do a lot of traveling to visit children and grandchildren. They're scattered all across the United States, from California to Texas to Minnesota, as well as Wisconsin and Missouri.

But our private joke when we plan one of these visit-the-kids adventures is, "Let's go visit our furniture".

That's because in the slow process of downsizing to a cozy home that's the right size for the two of us, we've disposed of lots of furniture.

Most of it was welcomed by our children, but we've discovered that furniture, just like former homes, holds memories that are very dear to us.

I expect *my* parents felt the same way, too. When I returned from World War II and resumed college as a married person, our furniture inventory was zero...a precise match with our bank account.

Mom and Dad came to the rescue, bequeathing to us what had been the guest-room double bed and matching dresser. It was nothing to brag about even when new, because Dad firmly believed a guest room should never be *too* comfortable, lest visitors stay overly long.

Time had not improved either the bed or dresser. Nevertheless, they served us well during our starting-out years—despite an annoying habit the bed had of coming apart with no provocation in the middle of the night and dumping us on the floor with a bone-jarring jolt.

Eventually, Mom and Dad also gave us a splendid maple cabinet and later a handmade walnut table with a marble top that had belonged to my grandmother.

Whenever Mom came to visit, she couldn't resist gently touching the maple cabinet as she walked by, as though it was giving off secret and precious memories stored in the wood itself. Dad, once again, would relate how the little table came down the Ohio River on a flatboat, then traveled in a horse-drawn wagon up to Illinois.

Now I know how they felt. It happens to me whenever we visit my oldest child in Houston. In Dianna's breakfast nook are the round maple table and matching chairs our family used for most of our meals. Sitting at it, I see my children as kids again…gobbling down cornflakes before the school bus arrived, apprehensive about a geography test scheduled that day or excited about a class trip to the zoo.

But mostly I remember our suppers, when everyone took turns telling their adventures of the day. (I was under firm orders to keep things light and resist my fatherly impulses to become a prosecuting attorney when a tiff with a teacher or a bad grade was mentioned.) Deal with problems later. Meals were to be enjoyed, not dreaded.

Later in the evening, that same table was where we tried to help with homework problems. Well, most of them. I never did get the hang of the "new math" popular then.

Dianna also has a special family treasure. It's an elegant golden oak Regina music box. It sits atop a matching cabinet that houses over 100 16" steel discs, which play everything from *Listen to the Mocking Bird* to excerpts from *Lohengrin* and even a couple of Sousa marches. Collectors have offered a lot for it, but nowhere near what it's worth in memories.

The music box belonged to my grandmother and sat in an alcove off her living room. As a small child, it was the benign blackmail that kept me from becoming too rambunctious or whiny. "If you're real good, you can play two pieces on the music box before you leave," Gramma would say.

What worked for Gramma also worked for me a generation later. By strict family tradition, the music box has been passed down from oldest child to oldest child, so I know someday grandson Tim will tell *his* children how Grampa only let him play it when he had been very, very good.

Two years ago, we ate our Christmas feast in the home of a daughter in Milwaukee. The dining room holds the table and chairs that were in the home from which all the kids left the nest and flew off to start their own lives.

Sitting around that table almost brought more memories than my heart could handle—all those happy years when my daughter and her brothers and sisters turned into young adults before my eyes ...and of the Christmas dinners.

My mind filled with images of Mom and Dad, supremely happy, surrounded by their beloved grandchildren as they posed for the annual Christmas photo. (Like most dads, I was the official photographer and never appeared in a single one of them. Future generations will incorrectly deduce that my kids grew up fatherless.)

At one time or another, that table was host to all my favorite people—Mom and Dad, sister Mary, Aunt Grace, Uncle Earle and dozens of good friends. I can see them all and hear fragments of our happy conversations.

At son Fred's home, I can revisit two special chairs, originally a gift from a rich aunt to my grandmother, then passed along to my mother and eventually to me. The chairs graced our living room as I grew up and were the only "grand" furniture we had in the '30s.

One was a platform rocker, and its matching mate was of the conventional four-legged variety. They were on the fragile side, so heavy-set guests were gently steered to sturdier chairs. Both were made of rosewood with inlaid accents of ivory on the arms and the chair back. The upholstery was a rich tapestry fabric.

"Aunt Annie's chairs" had once graced a mansion on Fifth Avenue in New York, allegedly just a door or two away from a Vanderbilt home. (Alas, while Aunt Annie's chairs passed along to the family, none of her considerable wealth did.)

I regarded those chairs with considerable awe, in light of their high society pedigree. Was it possible that a Vanderbilt or Rockefeller actually sat in one? And how did the chairs feel about finding themselves in our humble farm home?

Whenever Gramma Stevens came to visit, she usually sat in the platform rocker, perhaps to get in touch with her own private memories. I can't resist doing the same thing, because when I sit in one of them I'm again back in my childhood, listening to *Vic and Sade, Fibber McGee and Molly,* Edgar Bergen and Charlie McCarthy, or Fred Allen on our Silvertone radio.

On our most recent visit to son David in Minneapolis, we put up the Ping-Pong table that had been in our home while he was growing up. Instantly, I was transported to a former basement, where my sons and I played feverish games with such intensity that a newcomer would have sized us up as mortal enemies.

After Dave and I worked up a serious sweat battling each other again, you probably can guess how full my heart was when I introduced grandson Brian to the game.

The only furniture missing on these visits is the stuff from our early child-raising days. Those were the years when furniture was selected for "childproof" qualities rather than elegance. Tables were veneered with Formica, not teak or mahogany or maple.

Most of the bedroom furniture came from unpainted furniture stores and was designed to be repainted from time to time, rather than lovingly preserved with wax and polish.

We weren't buying heirlooms—just durable stuff that could withstand little savages and their toys. When it was finally carted off by the junk man, no sentimental tears were shed.

"Let's go visit our furniture" doesn't mean we aren't eager to see the kids and grandchildren. It means we again look forward to visiting all those hand-me-downs...saturated with the history of generations and absorbing more with each day.

Supper at the Table Served Families Well

Linda Cyers/RP

PLEASE PASS down the stories! When folks sat at the table for supper, kids enjoyed hearing Mom and Dad's family lore, which also taught valuable lessons. This 1956 shot was shared by *Reminisce* reader Linda Cyers—her husband is the cute big-eyed baby.

A popular mystery these days is who, or what, is to blame for the breakdown of the American family.

Unlike cars that break down, you can't issue a factory recall and bring all the "broken" families back to the dealership for repairs. And there's pretty good evidence that another federal or state Department-of-Something-or-Other won't provide any solutions.

We have no shortage of speculation as to what went wrong, but I'd like to toss my own theory into the hat: *The downfall of the American family as we knew it can be traced directly to the invention of the TV tray.*

I know—it sounds odd—but just hear me out. Before the invention of the TV tray, where was the family at suppertime? Of course! We were all sitting around the kitchen or dining room table. Mom, Dad, Sis, Bud, and right beside the table, tail thumping the floor, was loyal old Rover.

Today, come suppertime, where is the family? Well, Sis and Bud are probably sitting on the floor in the family room, plates on their laps, while Mom and Dad are in their Barcalounger recliner chairs with TV trays beside them. And everyone is watching television.

That's how it is, unless both Mom and Dad are away on business trips or working a second job at Wal-Mart or sacking groceries at Albertson's. If Mom and Dad are lucky enough to be home, Sis has gone to her ballet lesson and Bud is playing Little League baseball.

The problem is families don't get together much as families anymore, particularly around the supper table. There just isn't enough time.

Okay, I know what you're saying. There are still lots of families that share the supper hour. And not having meals together

doesn't explain *everything* that's wrong—but stick with me a little longer.

Some of my very best memories of growing up center around family meals we shared, especially at suppertime. (A note for city folks: On the farm, the evening meal was called *supper*. We ate *dinner* at noon, which was the big meal of the day. For years I was a little uneasy when invited to another home for "dinner". Should I arrive at noon, or did they mean 7 in the evening?)

Our family always sat around the oilcloth-covered table in the kitchen. The dining room table was reserved for three things: sorting laundry, doing homework and (very rarely) when company came for a meal.

Many of the useful and truly important things I know today were learned at our kitchen table, where we lingered long after the plates were scraped clean.

I found out about my ancestors there. Mom would share her memories of the Stevens side of the family and tell what it was like growing up in "my day and age".

I discovered how Grampa Stevens worked as a cabinet maker in a hearse factory, back when funeral carriages were ornately carved vehicles painted jet black and drawn by a team of horses. He worked 12 hours a day, 6 days a week, and walked 3 miles to the factory.

In his "spare" time he tended a huge garden which was critical to feeding his family of five kids. Mind you, Mom was telling these tales in the dismal days of the Depression, but she was remembering how much *worse* things had been 30 years earlier!

She also stressed how important an education was and how she had attended Dekalb Normal School for 2 years to get her teaching certificate...against her father's strenuous objections.

Then, at age 20, she got a job teaching 15 students in a one-room schoolhouse. Two of the boys were bigger than she was, so I asked how my 5'2" mother kept them in line. "It was no problem," she briskly answered. "Their parents saw to that."

The first year, Mom walked from home—4 miles on a gravel road, regardless of rain, sleet or blizzards. She arrived before the students so she could start a fire, pump water, chase a snake out of the schoolhouse or do whatever else was necessary.

Now stop a minute and think about what I was learning. It

was a lot more than family history. What I really learned was that life might be tough, but you could have what you wanted if you tried hard enough. Part of the key was a good education.

Dad, meanwhile, was a regular library of legends about the Strock family. His branch was a quarrelsome tribe that traced its roots back to 1757, when a 9-year-old arrived from Germany and was immediately indentured to a man near Philadelphia to pay for his boat passage. Essentially, he was a slave to this harsh man until he reached 21.

He also told how his grandmother had come down the Ohio River on a flatboat, then walked over land with her family to eventually end up in Illinois as a pioneer settler.

Dad loved to share his experiences from World War I. It had been the adventure of his life. He entered the Army at Camp Grant, Illinois at the height of the great flu epidemic sweeping the country. If you lived through Camp Grant, you had little to fear from the Hun.

From there he went to Kansas City, then a camp in Georgia and finally to Fort Dix, New Jersey before boarding a ship for France.

What an experience for a lad who'd never set foot outside his county! Dad didn't have a high regard for the French, but all he saw of France was the rural countryside. The old song about "how you gonna keep 'em down on the farm after they've seen Paree" didn't mean much to him, because he never saw "Paree".

Dad's big regret in life was that his education stopped at the eighth grade. He started high school three times only to be pulled out by his father, who didn't think an education was important for farming.

Dad did manage to educate himself over the years by subscribing to a half dozen magazines and checking out two or three books every Wednesday night at our local Carnegie library.

Dad also remembered hearing a terrible clatter coming up the road when he was a youngster. It was a noise like none he'd ever heard before and turned out to be a "horseless carriage," the first in our town. He had seen the future, but scarcely realized it at the time.

In fact, he had a front row seat for most of the astounding advances that tumbled out during this century.

So, my sister and I learned a lot of important stuff after the dishes were cleared from the table. But it wasn't all one-sided.

We were gently quizzed about our own activities of the day. How were we doing in geography? Were we ready for the next arithmetic test? Why didn't we like our teacher, and what should be done to improve things?

The latter subject was a risky one, because Mom and Dad were in solid agreement that the teacher was *always* right. Always! And if we were punished at school, we were punished again at home. There was no sense in appealing the verdict or trying to explain our side. We didn't *have* a side. The teacher was right.

The supper table was also the proper tribunal for decisions you needed. You didn't go to Mom and Dad separately, trying to play one off against the other. "Dad said it was okay" was not a bargaining chip; it was a serious crime.

Too often, the after-supper conversation turned to the grim subject of economics. Dad and Mom didn't just tell us we couldn't have a new pair of shoes. They took the time to explain *why* we couldn't. It didn't provide new shoes, but at least we knew the reason.

My sister and I also learned table manners and limited social graces. We were taught the difference between right and wrong, and I recall the Golden Rule being mentioned more than once. We were encouraged to set goals and told again and again that anything worth having would take hard work and persistence.

Mom and Dad made it clear we must *never* bring shame upon the family. It was critical that everyone in the family, including grandparents, aunts, uncles and cousins, be proud of us. We had a family obligation to excel at everything we did.

School helped prepare my sister and me to make a living. The supper table sessions taught us the proper way to *live*.

I refuse to believe such fundamental values can be learned watching *Wheel of Fortune* while eating off of a TV tray.

When Families Made Music Together

All of my children and grandchildren find it hard to believe there was a time when you didn't need a wall full of electronic equipment to fill the house with music. They've become accustomed to music on demand since nowadays

Ewing Galloway

TICKLING the ivories brought laughter to everyone in the house before modern-day stereos entered the scene.

you can tune in dozens of radio stations playing everything from classical to country, religious to rap, Top Ten to Golden Oldies.

And if you still can't find what you want, just slip in a CD that sounds so real, it's like listening to a live performance in your living room. What an improvement over Grampa's crank-up Victor Victrola, with a wooden needle cut from a thorn apple tree!

Some of today's music is wonderful, some is terrible and most of it lies somewhere in between. But it's always there and it's always effortless.

Youngsters find it hard to imagine a time when families made their own music—and had fun doing it. They're almost embarrassed when I tell them about our Sunday night sing-alongs with Mom at the piano. *How corny!*

But lots of families did it, gathering around the Story & Clark or Knabe upright piano to join voices in singing the latest popular hits as well as the old favorites. We'd warble *Red Sails in the Sunset, The Isle of Capri, Deep Purple, Carolina Moon, Chapel in the Moonlight* and other current tunes. Then we'd finish up with some of Mom and Dad's favorites from their younger days... *There's a Long, Long Trail a-Winding, Irish Lullaby* and *Roses of Picardy.*

It was fun. It was free. And it was something the whole family could enjoy *together.* We made music part of our everyday lives back then. Lots of families did. You could walk around the block on a warm summer evening and hear family choruses coming from window after open window.

I can't think of any other single thing that brought Mom and Dad as much joy as music. Nor can I think of a type of music they *didn't* love. My sister and I were lucky to grow up in a home like that.

Although it was a major sacrifice, Mom saw to it that both of us kids received piano lessons at an early age. I'll never, ever forget the lady who taught me. She was a tiny, grim woman who lived in a little cottage with perpetually drawn curtains. The inside was so dark that you had to be wary of bumping into furniture or one of her several cats.

Her piano was in the dining room, and the sole source of light was a reading lamp sitting atop the instrument. I'd give the piano seat a few whirls so my legs could reach the pedals and then go through the lesson assigned last week.

Meanwhile she sat, nearly invisible, outside the small circle of light. She was of the school that insisted you play with perfectly rigid wrists parallel to the floor. To encourage the stiff-wrist technique, she placed a rubber eraser on each of my wrists. Should an eraser fall off, punishment was swift and immediate. Out of the darkness, fast as a striking cobra, would come a ruler that delivered a stinging blow to the offending wrist.

(Even today, six decades later, both my wrists are stiff as boards as I sit here typing. You could balance a long-stemmed crystal goblet filled to the brim with water on each wrist and nary a drop would be spilled. The fear that her spirit lurks nearby, ruler at the ready, persists.)

Remember that great musical show, *The Music Man?* I don't know what inspired Meredith Wilson when he wrote it, but an honest-to-goodness Music Man came to our town when I was a fourth-grader.

Unlike his Broadway counterpart, our Music Man wasn't a charlatan. His name was Carroll Parkinson, and he and his family promoted "The Parkinson System of Music". The fact that they were successful during the depths of the Depression is great testimony both to the system and their salesmanship.

After receiving the blessing of the local school system, Mr. Parkinson set up talent tests for every interested schoolkid. Fortunately, you didn't have to be a budding Heifetz or Paderewski to pass the test...even I was deemed to have promise as a musician.

After checking my teeth and fingers and ability to tell a high note from a low one, Mr. Parkinson decreed that I was destined to become a trumpet virtuoso. Long-armed kids were steered toward trombones. The tone-deaf became drummers.

Amazingly, the only rich kid to take the talent test was pronounced a natural for the bassoon...an instrument that just happened to be awfully expensive.

I know you'll not be stunned to learn that the Parkinsons also

HIGH MILEAGE FROM MUSIC. *Reminisce* reader Owen Carpenter of Tucson, Arizona shared this 1955 slide of his dad playing the tuba in a July 4th parade. George began playing this instrument in 1898 at age 14 and continued off and on for 60 years.

sold trumpets, trombones, saxophones, bassoons and every other instrument needed for a proper band.

All that stood between me and musical greatness was the $30 needed for a trumpet. That was in 1935, the year when Dad's dawn-past-dark farming labors would result in a $400 loss after the drought, bugs, hail and various other disasters were through with him. But he and Mom somehow came up with the money. So did lots of other parents, at a time when only the fortunate had jobs—and the jobs paid just two or three dollars a day.

The single most memorable event of my boyhood was when Mr. Parkinson arrived at our door carrying a shiny black, pebble-grained leather case with chromium hinges and clasps. I'd never seen anything so grand!

He opened the case and there it was, softly cradled in a purple velvet nest like the crown jewels of some mythic emperor—a gleaming trumpet with mother-of-pearl keys and a golden bell. It was so beautiful I was afraid to touch it.

Mr. Parkinson made deliveries to 40 or 50 other homes in town and a schoolteacher, Gunnar Benson, was named conductor. (Bless him, we rediscovered each other through *Reminisce* and exchange letters every now and then.)

Thanks to the tireless efforts of the Music Man, Sterling had its very own school band. It started out loud and bad, but the patient Mr. Benson gritted his teeth and turned us into a source of pride for parents and grandparents.

Dedicated band mothers soon decided we needed uniforms. They raised funds through a giant bake sale, using the money to buy material which they painstakingly sewed into handsome capes of royal blue with gold satin linings. They even turned out jaunty blue berets for everyone.

After donning those capes over our basic uniform of white duck pants, white shirts and black clip-on bow ties, we were the proudest small-town band on the face of the earth!

We learned to march to our music and even maintain reasonably straight ranks and files. What a thrill to lead the Fourth of July parade through town...or tune up on the bandstand in Lawrence Park on a Sunday afternoon as our families dragged park benches near for a choice spot. Hey, this was show business! And we were the show!

Eventually an orchestra was formed, too, and Dad scraped up the money to buy my sister a second-hand violin. If you peeked inside the hole beside the strings, you could see a yellowed piece of ancient parchment with the maker's name written on it. Dad harbored hopes that he'd acquired a genuine Stradivarius.

Years later when the paper finally came unglued and slipped out, we learned that the violin had been made by someone in Newark, New Jersey.

So now the house was filled with music every day, my sister diligently sawing away on her violin and me doing compulsory exercises on the trumpet as a relentless metronome ticked out the tempo. No wonder Dad seemed to be spending more time in the fields!

But there was a good side, too. Eventually our family sing-alongs became a piano-violin-trumpet trio, with Dad's bold baritone blending in with Mom's soprano voice. What joyous times they were!

Back then, amateur entertainment of all sorts drew enthusiastic crowds. Parents looked forward to school concerts as a source of joy and pride and didn't go just out of a sense of duty.

Today's easily available, high-quality entertainment has raised our standards, no doubt about it. Once you've heard Pavarotti in concert, it's hard to be impressed by a local 15-year-old tenor.

I am truly grateful for our abundance of musical riches. But I'm not sure I'd appreciate them nearly as much were it not for those family sing-alongs, the Music Man and Gunnar Benson...or even the little bitty lady with the fastest ruler in town.

Gimme That Old-Time Hearty Cooking

SuperStock

Mom was never one to latch onto newfangled things in a hurry. Take the electric mixer Dad once gave her hoping it would make her kitchen chores easier. She eyed it with vast suspicion and wouldn't use it for *years*.

It was her belief that mixing, creaming or whipping could only be done properly by hand, not with some machine. Besides, she was sure the gadget would whack off her fingers.

Crisco and other "artificial" shortenings weren't allowed in Mom's kitchen, either. A good cook used *lard*, especially if she wanted to be sure she'd get a decent pie crust.

Cake mixes were equally unwelcome. Mom used her "from scratch" recipes, and nothing else would do.

I never tasted a "box cake" growing up, and even after I'd left the nest and taken a job at General Mills (home of Betty Crocker), Mom remained unconvinced.

Yes, she liked things plain and simple, and these days, the more I see of modern foods, the more I think she was right.

This morning, for instance, I breakfasted on flour, barley malt, niacin, thiamin mononitrate, riboflavin, corn syrup, wheat gluten, soy fiber, soybean oil, lactose, calcium sulfate, ethoxylated mono- and diglycerides, calcium propionate, sodium stearoyl lactylate and ammonium sulfate. The wrapper called it "bread".

It looked like bread and tasted a little bit like bread. It was even purchased in the bread aisle at the supermarket. My mistake was taking time to read the label and discovering that I'd munched on the contents of a chemical lab!

Mom would have had a conniption.

Once upon a time, when you and I were kids, we knew for sure what we were eating. Bread was simply flour, yeast, sugar, salt, milk and lard or some other shortening. Period.

Mom's arsenal of "chemicals" was limited to baking powder, baking soda, a few favorite spices and not much else.

Our vegetables came from the garden or a mason jar, not a can or freezer bag. We ate eggs every day of the week, and our chickens roamed free, snacking on unlucky grasshoppers and whatever else they happened across.

Each autumn, we filled two big wooden barrels with apples and kept them in the basement. The ones that weren't nice enough to store became cider and apple butter. Carrots, turnips and potatoes were covered with sand in the root cellar and kept nicely till spring.

Plums from our orchard produced tart plum butter, and the Concord grapevines that created a shady arbor all summer yielded a harvest of grape jelly and grape juice in fall.

Despite the Depression, we ate well. We bought little more than staples like flour, sugar and salt at the tiny grocery store we patronized. The era of supermarkets with 35,000 different items had not yet arrived. Our meals weren't prepared in some faraway factory where tomato soup was turned out by the tank car.

Then along came make-believe butter in the form of oleo. It was for our own good, they said—we'd be healthier staying away from the real stuff. Maybe so, but oleo was the cause of a childhood social boner that was burned into my memory back in 1932.

The occasion was a Saturday night visit at the home of town-dwelling friends. They had popped an enormous bowl of popcorn for the evening's treat, but I took one taste and whined, "Ugh, this tastes funny!"

Dad instantly nailed me with his 1,000-megawatt death-ray glare, reserved for my most serious transgressions. I knew I was in big trouble.

On the way home, Dad explained that, yes, the popcorn did taste awful, but that was because the family was poor and they could only afford something called oleo.

My outburst had embarrassed them and shamed our family. He'd hoped even an 8-year-old would know better, and he was right, of course. But I still gag when anything other than butter flavors my popcorn.

For my tastes, oleo was just the beginning of what I view as a lot of bum ideas. Eventually we were introduced to pretend sugar, fake eggs, sausage made from soybeans, phony crabmeat—even imitation bacon. All for our own good.

Now there's even phony fat from a company famous for its skill in making soap. We'll be able to gobble up a bag of potato chips without cholesterol, calories or guilt.

Much of the blame for this fake food goes back a decade or so to when a lot of North American scientists went on a nutrition crusade. Food experts decided that eggs and dairy products were a health hazard. Nix on eggs and butter. Then we were told that beef and pork were no-nos...but chicken and fish were okay.

Oops! But be wary of fish, because it might contain mercury. And on second thought, hold the chicken—it could carry something nasty called salmonella.

"See, we were right!" crowed the vegetarians. Then came concerns over pesticides used on apples and oranges and cherries. Eventually there was no such thing as eating without fear or guilt. Everything was guaranteed to do you in—you even had to be wary about the water you drank.

And it's still going on. Pick up the newspaper any day, and you discover that yet another scientist has found something else we shouldn't eat. But turn the page, and you'll likely find some new research proving that the stuff they warned us about 10 years ago really isn't so bad after all.

"Go ahead and have some eggs for breakfast," they say. "Put a little red meat back in your diet." I do, and those are the days that make me especially happy.

What keeps me so skeptical of all these well-meaning nutritionists is remembering the way we ate before we were blessed with so much science.

Dad's side of the family came from Pennsylvania Dutch country, where a typical breakfast *had* to include bacon or sausage, fried eggs, pancakes, raw-fried potatoes and hot biscuits...plus a slice of cake or pie.

When noon came, the *serious* eating took place. There were mashed potatoes whipped up with whole milk and a big lump of butter...thick gravy made of pan drippings from a guinea hen, goose or ham...string beans laced with bacon fat...baked apples flavored with brown sugar and cinnamon. And of course, all this was topped off with more pie or cake.

Dad's lifelong eating habits were atrocious by any standard. His idea of a breakfast treat was a big slice of last night's chocolate cake *liberally spread with butter.*

He selected only well-marbled steaks with plenty of fat, which he never trimmed away. His favorite bread spread was a 50-50 blend of butter and blue cheese. The candy jar was perpetually filled with cheap sweets sold in bulk at the grocery store—chocolate peanut clusters, chocolate-coated raisins, chocolate stars, malted milk balls or peanut brittle.

Dad's Saturday night snack was popcorn dripping with melted butter and a big pan of fudge spiked with peanut butter.

Our ice cream was made using pure cream skimmed from the top of tall cans filled with the rich milk of our Jersey cows. Dad also made cottage cheese from whole milk, and I've never tasted any store-bought variety that was half as good.

Dad lived to be 79. I wonder how many years wheat germ and artificial milk would have added to his life.

My Grandmother Stevens fixed the best roast pork loin I've ever tasted, liberally coating it with salt, then basting it with the drippings every half hour or so. The roast came out of the oven covered with a crisp, salty, fatty crust that was even tastier than the meat itself. I expect it wasn't so "good" for us, either. But Gramma made it to 97.

Later in life, I discovered ethnic food. Whether Italian, Greek, Irish, Jewish, Chinese, Hungarian or Spanish, it's always hearty, tasty fare with a splendid disregard for all the dietary things we seem to fret about nowadays.

What would borscht be without a delicious dollop of sour cream on top? Spaniards devour roast suckling pig without a qualm about fat and calories. And every Hungarian recipe seems to start with, "First, melt a half pound of butter..."

Each culture has its specialties, which are usually recipes created hundreds of years ago. Generations have been raised on them. Meanwhile, everyone seems to grow up hale and hearty, despite ignoring the latest advances in nutritional research.

I doubt most folks spend much time standing in the grocery store intently scanning the mandatory information on packages that tell you how many calories are in a bite, as well as how much potassium, unsaturated fat and vitamin C.

I'm sure it's valuable information, but who really wants to know about it when they dig into a slice of shoofly pie or a mouth-watering helping of stuffed cabbage?

Me, I'm more concerned about the "contents" information and why I'm ingesting mono- and diglycerides, sodium benzoate, ammonium sulfate, potassium bromate and a half dozen other chemicals.

What I want is chicken mushroom soup—which once upon a time contained chicken stock, mushrooms and a cream sauce—accompanied by a piece of toasted homemade bread. Now *that's* good eatin', just like we had around the kitchen table 60 years ago.

Shopping Was Simple Before Big Supermarkets

Brown Brothers

Every now and then, our government tries to impress some group of visiting Russian or Chinese dignitaries by showing them such spectacles as Disneyland, Old Faithful, Manhattan's skyscrapers or a big Iowa farm.

But what usually makes their eyes really bug out is an American supermarket. No country on earth has made good eating so available and affordable to so many. Regular soups, chunky soups, homestyle soups and heart-smart soups. Hundreds of kinds of cookies and candies. Frozen creamed onions as well as waffles and pies and fish sticks. The produce section offers fresh vegetables all twelve months of the year, even if we have to bring them in from Chile, Mexico, Hawaii and Honduras.

But it wasn't like that when I was growing up. The local grocery wasn't much bigger than today's "family room" and only stocked the basics—flour, salt, baking powder, cornflakes, boxes of dried and salted codfish, P&G soap and a few glass-topped boxes of bulk cookies.

You simply called off the items on your list, and the grocer would move around the shelves, using a claw-like gadget on a pole to fish down the products perched on higher shelves.

Then he added everything up on his pad. No scanners or fancy cash registers in those days. If you had the money, you paid him in cash. Most often, though, he "carried" you until next payday. During the Depression, that could be months in the future, though. Who knew when there would be another payday?

You could also phone in your order, because grocers delivered back then. In an hour or two the "grocery boy" would wheel up your sidewalk on his bicycle, come around to the back door, knock, walk in and deposit everything on your kitchen table. He could get in even if you weren't home, because who bothered to lock doors?

Next door to our corner grocery was a butcher shop, presided over by a portly man with a thick German accent. If you wanted something in the meat case, he'd go into the cooler and cut it precisely to order.

More often than not, all we could afford were wieners and sausages, but this was scarcely a big sacrifice. His were the best I've ever tasted.

If you were a regular customer, he'd also throw in a bone or two for your dog. (Sometimes the dog had to wait a day or two until Mom made vegetable soup with it.)

We ate well and we ate hearty, partly because many a delicious meal actually had its start back in February when the first seed catalogs arrived. That's when Mom and Dad decided what to plant in our big garden. We enjoyed fresh garden produce through the summer and early autumn and canned what was needed to hold us through winter.

In fact, one measure of a good homemaker was how many jars of vegetables, fruit, jellies and preserves she had "put up" by October. (Whenever you went visiting in autumn, a trip to the pantry or basement was mandatory because you were expected to "ooh" and "aah" at the bounty.)

Mom could hold her head up with the best of them, because her shelves in the basement were lined with rows of Mason jars holding green or yellow string beans; kernel corn; tomatoes; peaches; apple sauce; apricots; watermelon pickles; grape, raspberry and

A.M. Wettach

TO DISPLAY a fully loaded larder was much like showing off a prize-winning heifer when friends or neighbors visited. After a summer of gardening and canning, those shelves packed with colorful jars were a source of pride for those who'd worked hard to "put them up".

strawberry preserves and rhubarb. There were also sweet and dill pickles as well as sauerkraut in a ceramic crock.

Everything came from our garden and orchard, which meant hours and hours of gardening, picking, preparing, sterilizing jars in a sweltering kitchen, melting paraffin on the iron cookstove to seal the top of jelly jars and then toting everything down to the basement. The whole family pitched in.

Back in those days, even many folks who lived in town kept a few chickens. We had considerably more than most because an important piece of our family's income was from the eggs and broilers we sold.

Dad bought his baby chicks from a mail-order hatchery in Indiana. Sometime in March, he'd get a call from the Railway Express office. "Oscar, your baby chicks are here."

It didn't occur to me then, but baby chicks seem to be nearly indestructible. Their winter trip from Indiana—with a change of trains in Chicago—must have taken at least 36 hours. Yet, when we opened the perforated cardboard boxes, those lively yellow balls of fluff would be cheerfully cheeping and peeping.

We'd take each of them out one by one, quickly dip their beaks into a pan of water for a drink and then turn them loose. In no time, they'd find their way to the comforting heat of the "brooder stove" in the middle of the special building where we started our new chicks.

Eggs were a mainstay of our diet. We ate them poached, fried, scrambled, deviled, soft-boiled and as omelets. Fortunately no one knew about cholesterol yet, so we indulged guilt-free and seemed to thrive on it.

I always knew times were tough when we had chicken more than once a week. You see, to Dad, those birds were a bunch of two-legged egg factories producing eggs that, even at 20 cents a dozen, were crucial income. You just didn't slaughter your golden goose willy-nilly.

We also swapped chickens and eggs for home-rendered lard, headcheese and pork chops produced by neighbors who butchered their hogs. (Dad was a "chicken man", not a "hog man.")

It's hard to beat a dinner of pork chops, savory gravy, buttered potatoes, crusty bread warm from the oven, canned green beans and a tart, flaky pie made with apples from your own orchard. Now *that* was a meal.

(An important note for all of you who grew up in the city: "Dinner" on the farm was the day's big meal and served at noon. "Supper" was served after the day's work was done and was more likely to be macaroni and cheese, homemade vegetable soup or just sandwiches.)

Like most people of that era, Mom wasn't into fancy cooking. Shredded carrots floating in lime Jell-O was her major "gourmet" dish. And when company came, she sometimes went all out and stuffed celery with pineapple cream cheese from those little ornamental jars we later used for juice glasses.

Plain cooking. No arugula, jicama, portabella mushrooms or exotic spices from the South Seas. I'm not even sure she owned a recipe book, although she did swap cake recipes with her sisters.

And isn't it interesting that "plain cooking" is making a comeback? People want recipes that only call for three or four ingredients and can be put together in a few minutes—despite all those TV cooking shows that feature French and Italian chefs showing off their exotic tricks.

Today is also the age when eating out is more common. Whether we're in the mood for Chinese, Thai, Italian, Mexican, Southwestern, Greek or a burger and fries from the drive-through window, the choice is endless.

It certainly wasn't that way in pre-World War II days, though. Our town had a few "luncheonettes" where you could get the Blue Plate Special (overcooked slices of beef, canned peas and mashed potatoes covered in gravy) or a hamburger with french fries and a chocolate malt.

As best I can recall, the entire state of Iowa only had two renowned places for eating out. One was Stone's, under the railroad trestle in Marshalltown. The other was a splendid steak place in Des Moines. People traveled for miles to enjoy a "special dinner" at either place.

When you were traveling and came into an unfamiliar small town, the trick was, you looked for the "Eats" sign that had the most pickup trucks parked near it.

The culinary Disneyland in our part of northern Illinois was Bishop's Cafeteria in Rockford. Whenever a special occasion warranted, Dad loaded us in the car and drove the 45 miles of winding, two-lane road. The food array was dazzling. We faced an agony of indecision as we moved our trays along the buffet line. There were a half dozen different kinds of meats, mashed potatoes *and* au gratin *and* home fries and even sweet potato soufflé with melted marshmallows on top.

Not only that, there were dozens of desserts. But what pleased Dad the most was Bishop's "bottomless cup of coffee". Each table had a tiny electric lamp. Switch it on, and a waitress immediately appeared to refill your cup.

Dad couldn't understand how anyone could make a profit with such largesse. Of course, if all the customers were like Dad, they wouldn't have!

And then sometime in the mid-'30s, our town got its first supermarket. It was an A&P store that moved into what had been a furniture store next to the Congregational Church.

Small by today's standards, it seemed huge to us. Instead of two walls of shelves, there were eight long aisles filled with food. Instead of waiting for a grocer to get around to you, you just grabbed a cart and filled it yourself.

And there was a produce department with fresh fruits and vegetables throughout the year. We could enjoy bananas and pineapples, lemons and oranges as well as lettuce, carrots and radishes even when there was snow on the ground.

It was the beginning of a food revolution that continues to this day. Nevertheless, there's a lot to be said for the simple shopping and plain home cooking of yesteryear.

Hitching a Ride Was A Thumbs-Up Way to Go

Columbia (Courtesy Kobal)

THUMBING a ride was easy for Clark Gable in *It Happened One Night* with Claudette Colbert along. Movie fans will recall she also used a shapely ankle to snare drivers.

There I stood alongside the highway somewhere between Houston and Palacios, Texas. Talk about barren and flat! You could see for 2 full days before you got to the horizon, and there was no sign of human life anywhere.

Ah, the perils of hitchhiking.

I was 19 years old. Far down the highway, I could spot a slow-moving object creeping into view. The vehicle was moving in the same direction I was headed. Eventually it reached me and shuddered to a stop—an ancient Model T coupe, crudely altered into a pickup truck of sorts.

"Hop in, sonny!" the elderly driver said. He was a tall, lean, whippy Texan who appeared to have been left out to sun-dry for several decades.

He let in the clutch, and soon we were roaring along at 20 miles per hour. But I wasn't complaining—any ride was a good ride.

Then he started talking. It seemed he had been Teddy Roosevelt's baby-sitter. Good kid, Teddy, although a trifle rambunctious.

I was vague on TR's date of birth, but as best I could recall, it had been in the late 1850s or early 1860s. It was now 1943. Hmmm...another Texas tall tale?

"Yep," the driver said, "I've known 'em all—Abe Lincoln, Thomas Jefferson, Davy Crockett. Good men, every one of 'em." Then he grabbed my wrist with his enormous hand. "Here, feel my head. Feel that hole?"

No, I didn't...but I wasn't about to say so.

"They've tried to drown me three times, but the water always runs out, and that's why I'm here today."

OK, so not every ride was a good ride. When we came into a tiny crossroads settlement, I vaulted out, not even bothering to open the door. I was prepared to settle down and spend my life there, if necessary.

Texas hitchhiking had perils I hadn't counted on, but hitchhiking was my primary means of transportation for years. You definitely couldn't beat the price, and you met nice people most of the time.

Of course, that was in an era when there were lots of hitchhikers, and for the most part, people didn't hesitate to pick them up.

How times have changed. Recently I saw a highway sign that said WARNING—Hitchhikers may be escapees from the state work farm. For the next 50 miles, I wouldn't have picked up Jimmy Carter!

Years back, you didn't have to worry, and if you traveled by thumb, you gradually learned the tricks of successful hitchhiking. The first rule was to be neatly dressed. Most people wouldn't stop to pick up bums, and there were plenty of those on the road.

If the weather was chilly, it helped to look as cold as possible. A light rain increased your chances, too. But heavy rain worked against you, because no one wanted a soaking-wet stranger sitting on the upholstery.

You also needed to experiment until you learned the best technique for using your thumb. You had to lean into the highway just a bit and make a full swing with your arm, thumb pointed down the road. A big friendly smile was essential, too—people didn't pick up scowlers.

Another important rule was to find out the driver's destination before accepting a ride. I learned this lesson (like almost all important things) the hard way. A kindly stranger who picked me up outside Columbus, Ohio took me all the way to Aurora, Illinois. So far, so good—I was less than 80 miles from home. But he was headed for Wisconsin, so this was the end of the ride for me.

Unfortunately, it was 11 p.m. and I was in downtown Aurora. There was lots of traffic, but all of it local. There I sat on the curb until 7 the next morning. I made the last 80 miles in town-to-town hops and didn't reach home until noon.

That's why smart hitchhikers carried signs with their destination printed in large black letters. As in the restaurant business, location was everything. You had to pick a spot where drivers could get a good long look at you so they'd be able to slow down and stop. Intersections with stop signs were the best, of course...but the competition for rides was stiffest there.

And while company is nice on a trip, hitchhiking was most successful as a solitary pursuit. Folks were leery of picking up more than a single stranger.

Some of the people who stopped for me were just plain good-hearted. Others—traveling salesmen, for example—were lonesome and wanted someone to talk with. Several times I was picked up by a driver who was tired and wanted to take a snooze while I drove.

A friend of mine found his life's calling thanks to hitchhiking. He was picked up by a sharply dressed man driving a pricey new car. My friend asked the man what he did for a living.

"I'm a salesman," he said. During the rest of the trip, my friend discovered that the man got a new car every other year, had a generous expense account and made what sounded like a princely income.

"Right then and there, I decided to become a salesman," my

friend says. And he did, moving up through management until ultimately he was able to start a company of his own. Being poor and forced to hitchhike made him a wealthy man. (Yes, and being smart helped, too.)

Whether your destination was the next town or Los Angeles, you could always find a ride…eventually. Sometimes you even got where you were going faster than you would have by train or bus. (And other times you spent the night in Aurora.)

During the Depression, another form of hitchhiking became widespread. It was called riding the rails.

I remember our family sitting at a railway crossing while a long freight rolled by. My sister and I tried to count the hoboes and came up with more than 100—and those were just the ones we could see.

Lots of hoboes rode on top of loaded coal cars. They threw lumps of anthracite down to kids standing by the tracks, knowing they were helping a family keep warm for another night.

A surprising number of *Reminisce* readers have shared stories of how they "rode the rods" in those days, ate in the "hobo jungles" when they were hungry and took their chances with men who were not always the cream of society.

But to a youngster with no prospects in the old hometown, it was a grand adventure well worth the occasional danger. Often as not, they had no idea where the train was headed when they jumped aboard. Frequently flat broke and hungry, they were able to exist thanks to the kindness of strangers.

Then came World War II. If you were in uniform, hitchhiking was a cinch. Only the stoniest-hearted would drive past a serviceman in uniform with his thumb stuck out. Not only that, they'd often treat you to lunch or even take you home for a meal.

That's how I met that great big old Texan who claimed to know Teddy Roosevelt. It's also how I met another Texan who insisted I join him on a nighttime rattlesnake hunt. That was about as interesting an evening as I've ever had, if you don't count driving home with a gunnysack full of rattlers in the backseat.

If I was anywhere near an air base, the best bet of all was to hang around the Operations or Weather offices and hitch a ride with a training plane going somewhere. I imagine it was against military regulations, but I often lucked out.

I never did stop to think that the pilot probably had less experience flying a plane than he did driving the family car. What counted was that I could be in Atlanta or Chicago or Denver in 2 or 3 hours—for free.

It was especially comforting when I knew it was going to be a round trip. Missing a ride back to where I was stationed meant trying to talk my way out of AWOL charges.

The lucky pilots, most of whom had managed to schedule their cross-country training flight so it took them to their own hometown, soon learned of a simple way to add another day to their layover. All it took was a swift kick to the aircraft's radio just before takeoff. Rarely could a radio be repaired in less than 24 hours.

Now you hardly see hitchhikers anymore unless it's some poor soul who's run out of gas. These days, picking up strangers is downright dumb.

But there's still something alluring about hitching a ride. So, instead of sticking out my thumb to find a free ride, I try to pile up Frequent Flyer miles with an airline.

A few years back, I had enough mileage to earn two first-class tickets from St. Louis to Maui and back.

As we lounged in our spacious leather seats while being pampered by our very own attendant, my wife sighed and said, "Now this is the way to travel."

"No," I told her, "this is the best ride I've ever hitched."

A HANDY idea for hitchhiking was a destination sign. Otherwise, you might end up in a desolate area with no chances to get another ride!

Remember the WLS National Barn Dance?

Courtesy of Ruth Protz

READY, HEZZIE? The Hoosier Hot Shots played foot-stompin' tunes with whatever was handy when they appeared on the popular WLS Saturday night *Barn Dance*.

One of my earlier columns in *Reminisce* magazine mentioned the WLS *National Barn Dance,* and I asked if anyone remembered which character on that famous radio program said, "Give me a toot on the tooter, Tommy." Well, did I ever get answers!

Lots and lots of *Reminisce* readers have shared memories of that great Saturday night radio broadcast from Chicago, which hit its peak of popularity in the '30s.

Though I normally write about memories of my own, I thought it might be a good idea to step back for a moment and let the readers talk about their happy memories of this popular program.

Helen Linhart, from Grafton, North Dakota, lived on a small farm back then. She writes, "I well remember how Mother and I sat up until midnight every week to listen, hoping the radio batteries wouldn't go dead."

Helen's late-night listening left her with cheery recollections of the Hoosier Hot Shots, the Prairie Ramblers, Arkie, the Arkansas Woodchopper and Patsy Montana singing *I Wanna Be a Cowboy's Sweetheart.*

"I remember when Lulu Belle and Scotty's little girl, Linda Lou, was born," Helen says. "It was as if a member of our own family had a new baby. These WLS folks were our family!"

We also heard from Warren Harding Edgar of Parry Sound, Ontario.

"'Give me a toot on the tooter, Tommy' was said by Uncle Ezra just before he'd go into one of his clippety-clop dance steps," Warren remembers. "I believe he was speaking to the Hoosier Hot Shots, who played a great array of tooting instruments, washboards and so forth.

"We had a Northern Electric 'Lucerne' radio," Warren adds, "and the Barn Dance just came booming into our home. Our neighbors listened on Atwater-Kents, Radiolas, Kolsters, Crosleys and other popular radios of that era."

Warren's mention of those radio brands sure brings back some memories for me. Our radio sat on the "library table" in a tiny room we called our den. It was powered by a half dozen or so humming batteries on a shelf in the basement.

I have no idea what brand it was, but it featured an ominous-looking array of knobs that only Dad was allowed to touch. When operating it, he looked a bit like those old images of the radio operator on a sinking ocean liner, frantically sending out an SOS.

Perched atop it was a giant "tulip-horn" speaker, from which came squawks and buzzes and crackles and—when everything was adjusted properly—actual broadcasts.

Beside the radio was a notepad on which Dad carefully logged the stations he'd captured, much like a bird-watcher recording rare species on his "life list".

"Imagine, KDKA in Pittsburgh," Dad would marvel. "And WLW from Cincinnati!"

Like millions of families, the one show we always looked forward to was the *National Barn Dance*. Nothing else could match it for variety and talented performers.

WLS was a powerful 50,000-watt clear channel station that could be picked up over a large part of the United States and Canada, especially on cold winter nights when reception was good.

The show was also carried by more than 60 NBC stations, so it truly had national coverage. The *Barn Dance* was aired from the Eighth Street Theatre in Chicago, where the entire stage was transformed into a hayloft every Saturday night.

The first show was broadcast in April of 1924, even though some of the station's executives were skeptical about its chances for success. Ringing cowbells announced that the show was on the air.

Back then, WLS billed itself as "The Prairie Farmer Station", and its programs were aimed at a farm, home and family-oriented audience. Morning devotions led by Jack Holden began each day, and on Sundays, Dr. John Holland conducted "The Little Brown Church of the Air".

The *Barn Dance* performers all had weekday shows, too. But, as Ruth Protz of Oshkosh, Wisconsin recalls, "On Saturday nights they'd all gather for the *Barn Dance*. Their picking and singing, fiddling, stomping and ringing cowbells lifted our spirits and brought joy to our lives in those dreary Depression days."

Ruth also points out that "no Midwest state fair was complete until the famous *Barn Dance* was broadcast live in front of a packed grandstand."

Was she ever right! An astounding 110,000 fans turned out when the cast was on hand for the 1935 National Corn Husking Contest in Newton, Indiana.

Members of the *Barn Dance* troupe also made personal appearances at county fairs and year-round in small-town theaters, schools and community festivals such as Illinois' Watermelon Day in Thompson and Sauerkraut Festival in Milledgeville.

Yes, the *Barn Dance* was broadcast from the Illinois and Indiana state fairs, from a water-supply structure 2 miles off Chicago in Lake Michigan and from the Century of Progress Exposition, where throngs of 30,000 crowded the Court of the States to see and hear the Barn Dance stars.

This, of course, was also known as the 1934 World's Fair, and on one night the Hoosier Hot Shots broadcast their part of the show from an airplane—wow!—soaring over the exposition grounds.

The *National Barn Dance* became a launching pad for many soon-to-be-famous entertainers, such as the 12-year-old with a beautiful choirboy soprano voice who joined the show in 1933.

"The Little Cowboy", as he was called, grew up to become comedian "Lonesome George Gobel", who had his own television show and a fictional wife he called "Spooky Old Alice".

A young pal of his on the show was squeaky-voiced comedian Pat Buttram, the son of an Alabama circuit-riding preacher. Pat later enjoyed a successful career in the movies and on TV.

Gene Autry, the Singing

COLORFUL CAST. Patsy Montana and the Prairie Ramblers (top) were *Barn Dance* stars, as was Gene Autry (top). George Gobel (bottom right) also got his start on the *Barn Dance*. Lulu Belle and Scotty (center) and Grace Wilson (bottom left) were longtime favorites.

Cowboy, was also part of the cast. So was Red Foley, later to become Pat Boone's father-in-law and Debby Boone's grandpa.

A special favorite of mine was Rex Allen, a man gifted with one of the great voices of this century. By a strange quirk of fate, I had the joy of working with him nearly 50 years later.

The years had been kind—his voice just got better with time. But fame never went to his head—he was as friendly as your favorite neighbor and as hardworking as the day he broke into show business.

Holding everything together was master of ceremonies Joe Kelly, a man with a hearty laugh and obvious affection for the members of the cast.

From announcers to stagehands, it took lots of talented people to put on the 4-1/2-hour *Barn Dance* show. Warren Edgar's letter included a photo of the entire crew—98 people, if my count is right.

It shows the Hoosier Sod Busters, two men who teamed up to play a 3-foot-long harmonica, as well as a five-member German Band. There's Grace Wilson, a singer called "The Girl with a Million Friends", and Uncle Ezra, "The Old Jumpin' Jenny Wren", whose real name was Pat Barrett.

Verne, Lee and Mary, "The Three Wisconsin Honey Bees", were Saturday night regulars, as were The Hometowners, a male quartet. Patsy Montana sang with the Prairie Ramblers, four young men who had been born in Kentucky log cabins.

Why was the show so popular? Maybe its appeal was nostalgia. One fan wrote, "The listener will hear the songs of cradle days. Once again, he will see Mother sitting in the old wooden rocker beside the drop-leaf table, on which sits the lighted kerosene lamp, while the blazing fire in the old-fashioned stove throws wavering shadows on the clay-plastered walls."

Nowadays, country and western music has two "capitals"—Nashville, Tennessee and Branson, Missouri. It's as popular with city people as with country folks. The basic *Barn Dance* appeal is still there—foot-tapping music and lyrics that tell of home, true love, heartbreak and coping with life's problems.

It all started with the WLS *National Barn Dance*. I know… through the magic of radio, I was there.

$\mathcal{T}$he Best Fun Was Always Free

Julie Habel

Sometime during the mid-'30s—as if the Depression and killer droughts weren't enough —a baby tornado had touched down and destroyed a machine shed on our northern Illinois farm.

That was the only bad news. The good news was that all the nails that were used to fasten down the corrugated metal roof and sides had lead washers to thwart leaking during rainstorms.

I spent the better part of 2 weeks scrumbling through the wreckage of the machine shed, salvaging those precious washers. Eventually I accrued more than 10 pounds of lead.

This unseemly ambition was motivated by the fact that the minister's son down the road owned dozens of the metal molds used to make lead soldiers.

So we made a deal: I'd provide the lead and he'd melt it down and pour it into the molds. Then we'd split the output. (That was my introduction to capitalism. He owned the "factory" and I furnished the materials.)

I ended up with a regiment of soldiers. Some marched; some

knelt to fire rifles or pistols; others sat astride horses. There was also a rampaging band of Indians armed with bows and arrows, tomahawks and spears.

Mom set up a card table in a corner of the dining room, and my sister pitched in to help me paint my army and its bloodthirsty enemies. Those lead soldiers and Indians brought me hundreds of hours of pleasure...and didn't cost a cent.

My, how times have changed. Anyone who's purchased a toy for a grandchild recently knows that there's nothing available for less than $19.95. Fun isn't cheap these days.

There's not much good you can say about hard times, but at least they taught kids how to have fun for free. Necessity may be the mother of invention, but so is poverty.

Consider an inner tube, for example. There aren't many to be had nowadays, but 50 years ago every tire had to have one. An old discarded inner tube was quite a find for a kid, even if it needed some patching.

Blow it up and you could spend hours floating in the creek or lake. Cut it into strips and you had giant rubber bands that could hold together a broken scooter. Best of all, you had the beginnings of a good slingshot.

More free fun could be had with two thin sticks, some string, a sheet of newspaper and paste made from flour and water. That's all you needed to construct a fairly decent kite. It didn't hold up too long, but it worked as well as the kites sold at Woolworth's for a dime. One kid I knew even made his own box kite. (Later he became a test pilot for Boeing.)

My own flights of fancy took a different turn after some barnstorming aviators came to town. They performed breathtaking loops, spins, dives and wing-walks, and the grand finale was a thrilling parachute jump. We strained our eyes as the plane climbed higher and higher, then gasped as a tiny figure leaped out. Everyone *oohed* as the chute opened and the man drifted down.

Oh, to be a parachute jumper! As soon as I got home, I "volunteered" one of those lead soldiers from my toy army for parachute duty. All it took was a square of cloth from a feed sack and four pieces of string.

I'd carefully fold his chute into a tidy bundle and then fire him aloft with my slingshot. When things worked right, the chute unfolded and the soldier drifted gently back to earth. But the failure rate was high. (Maybe I didn't want to be a parachute jumper after all.)

My fascination with skydiving was short-lived, thanks to Indy 500 drivers such as Wilbur Shaw, Floyd Roberts and Louis Meyer, who topped the 100 mph barrier at the Brickyard, capturing the imagination of every young boy.

Most of us decided to build our own racers, powered not by Offenhauser engines, but by our feet and gravity. We scavenged the necessary materials from garages, basements and even the city dump. Before long, communities were holding sanctioned "Soap Box Derby" contests, and the winners went to a national competition in Akron, Ohio.

Those also were the days when Gar Wood was making headlines with his powerful speedboats. Using a picture from the newspaper as a guide, I began making miniature speedboats from scraps of lumber carefully shaped, planed, sanded and painted. Soon I had a fleet of my own, which I "raced" in the horse tank.

Boys weren't the only ones who made their own toys. My sister, Mary, roamed the fence rows and ditches to gather milkweed pods. She laboriously extracted the floss to stuff a mattress for her doll cradle. No doll ever slept in such comfort!

Mary also made necklaces from dandelion stems looped together and whipped up tasty salads for her doll family from weeds and wildflowers.

Speaking of flowers, when our "tulip-horned" battery-powered radio was replaced with a new Silvertone Super-Hetrodyne 12-tube console, Dad let me dismantle the old relic. Purely by accident, I discovered that the headphones and speaker could be turned into crude telephones, connected with nothing more than a piece of electrical wire.

Soon Mary and I were a two-person AT&T, with a far-flung communications system that stretched all the way from the chicken house to the barn. (We also can claim to have created the "Friends and Family" phone plan, since we insisted that all our friends and family try out our new marvel.)

I may have had my own phone, but I still envied the more affluent boys at school who owned BB guns. Then one day I discovered that Swartley's Greenhouse used slender bamboo sticks to stake up their tall-growing plants. The bamboo had a hollow core just the diameter of a grain of rice. That gave me an idea.

I cut a section of bamboo about 8 inches long and became, briefly, the terror of the fifth grade, using my blow-gun to fire grains of rice from my seat in the back of the classroom at unsuspecting classmates.

It didn't take the teacher long to make the connection between students yelping "Ouch!" and the dozens of rice grains on the floor. After that it was just a matter of her waiting for the culprit to get careless. (I never was crafty enough for a successful life of crime.)

As far as I'm concerned, the luckiest kids were those who grew up close to a woods, the way my wife did. Nothing frees up a kid's imagination more than a forest.

Find a large fallen tree and you had a pirate ship ready to sail the bounding main in search of merchant ships to plunder. The only decision was who would climb up into the crow's nest to watch out for hostile ships.

You could build hideouts in the woods, stalk fearsome wild game such as gophers and squirrels and, if you were especially lucky, get just lost enough to scare you for a few minutes.

One of my favorite examples of dirt-cheap entertainment isn't a memory of my own. It was shared in the April 1993 issue of *Reminisce EXTRA* by Ed Knapp, a frequent contributor who lives in Three Rivers, Michigan.

"I Flew the Amazing Dirt Airplane" was Ed's whimsical tale of the "airplane" he made as an enterprising 9-year-old. Inspired by the comic strip *Tailspin Tommy*, little Ed made himself a backyard biplane. All it took was a shovel and permission to dig a hole next to the garage. Inside that "cockpit" he used a mound of dirt to shape an instrument panel.

An odd collection of thread spools, string, sticks, nails and stones became flying instruments—altimeter, speed indicator, fuel gauge, compass and starter switch. Ed topped it all off by jamming an old plunger handle into the ground for a "joystick". Most of those things were located in trash piles.

Ed soared high and flew far in his "dirt airplane". He did daring aerobatics and battled the Red Baron, all while hunkered down in his hole-in-the-ground cockpit.

There's no such thing as trash when you're a kid with an active mind and no money. Discarded alarm clocks, radios, spark plugs,

GOOD, CLEAN FUN. When skies cleared and the sun came out after a brief summer shower, the kids came out for a rousing afternoon of puddle-stomping.

fan belts and toasters are instantly recognized as potential airplanes, space ships, racing cars and such.

Now, don't get me wrong. I know that my remarkably good-looking and unnaturally intelligent grandchildren (and yours, too!) have lively imaginations and creative minds. But have you checked their rooms lately?

Who needs to dream up a dirt airplane or make a mattress from milkweed silk when the folks at Sega and Sony turn out such sleek, glittering diversions?

Why build a soapbox racer when you've got a $150 pair of Roller Blades? Why captain a pirate ship in the woods when you can save a princess guarded by dragons in the world of Nintendo?

Today's pricey store-bought toys are great. But as many of us know, the greatest toy store of all was in our own imaginations. It was open 24 hours a day, and the price was always right.

Spring Cleaning Took Teamwork

H. Armstrong Roberts

It was like clockwork. Every year in late April or early May, when the forsythia came into bloom and the irises beside the driveway were pushing up, Mom would announce it was time for spring housecleaning.

Timing was critical for Mom—she had to be sure winter was entirely over, but she couldn't wait too long or Dad would be itchy to get in the fields to start spring plowing.

Back in those days, when furnaces didn't have filters and you swept the rugs with a Bissell carpet sweeper, spring housecleaning was a large-scale project requiring the services of the entire family. That meant scheduling the job for a long weekend when my sister and I had some days off school.

First the furniture was moved so Dad could roll up the carpets and carry them outside. He'd drape them one at a time over a sturdy rope strung between two trees, and I'd go to work with the carpet beater.

Carpet beaters came in many styles, and every family had its favorite. Ours was made from rattan with an elaborate four-leaf clover design at the business end. It had an agreeable "whippiness" and delivered a satisfying *smack* when swung properly. Every stroke raised a big puff of dust that floated off on the springtime breeze.

I'd pretend I was Gabby Hartnett, Phil Cavarretta or one of my other Chicago Cubs heroes, standing at the plate in Wrigley Field with the game tied and two out in the bottom of the ninth. The dreaded Carl Hubbell, ace pitcher for the New York Giants, would scowl from the mound, then rear back and toss one of his terrifying screwballs over the plate. *Wham!* I'd send the ball back, back, back and over the fence.

By the third carpet, however, baseball didn't seem like such a wonderful career anymore. My winter-softened hands were sprouting plump red blisters...and Dad was still carrying carpets out to me.

Meanwhile, inside the house, the oak floors were scrubbed and waxed. In some of the areas that took a lot of traffic, Dad would sand the worn places and administer a fresh coat of varnish.

(Things were even more involved back in *his* childhood, Dad assured. His mother put down a thin layer of straw under the carpets for winter insulation, so a big part of spring housecleaning was spent getting the straw swept up and taking the corn-shuck mattresses outside for airing and fluffing.)

Next, all our curtains came down and went into the Maytag washing machine. Then, still damp, they were put on a curtain stretcher. Ours was simplicity itself—two steel rods. One went through the top hem and was hung in the archway between the living and dining rooms. The other rod went in the bottom hem and was weighted with bricks or flatirons. Spring breezes blowing through the house dried the curtains wrinkle-free in a jiffy.

Cushions from the sofas and chairs were also taken outside to beat, and I had to be careful not to hit hard enough to rip the ancient upholstery. No more home runs over the left field fence.

Sometimes a room or two had walls that needed washing or a fresh coat of paint or wallpaper.

Finally, it was time to put up the curtains, bring in the carpets, move the furniture back into place, rehang the pictures and admire our clean-smelling home.

Every 2 or 3 years, we had the extra excitement of putting fresh linoleum in the kitchen. This meant a trip to the furniture store, which was owned by the same family who operated the mortuary.

Dozens of rolls of colorful linoleum in a wide variety of designs were displayed. After much family discussion, Mom made her selection. The clerk cut off the proper length, and we'd head home with the roll tied on top of our car.

After the linoleum was installed, Mom predictably announced that *now* we needed new oilcloth for the kitchen counters. She would then head back downtown to Woolworth's, which had a whole section of nothing but oilcloth.

She'd fuss and fret, trying to decide which color and pattern went best with the new linoleum. While she was gone, Dad stripped off the old oilcloth, carefully saving the brass upholstery nails that held it snug.

When Mom returned, Dad measured and cut the new cloth, then tacked it in place with the salvaged upholstery nails, mumbling and tugging while he worked out all the wrinkles.

At last, the family assembled to admire the new linoleum and fresh countertops, always agreeing that the changes "made the kitchen look just like new".

The best spring of all was when our old kitchen range was replaced by a Perfection kerosene stove. Wow! The kitchen looked as big as Wrigley Field without that old cast-iron monster. (Eventually, some of the extra space was occupied by an electric refrigerator to replace the icebox on the enclosed back porch.)

Warming weather also meant taking down storm windows and putting up screens. Dad used the extension ladder to reach the second-floor windows, with me inside the house to unhook the storms and carefully push them out so he could haul them

FRESH AS A BREEZE. The warm, spring air made a perfect time for hanging out wash or beating the dust from household rugs and furniture cushions that had sat inside all winter.

down. This always required a certain amount of finesse.

Those were the days before aluminum or plastic screen mesh was available, so screens usually had to be painted—not just the frames, but the wire, too.

Before we painted, Dad patched any holes by weaving in a small piece of screen wire. It was a tedious job, but it saved buying new wire for the entire screen.

Painting was a chore, too, because the paint had a nasty tendency to plug up the screen holes if you tried to work too fast. A small pad of old carpet dipped in the paint seemed to work better than a brush, but it was slow going. When all else failed, you'd

Harold M. Lambert

have to use a pin or small nail and painstakingly unplug the blocked-up squares.

Along with exchanging storms for screens went window-washing, still my least-favorite household chore. Mom's mixture of ammonia and vinegar worked better than any of the high-priced bottled stuff at the supermarket today, which seems to be mostly water with a few drops of blue dye added.

Finally, there was just one job left—readying the front porch for summer. First came a fresh coat of gray enamel paint on the porch floor, which stretched across the entire front of our farmhouse.

Once the paint dried, the ceiling-hung "glider" came out of storage. The cushions were washed, and the glider was installed at one

ELBOW GREASE and a mix of vinegar and ammonia made windows sparkle.

end of the long narrow porch.

At the other end went a small daybed, and in between were two canvas deck chairs. A woven-grass carpet covered part of the floor, adding a nice homey touch.

We practically lived on that porch in decent weather, often eating supper out there and sleeping on it during the hot nights of July and August.

At last, our work was finished. How satisfying to savor a sparkling, clean house, with fragrant spring breezes wafting through the windows, bright green grass poking up in the lawn, new-born leaves on the maple trees and elms, lilacs bursting with plump buds, baby calves frisking in the orchard and rhubarb making its cautious appearance in the garden.

The whole world was fresh and new, it seemed, and life just couldn't be much better.

~ *C*an You Recall the ~ Early Days of Television?

Archive Photos/Lambert

Up until 1948, the lives of most Americans didn't stretch much beyond the immediate horizon. I remember a friend of mine asking why in the world I was planning a trip to Mexico. "Gosh," he said. "I haven't even seen all of Iowa yet."

Then along came television.

Edward R. Murrow put it just right in 1951 when his new program called *See It Now* debuted. On the screen came a live shot of the Atlantic Ocean, followed by one of the Pacific. "We are impressed by a medium through which a man sitting in his living room has been able for the first time to look at two oceans at once," he marveled.

Suddenly, no place on earth, no important event, no notable person was farther away than our television set.

Up until then, we had entertained ourselves. We read books, pored over the daily newspaper, played cards with friends, gathered around the dining room table for a game of Monopoly, looked forward to the home-talent performance of *H.M.S. Pinafore* in the high school gym, went to band concerts in the park or—imagine it!—just sat around and talked.

How quickly we changed from amusing ourselves to being entertained. And how seductive it was. Like most Americans, I had never seen major league baseball, professional football, hockey or a golf tournament. Now I could, and from the best seat in the house.

I sat at ringside (my easy chair) and saw championship boxing matches, including everyone's hero, Joe Louis. I had the choice seat at national political conventions, only to discover that they were mostly bombast and baloney. Nevertheless, commentators like David Brinkley, Chet Huntley and John Chancellor managed to give me a sense of what chicanery was afoot behind the scenes.

John Cameron Swayze and Douglas Edwards delivered the day's news to my home, and a feisty, rude young reporter named Mike Wallace made self-important people uncomfortable with his blunt questions on a show called *Nightline*.

Being entertained by the biggest and brightest stars in show business became irresistible. Who wanted to play cards when Milton Berle or Jackie Gleason could be summoned by a flick of the "On" button? Neighborhood get-togethers came to a dead stop while everyone crowded around the television set to watch *The Show of Shows*. And why not? Look at the talent! Sid Caesar, Imogene Coca, Carl Reiner, Art Carney, plus an endless parade of big-name guest stars.

The king of daytime radio, Arthur Godfrey, quickly became the king of television, too. Hawaii enjoyed a giant tourist boom thanks to Arthur, his ukulele and glowing tales of his own vacations in the islands. Arthur was our pal, our buddy, the slightly naughty scamp who was the son we wished had been ours. He could sell us anything—a fact not lost upon eager sponsors of his show.

We were like kids locked in a candy store. TV's beguiling feast of amusements and diversions provided more goodies than we knew what to do with. Studies showed that we watched TV more than 5 hours a day, a figure I've always viewed with great suspicion. (Somehow, admitting how much television you watch has always seemed like owning up to a serious character flaw.)

We arose to turn on the early-morning *Today* show, co-hosted by Dave Garroway and a chimp named J. Fred Muggs. You got news, celebrity interviews, the day's weather and entertainment—right along with your corn flakes.

Later in the day, television brought new reality to our soap operas. *Search for Tomorrow* was the first solid success, followed by *The Secret Storm, Portia Faces Life, The Guiding Light,* and the durable *As the World Turns,* just to mention a few.

Those were the days when all television was broadcast live, with no chance to reshoot bloopers. It wasn't unheard of for a recently slain corpse to be seen crawling off the set, unaware he was still in the picture!

And no wonder. I had the chance to attend one day's episode of a highly popular soap opera. It was a scene of casual chaos as the performers wandered in, glanced at the day's script (no teleprompters or cue cards then) and mostly ad-libbed the day's action. The only organized, rehearsed person I noted was Adelaide Hawley, who played the on-screen persona of Betty Crocker.

Every day we hurried home from work to catch the evening news, followed by comedies, celebrity-packed variety programs, dramas and quiz shows. We even bought TV trays so we could eat in front of the family shrine and not miss a moment.

Nor could we resist staying up late for Steve Allen's *Tonight* show, which turned out to be a launching pad for a dozen young singers (Steve Lawrence and Eydie Gorme, Andy Williams) and comedians like Don Knotts, Tom Poston, Louis Nye and Bill Dana.

We were hooked. Entertainment-addicted. Enslaved dawn to midnight by a mind-numbing cornucopia of entertainment and information.

Meanwhile, great magazines such as *LIFE, Saturday Evening Post, Look* and *Colliers* closed down as advertising revenue was diverted to television.

Soothsayers predicted the demise of radio, too, but that hardy medium adapted to the changing times, and it has now reached the point where you'll find a lot more radios in households today than in the "Golden Age of Radio".

The motion picture business also suffered. Why go to theaters when there was more entertainment at home than anyone could consume? The big studios had lean years, but a few survived, emerging stronger than ever. Unfortunately, those great ornate cinema palaces became dinosaurs, replaced by today's grungy 8-screen Cineplexes.

Another watershed change took place at about the same time when the era of Big Bands came to an end. The legendary great ballrooms weren't drawing crowds anymore, and band tours had become prohibitively expensive. There were no extended bookings into the 5,000-seat movie theaters either because they had closed their doors.

A few played on, notably Woody Herman, Stan Kenton, Count Basie, and an ersatz Glenn Miller group—but only one flourished: Lawrence Welk. The corny North Dakotan with the comical accent was, deep down, a shrewd businessman. He moved into television without missing a single "a-one...a-two...a-three" beat.

Welk had a big band, yes, but he enhanced it with singers and dancers, then featured musicians playing everything from the accordion to the musical saw. He put on a show!

So-called sophisticates sneered, but to millions it was just the best down-home Saturday night talent show there ever was. Welk claimed he simply put on a show that his mother would like.

Obviously there were a lot

Archive Photos

Archive Photos

FROM LAUGHTER TO TEARS. TV personalities Milton Berle (left), Ed Sullivan (above) and Lucille Ball gave folks a variety of reasons to stay home and sit in front of the tube.

of people like his mother out there in TV land. In the end, his was the only band to conquer, rather than be conquered, by television.

Certainly the passing of the Big Bands was a tragedy, but something wonderful emerged from the ruins. A whole new crop of talented male and female singers appeared.

I still remember the first time Eddie Fisher appeared on *The Ed Sullivan Show*. Gosh, how this good-looking kid could sing! *Any Time* was the perfect song to showcase his pure, sweet voice.

Frankie Laine rode into our lives aboard his mega-hit, *Mule Train*. Guy Mitchell, Andy Williams and Johnny Mathis (*Chances Are*) blazed to the top in record sales.

Bearded Mitch Miller gave us television sing-alongs, while master-minding the careers of a score of before unknown young singers. Meanwhile, Rosemary Clooney urged us to *C'mon-a My House*, and Patti Page warbled about *Mockin' Bird Hill*. Kay Starr (*Wheel of Fortune*), Jaye P. Morgan, Jill Corey, Gogi Grant (*Wayward Wind*), and Teresa Brewer (*Music! Music! Music!*) filled the airwaves with their fresh voices.

I was a commuter in Detroit during those days, and never has the tedium of traffic backups been more enjoyable. It was a daily feast of memorable songs and exciting new talent, not to mention great melodies and lyrics.

We went from entertaining ourselves to sitting back and *being* entertained. We dropped our magazine subscriptions and bought reclining chairs. We didn't play sports; we watched them. We became voluntarily, happily housebound and, alas, broad of beam and short of wind. But wasn't the entertainment wonderful?

The years from 1948 to 1955 brought permanent changes in our lives. That's inarguable. Whether they made us better people or not is hotly debated these days, especially in discussing television's impact on our children. Nevertheless, it was a bloodless revolution, the likes of which has never been seen before or since.

And through it all, I had the best seat in the house.

ℒocal Entertainment
Was Simply the Best

A.M. Wettach/RP

Recently I saw an amusing television commercial for a pizza chain. It showed two adults so relishing their pizza that they were oblivious to everything else…including a baby singing a Broadway show tune while balancing a juggling cat on his head.

The scene sure caught my attention and probably sold plenty of pizza. But it also provided a wry commentary on how jaded we've become about entertainment. It's pretty hard to thrill us anymore.

Television brings into our homes the Boston Pops Symphony, the best tenors in the world, the finest dancers, the greatest actors and actresses of our time, world-class magicians and the best in sports.

From the comfort of our favorite chairs, we can see more fine entertainment in a week than most people half a century ago saw in a lifetime. Trouble is, we've become watchers instead of doers.

Back in the '20s and '30s, we were good at providing our own homegrown entertainment. The community productions we enjoyed were simple, but so much fun.

I can still remember the winter when a group of our parents decided to stage *H.M.S. Pinafore* at Central School in Sterling, Illinois. (No one knew why these eager Midwestern amateurs selected a musical with tricky lyrics that demanded a cockney accent.) Undaunted, they joyfully plunged into it, making their own costumes and building all the necessary sets.

They rehearsed several evenings a week. Mom was nervous about driving home alone after rehearsals, so she insisted I come along. That's why, to this day, I can sing the lyrics to every song in that wonderful Gilbert and Sullivan operetta, including *I'm Called Little Buttercup*.

The performance turned out to be a standing-room-only hit. An encore performance was staged a week later, and it, too, packed the gymnasium. The show may not have been Broadway caliber, but it more than satisfied our entertainment-hungry town.

Between community theater events, some of the best entertainment we enjoyed came from the municipal band.

Back in the '30s, nearly every small town in our area had its own band. Arguably the best was in Mount Morris, where key positions were filled by musicians who, prior to the Depression, had played with the great military bands of Sousa, Goldman, Karl King and others.

A few in the Mount Morris band were also alumni of the Barnum & Bailey Circus band, every one a top musician with a "leather lip" and strong lungs.

Our Sterling band had a few circus veterans, too, drawn there by J.J. Richards, who had been conductor of the Ringling Brothers Circus band.

Every band played a few winter concerts and marched in all the parades. But the "band season" was really in summer, with weekly concerts in the park. These programs invariably featured Sousa marches along with familiar light classics such as *Poet and Peasant Overture*, *March Slav*, *The Soldiers' Chorus* from *Faust* and excerpts from *Lohengrin*.

For better or worse, every concert also featured a local vocalist. Men seemed to favor *Asleep in the Deep* and *Old Man River*, while the female singers could be counted on for songs like *Mighty Like*

MARCHING DOWN MEMORY LANE. Parades meant fun for spectators and local band musicians—plus a chance for neighbors to meet along the street.

a Rose and *Summertime*.

The Sterling and Mount Morris musicians performed in snazzy band shells, while the Dixon band played on a platform in front of city hall. Franklin Grove's band used a hayrack festooned with Christmas lights.

Whatever stage they may have used, bands were really at their best marching in parades, which were great community entertainment in the 1930s.

It seems to me that parades were considerably more grand in those days. I still recall one in Rockford, Illinois, sponsored by the *Morning Star* and *Register-Republic* newspapers to honor their carriers.

This event brought together school bands from all over the northern part of the state and attracted a huge crowd that lined the street for miles.

Every town had a Fourth of July parade that always ended in the park, where some politician of note delivered an hour-long oration. Those were the days when "rock 'em sock 'em" oratory—delivered without a microphone and loudspeakers—was still an art form.

In addition to parades, most towns, no matter how small, found some sort of excuse for a summer festival. Sauerkraut Day, Cheese Day and Watermelon Day were three big ones in our part of the world. These events didn't cost a lot to attend (how much can you spend on sauerkraut in one day?) and included the predictable profusion of carnival rides at 5¢ per ticket.

Another popular diversion was Golden Gloves boxing. Local

lads, some of them neighbors, whaled away at one another while the crowd cheered (or booed) their favorites.

I recall one ponderous heavyweight apparently born with a granite jaw. His opponents wore themselves into exhaustion flailing away at this local Mt. Rushmore. He eventually made it all the way to the Illinois finals in Chicago.

For those who didn't care to watch pugilists dancing in the ring, there were foot-blistering dance marathons. Halfway between Sterling and Dixon was a large dance hall where they were staged often. They drew big crowds eager to watch exhausted contestants trudge around the floor in the hope of winning a $100 prize.

The real lure for the audience was the same excitement that draws some to auto races—the possibility of seeing a "crash" as a weary couple collapsed in a snoozing heap.

Closer to home, there was always plenty to do in our new National Guard armory. It had a hardwood dance floor, large balcony, a stage and fully equipped kitchen plus a bowling alley in the basement.

During the winter, artists of some note appeared there in concert. Times were tough, and even towns as small as Sterling generated enough box office dollars to make a stop worthwhile for performers. One "big name" act I recall seeing was "Rubinoff and his violin". We'd heard him perform on the radio, and that made him a genuine celebrity in our eyes.

On top of the armory building was a "roof garden" with a small bandstand and a painted concrete dance floor surrounded by brightly painted wooden booths and colorful lights. The better Midwestern dance bands included Sterling on their circuit, so there was dancing under the stars every week of the summer.

The challenge for us high school boys was to sneak up to the roof garden and get in free. At first this involved climbing the fire escape, but that route was soon closed off.

After that, we'd pool our money so one of us could pay admission and get his hand "stamped" at the door. As quickly as possible, he'd come back outside, and we'd all go to work duplicating the stamp as best we could with pen and ink.

Sometimes that worked. Other times, we were rejected at the door and sternly ordered to go home. On those occasions, our single paying customer would open the fire escape door at the rear of the building on the sly and let the rest of our group inside.

From rooftop to basement, the armory hosted all sorts of fun. Money was not a big concern for those of us kids who visited the bowling alley in the basement—it was a simple matter of work-for-play.

Before automatic pin-setting machines, you could set pins for an hour and earn a quarter. The two bits covered the cost of bowling three lines afterward. If you set pins for 2 hours, you could bowl three lines and have enough left over for a hamburger and a soft drink—an altogether satisfactory evening for a teenager in those days.

Finally, there was one form of free entertainment that persists even today—"cruising" Main Street. Back then this was an exclusively male form of recreation.

One of our group would convince his dad to let him use the car on Saturday night. He'd pick us up and drive downtown, where we'd cruise back and forth down one side of the street and back up the other.

The attraction, of course, was girls, who just happened to be out walking. A few whistles were mandatory on the boys' part, and pretending to be annoyed was expected of the girls. It was a harmless way to brighten up a dull Saturday night when you were too broke for a movie and too shy to ask for a date. I know...I was there.

SATURDAY NIGHT and square dancing went hand in hand when it came to having a good time, and what better way to hook up with that cute guy or gal you'd been eyeing!

ℬig City Visits Filled Us with Wonder

Before World War II, most of us lived in small towns or, like my family, out on the farm. We didn't stray far from home too much, because automobiles were pretty undependable and the roads were mostly gravel and mud.

That was OK, though, because our hometown furnished most everything we wanted. Whatever existed over the horizon was of no particular interest. Why, we wondered, would anyone want to live in a crowded, noisy big city?

For folks in tiny Sterling, Illinois, where I grew up, the "big city" was Chicago. Few of our neighbors had ever driven there, although some had taken the 2-1/2-hour trip on the Chicago & Northwestern Railroad.

Those who did "venture beyond" came back with some hard-to-believe tales. They said the city sat beside a lake so big, you couldn't see across to the other side. Supposedly there were buildings taller than a silo! And according to our local newspaper,

Chicago was run by a man named Al Capone who was prone to use a tommy gun on people who displeased him.

Our pigs and cows became pork chops and T-bone steaks at the Chicago Stockyards, and somehow the price for our corn and oats was decided upon in a mysterious place called the Chicago Board of Trade.

My primary interest in Chicago was that it was home to the Cubs and White Sox. There were divided loyalties in my family, and passions ran high. Grampa Stevens was a White Sox fan and Gramma rooted for the Cubs.

Grampa sat in a rocking chair beside his tabletop Atwater-Kent radio, intently listening to Bob Elson or Quin Ryan call the games. He always knew the batting order, the batting averages of every player and each man's strengths and weaknesses.

Those were the days of Zeke Bonura and Heinie Manush, Gabby Hartnett and Dizzy Dean. (What ever happened to all those vivid names ballplayers used to have? It's hard to get excited about guys named Clyde and Warren.)

When the White Sox lost, it was usually wise to leave the house for an hour or so. When the Cubs won, Gramma celebrated by doling out fresh-baked cookies. You guessed it—I was a Cubs fan.

In 1931, when I was 7, we made our first trip to Chicago, about 110 miles away. Mom packed sandwiches in a picnic basket and Dad squeezed a dozen lemons so we'd have lemonade in our big Thermos bottle. Somewhere around De Kalb or Sycamore, we pulled off the road and had lunch sitting on a blanket under a shady old tree. Dad checked the tires, radiator water and fan belts, then we resumed the trip.

We stayed with Aunt Florence, who lived in an apartment house on what was called "the near North Side". I soon determined that an apartment house was a place that smelled of cabbage and had no lawn to mow. It seemed to me like a bizarre, unnatural way for people to live.

I spent a sleepless night on the living room sofa listening to car horns, streetcars, sirens and people quarreling on the sidewalk down below. Didn't anyone in this town ever sleep?

The first thing we did the next morning was take a streetcar to the Tribune Tower, a skyscraper that housed the *Chicago Tribune*, which humbly called itself "The World's Greatest Newspaper".

This was the tallest building in the city at that time, and the elevator was considerably faster than the one in the 4-story Central National Bank building back home. Still, the ride seemed to last forever.

When the doors opened, we stepped outside onto the breezy observation deck. Wow! We could see most of North America!

To the southwest were the stockyards and the University of

HUSTLE-BUSTLE was a new concept for country folks' first visit to the metropolis. This vintage view of State Street shows Chicago as a vibrant "city on the move" in the early '40s.

Chicago campus. Homes and businesses stretched to the western horizon, and to the north we could make out apartment houses and hotels lining the lakeshore.

And it was true...even from this eagle's perch, we really *couldn't* see all the way across Lake Michigan.

Back down on the street, we hopped aboard one of the double-decker buses (affectionately called "rubbernecks" by the natives). We climbed the little spiral staircase to the open top deck and rode up Michigan Avenue until we reached the Lincoln Park Zoo, the first zoo I had ever seen.

Nothing in my schoolbooks had prepared me for the sight of giraffes, elephants and lions. We had lots of animals on the farm, but nothing like these exotic critters! I decided that zookeepers had the best job in the world.

Our next stop was the Merchandise Mart, billed as the world's largest building in terms of total floor space. Those were the days when the National Broadcasting Company had both a Red and Blue network. (If my memory isn't playing tricks, I recall both networks had studios in the Mart.)

Our tour guide let us peer through glass windows that looked down on a broadcasting studio. She pointed out celebrities who we had only known as voices coming out of the radio.

When we learned there was a soap opera in progress, everyone watched, fascinated, as the cast stood at microphones reading from their scripts. Off to the side, a sound effects man busily rang doorbells, slammed doors and made *cloppety-clop* footsteps with wooden blocks.

Radio would never seem quite the same to us again. Instead of seeing a galloping horse in our mind's eye, we'd now envision a man rhythmically hitting a board with two rubber cups.

Chicago, as many recall, was also the longtime home of the *WLS Barn Dance*, which in those days was a national showcase for country music talent. Remember George Gobel, Red Foley and others cast in the early days? It was our favorite Saturday night radio entertainment. Unfortunately, we couldn't get tickets for the show that night. No one warned us you had to reserve tickets *months* in advance.

After dark, before returning to spend another night with Aunt Florence, we walked to Grant Park and viewed the splendor of its incredible fountain. Seated on a bench, we marveled at the colored lights and changing water patterns. It seemed the grandest sight any of us had ever seen.

The next morning, we visited Marshall Field's department store. We couldn't afford to buy anything, of course, but just *seeing* the most famous store in Chicago was an adventure.

The first floor alone seemed to cover more area than all the retail stores in Sterling...and there were several more floors just like it. "Who in the world buys all this stuff?" Dad grumbled.

Later, we walked around the Loop, terrified by the overhead clatter and thunder of the El trains. I couldn't imagine risking my life on one of those clanking, speeding monstrosities.

Finally, it was time for the long drive home, but first we paused briefly so I could see the Vatican of Baseball and home of the Cubs, Wrigley Field. My Cubbies were out of town that week, but at least I got to see where they did battle with the fearsome Pittsburgh Pirates and the rowdy St. Louis Cardinals' "gas house gang".

Mom had come down with a bad case of pinkeye, and tears streamed down her cheeks as we left downtown and drove into the setting sun. The blinding glare also caused Dad to miss a stoplight, and he was flagged down by a grim-faced policeman.

The cop put one foot up on the running board, leaned down to look inside our car and sized things up at a glance. Here was an angry-looking man and a red-eyed woman with tears flowing down her face.

Obviously, a domestic tiff had been in progress. The officer hesitated for a few seconds, then patted Dad on the shoulder and said something about how he should keep his eye on the traffic and do his quarreling at home. He waved us on our way.

That may have been the only time a case of pinkeye helped beat a traffic ticket!

We got back late that night, having suffered just one flat tire on the way. The dogs came bounding out to greet us, then Dad and I changed clothes and went to the barn to do the milking.

The big city had been awesome and a lot of fun...but it sure felt great to be back home.

We All Fall For Tourist Attractions

Many years ago, I was driving across Ohio on old U.S. Highway 20, headed home to visit Mom and Dad in Illinois. Suddenly I noticed a sign that proclaimed: "World's Only Living Two-Headed Calf 10 Miles Ahead!"

What sort of swindle is this? I wondered. *What won't people dream up to bilk innocent travelers?*

Before long the next sign appeared: "See The World's Only Living Two-Headed Calf—Five Miles."

I'd been raised on a farm with cattle and had helped bring many a calf into the world—little ones, big ones, twins and a few that made their entrance backwards. But never a two-headed calf. Was it possible?

Probably not. I thought back years earlier when I'd been fleeced out of a quarter at the Illinois State Fair, lured in by the

164

promise that I would see a "Genuine Mermaid Living Under Water".

It had been a total fraud involving a young lady in a flesh-colored bathing suit and an optical trick that was apparent even to a 14-year-old. Not only that, the "mermaid" didn't even have a tail with flippers.

Then the next sign popped up, announcing that the genetic bovine marvel was but 3 miles away.

And then came the big sign urging, "Turn Here To See The World's Only Living Two-Headed Calf! Second farm on the left."

Well, home was still many hours ahead, and I wanted to arrive in time for supper. I drove on.

It's been at least 40 years since I saw those signs, and to this day, I wish I had turned down that gravel road. Maybe I missed out on seeing one of Mother Nature's true marvels. (Since writing this, three people have assured me that they saw the calf with their own eyes. It was, indeed, alive and had two heads.)

I'm sure you remember stopping at similar tourist attractions a half century or more ago. Those were the days before Disney World, Six Flags amusement parks, Dollywood, Silver Dollar City, Sea World and dozens of other mega-attractions. We were easily lured off the road for anything that promised to break the boredom of a long trip.

For sheer ingenuity, it was hard to top the Wall Drug Store in Wall, South Dakota. It hit upon the simplest, cheapest come-on in the world—free ice water. It was an irresistible lure to parched travelers in those days before air-conditioned cars.

I remember how excited my sister and I were when Dad stopped at a crossroads general store/gas station/post office in northern Wisconsin where a black bear was penned up. Buy him a bottle of Nehi soda pop, and he would swig it down while standing on his hind legs.

We had never seen a live bear...much less one that drank soda pop. I'm sure the man who owned the bear sold a lot more gas and groceries—not to mention Nehi—than he would have otherwise. That's how tourist attractions were born.

A popular summer destination in the Midwest was a place called the Wisconsin Dells. It was a pleasant area where you could take a boat ride on the Wisconsin River and view the magnificent rock formations along the shore on both sides.

There also were places where you could spread out your picnic lunch on a table under the trees. Nearby were a few booths and stalls where Indians sold moccasins, kid-sized feather headdresses, tiny birch bark canoes and little cloth bags packed with aromatic pine needles.

It sure was exciting to talk with a genuine Indian. Who could resist coughing up allowance money to buy one of their handicrafts?

But alas, life is filled with disillusions. Imagine my disappointment when I got home and discovered "Made in Czechoslovakia" stamped on the insoles of my new moccasins!

(See why I didn't stop for the two-headed calf?)

It also was in the '30s when Florida entrepreneurs discovered that Northerners would slam on the brakes and pitch the kids against the front seat to view *Live Alligators!*

That must have astounded Floridians, given that alligators were (and still are) common throughout the state. It was akin to an Iowan advertising *See Live Pigs!*

Despite the estimated 1,000,000 gators on the loose in Florida and the fact that the state maintains an alligator removal service in case one takes a liking to your backyard, they're *still* a tourist attraction. Imagine what a magnet they must have been 60 years ago, back before Disney invented mechanical alligators and an Abraham Lincoln robot.

To be fair, though, not all tourist attractions back then were as tawdry as the Nehi-swilling bruin. For reasons which escape me, Niagara Falls was the number one honeymoon destination.

Mom and Dad broke with tradition and went out West instead. One of Mom's most cherished treasures was a well-thumbed photo album filled with snapshots of their month in Estes Park, the old mining town of Cripple Creek and the wondrous Garden of the Gods.

They stayed in primitive cabins, took long hikes in the mountains and came home with a lifetime's worth of happy memories, despite a shortage of glitz and glitter.

The area in which I grew up was on the Lincoln Highway, America's only coast-to-coast route at the time. If you were traveling east or west, the Lincoln Highway was likely the road you took.

STEP RIGHT UP. Whether it was a honeymoon trip to Niagara Falls or the sideshow attractions at a county fair, folks had plenty they could marvel at in the good old days.

Nearby Dixon, where my grandparents lived, was also on Route 30. The town commissioned what I believe is one of the best statues anywhere of Abraham Lincoln, locating it on the site of one of the famous Lincoln-Douglas debates. It turned out to be a dandy attraction. It's still there, but you have to hunt for it behind a gaggle of taverns and filling stations.

Farther north along the Rock River, tourists pull off to marvel at the towering, magnificent statue of a brooding Black Hawk, scanning the river from a tall bluff on the far side. I can't think of a grander tribute to any major Indian figure.

If your destination was onward to the Golden West, those "genuine Indian souvenirs" places became more common. Somewhere out there was a legendary donkey that drank soda pop out of a bottle just like the Wisconsin bear.

Once you reached Los Angeles, you simply *had* to see Schwab's Drugstore where, legend had it, a very young Lana Turner in a very tight sweater was discovered by a talent scout.

Later you probably took a ride on one of the sight-seeing buses that promised to show you the homes of famous movie stars. And if you were lucky, you might even get to tour the MGM Studios.

167

On the way home, you made sure your route took you to Yellowstone National Park, established by Teddy Roosevelt. Just as today, you patiently sat on benches to wait for Old Faithful to erupt, Box Brownie in hand to photograph the grand moment.

You were in good company, though. Legend has it that when Daniel Boone was in his 70s, he *walked* from his home outside St. Louis all the way to Yellowstone to see if the tales trappers told of its wonders were really true. He, too, marveled at Old Faithful …and then turned around and walked back home.

One of the good things to come out of the Depression years was the development of our state and national parks, thanks largely to the Civilian Conservation Corps. It was a visionary idea that did a lot of lasting good for us all.

I have one special memory of the CCC. We took only two vacations while I was growing up, and one was to the Arrowhead country of Minnesota.

We were bumping along a narrow forest road in the Superior National Forest when an army truck loaded with CCC boys came toward us. Dad tried to make room for the truck but slid off into the ditch. We were miles from civilization.

No problem. The truck stopped, our family got out of the car and a dozen or so young men simply *picked up* our 1930 Willys and put it back on the road. That was the highlight of the trip!

By the time the Depression was over and the CCC disbanded, the United States was blessed with thousands of fine places where we could picnic, swim in a lake, splash in an ocean, camp on Cape Hatteras, wade in a creek or take long hikes through towering forests and up into the mountains.

What better tourist attractions could we have created?

Our ideas about what makes a good vacation continue to change. Although alligator farms and snake ranches still thrive, somehow too many of our tourist attractions seem awfully *organized* and *commercial* nowadays.

By the way, no matter how many grand places I've had the good fortune to visit, I still wish I had stopped to see that Live Two-Headed Calf.

$\mathscr{L}$odging Was Lacking for Early-Day Travel

In the '30s and '40s, when people were scratching hard to make a buck, nearly every town you passed through had homes along the highway with signs out front offering "Tourist Rooms". Remember?

Most of those places were nothing special—just a pleasant family abode a lot like your own. The homeowner had a spare room or two available and hoped to rent them out for whatever the traffic would bear. For a dollar or two, you got a clean room, a double bed and the opportunity to share a bathroom down the hall with the family.

Even in the early '50s, a few of these places still operated. I recall staying in a home near Ashland, Ohio back then. It was a great sprawling farmhouse with bedrooms furnished in fine antiques, reminding me of childhood visits to Gramma's house.

In the morning, I went down to an enormous cozy kitchen with a big round table and joined the family for a cooked-to-order breakfast. It was about as close to being back home as a traveler could get.

Those were the days before motels were common, although the first one had opened during the '20s in California. Instead, highway travelers often relied on "tourist courts"—usually a shabby huddle of tiny one-room dwellings with space for a couple of steel cots and a chair or two. The "facilities" were out back and down the path...just be sure to take your flashlight. The better tourist courts had covered parking spaces alongside each cottage.

Once while traveling on business, I stayed in a typical old-time tourist court on the edge of a small Kansas town. It was a hot night and there was no air-conditioning, so I switched off the light and opened the window above my bed.

A short time later, a cow blasted a plaintive *Mooooo* right in my ear. My heart stopped for at least 5 seconds. Why was there a cow in my room? When judgment returned, I realized that the cow wasn't really in the room, he was just peering through the window.

Looking around the next morning, I found that the back wall of the unit formed one boundary of a pasture full of cows. Apparently the one that startled me was just being friendly and wanted to say hello to a weary traveler.

Besides tourist courts, some small towns had at least one hotel. There were two in my hometown of Sterling, Illinois. One was typical of that era—a two-story building with a veranda across the front, right next to the sidewalk. That big porch was amply stocked with rocking chairs so guests could sit outside on nice evenings and watch the local folks stroll by.

In many towns, the local hotel dining room was the best place to go if you wanted something more than coffee-shop food.

Most salesmen knew the best places in town to eat and to stay, so hotels depended on traveling salesmen for their steady business. Even today, salesmen have a way of congregating where other salesmen stay. Like fishermen, they get together to boast of their successes and bemoan "the big one that got away".

Small-town hotels were friendly places, even if the rooms weren't anything to brag about. You cheerfully settled for cheap and clean.

I particularly remember the old Kankakee Hotel in Kankakee, Illinois, just across the street from the Illinois Central railroad station. It was a dandy place to stay and it had a first-rate restaurant.

There was one unnerving feature, however. The rooms had steam radiators, and tied to the leg of each radiator was a sturdy coil of rope with a knot every 2 or 3 feet. It was the fire escape.

Whenever I stayed

Ewing Galloway

TOURIST COURTS as pictured (left) provided cozy quarters for tired motorists and a "path out back" to the facilities.

Courtesy of the Peabody Hotel

GRANDEUR FROM THE PAST. The Hotel Peabody in Memphis remains an elegant symbol of yesteryear. Early-bird guests still enjoy seeing resident ducks waddle off the elevator from their rooftop pen and make the grand march into the lobby's fountain pool.

there, I said my bedtime prayers and added a special request that I wouldn't wake to discover fire trucks parked down below.

One hotel I'll bet lots of *Reminisce* readers recall was the one in Ogallala, Nebraska. Ogallala was a solitary oasis out in the middle of nowhere on Route 30, the transcontinental road known as the Lincoln Highway.

If you were heading west, it was where you branched south toward Denver or Los Angeles or straight on to San Francisco. After a long day of coping with two-lane traffic, Ogallala looked like paradise on the prairie.

The town's hotel hardly qualified as a restful haven, given the endless procession of cross-country trucks that rumbled past its windows. A busy railroad depot was just across the street, too, as I recall.

Despite the all-night racket, prudent travelers planned their trips to stay overnight in Ogallala. It was either that or else sleep beside the road.

Of course, lots of people did just that—they carried a tent and sleeping bags or cots and set up for the night along the road or in a town park. No one seemed to mind, as long as they tidied up when they left.

Big-city hotels were a whole different matter. They were majestic places with hustling bellhops, high-ceilinged lobbies and friendly people at the front desk who greeted you by name if you were a "regular".

I never frequented such fancy lodgings, but my bride and I did honeymoon at the old Stevens Hotel on Michigan Boulevard in Chicago during World War II.

Then the Army sent me overseas. When I returned many months later, my wife and I once again reserved "our" room at the Stevens to celebrate.

When I walked up to register, the desk clerk sadly informed us that he couldn't give us the room we'd had during our honeymoon because it was occupied. To make amends, he gave us a larger, nicer corner room and hoped we wouldn't mind too much.

Until someone comes up with a better definition of what makes a great hotel, that will do just fine.

Another hotel of distinction is the Peabody in Memphis, Tennessee, long known for the ducks that swim in the lobby fountain. Many guests wake up extra early to be on hand when the ducks get off the elevator (their pen is on the rooftop) and waddle across the lobby to begin their workday paddling around in the fountain's pool.

Lobby fountains and friendly service weren't the only attraction of some of the grand old hotels. Their ballrooms were home to many of the best Big Bands of that era.

There was the ballroom of the Chase Park Plaza in St. Louis "overlooking beautiful Forest Park"…the Starlight Roof of the Waldorf in New York…the Edgewater Beach ballroom on Chicago's north side…and the Roosevelt Hotel in New Orleans.

Every night, radio stations would carry live broadcasts from those magical spots, featuring the music of Shep Fields and his Rippling Rhythm, Benny Goodman, Lawrence Welk and Horace Heidt.

The big-city hotels were also proud of their fine restaurants. Eventually I got to visit a few of them in the waning days of the fine downtown hotels. They were every bit as good as I had imagined.

Nowadays, there aren't as many of those grand old urban hotels around, but a few of the pricier national chains have recently reinstated the splendor and service. What goes around comes around.

Motels now flourish at every major crossroads on the interstate. In recent years, many bare-bones motels have come along for economy-minded travelers who can do without a restaurant, swimming pool, exercise room and secretarial service.

But what I get the biggest kick out of is how tourist rooms have made a comeback. Today they're called "bed-and-breakfasts", but instead of a dollar a night, they charge up to $100 or more.

However, you still get to share a bathroom and eat breakfast with the family—just like that place outside of Ashland, Ohio I recall so fondly.

Downtown Was the Center Of Our Community

Let's go downtown....You don't hear those words a lot anymore, because too many places don't have much of a downtown these days. There was a time, though, when going downtown got the heart beating a little faster, because *everything* was there.

The only place I know where you didn't go downtown was Dixon, Illinois. The Rock River flows through the middle of the city, so if you lived on the north side of the river, you went "over town". I guess it's because you must go *over* the river on one of the city's two bridges.

Every "downtown" had its own special personality, and anything you needed was there. The dry goods store, the drugstore, the movie theater, bank, hardware store, jeweler, cobbler, clock repairman, the caramel corn shop and soda fountain, the music store and bakery...they were all downtown.

My favorite "downtowns" were built around a central square. In the South, there usually was a statue of a Confederate soldier in the middle. Squares in the North seemed to favor ancient cannons.

Lots of town squares had a gazebo where the local band

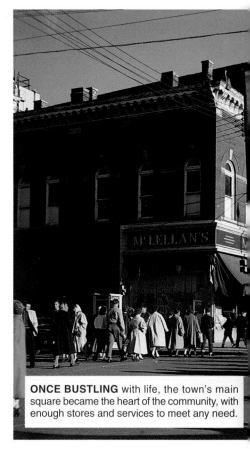

ONCE BUSTLING with life, the town's main square became the heart of the community, with enough stores and services to meet any need.

tootled once a week. Often the courthouse and the post office faced the square.

A smattering of places still have thriving downtowns and shady squares, and folks in Dixon still go "over town". But they're the exceptions, and it's a pity.

Downtown used to be much more than where you went to shop. It was the living, beating heart of your community.

Walk around downtown, and you might encounter the mayor. When adults met him they had a chance to say how things *ought* to be run.

You could complain about the newfangled parking meters and the hazards of angle parking or whatever else was on your mind. The conversation might not trigger changes, but it made you feel

better. You might even bump into the banker and, standing right there on the sidewalk, work out the details of a loan. "Just stop in tomorrow and sign the papers," he'd say.

You could even drop in at the utility companies, pay your bills and save a few 3-cent stamps. Where I grew up, you could even take in a paper bag full of burned-out light bulbs and get new ones—*for free!*

There was also a men's clothing store in our town that, to me, typifies what downtown was really about. On the main floor were suits, topcoats and accessories for men. Go up the creaky wooden steps to the second floor, and you were in the area for boys and young men. Down in the basement were OshKosh B'Gosh bib overalls, denim shirts, work jackets and sturdy boots.

The store was a cradle-to-grave supplier of male apparel. You and your favorite clerk went through life together—from your first knee pants and high-top boots to your high school sport coat to your wedding suit, slowly progressing from a "38 long" to a "54 portly".

Two blocks away was the shoe repair shop, a dark place filled with the aromas of leather and shoe polish. Not many people have their shoes repaired anymore, but back then the cobbler's store had piles of them waiting for new soles and heels and other disorderly piles of shoes waiting to be reclaimed.

As you walked inside, the owner would get up from his bench, wipe his hands on his apron and, through a mouthful of shoe tacks, ask what you needed. When you reminded him that you had dropped off your shoes last week, he'd look at the pile and say, "They'll be ready Tuesday" as he turned his back and went on working.

Sure enough, come Tuesday, there were your shoes with new soles and heels, a fresh shine and new laces.

We had a daily newspaper in Sterling, but if you wanted to find out what was really going on, you stopped by the barber shop. That's where the men who were serious about checkers, dominoes or pitch waged their endless battles. The shop was also a magnet for gossip and rumors. Some of what you heard was even true.

For the news about the world beyond Main Street, you stopped in at the newsstand and tobacco shop, always open on Sunday morning with plump Sunday editions shipped by overnight train

Harold M. Lambert

SIPPING A SODA or digging into a luscious ice-cream sundae was like the cherry on top of a delightful day downtown.

from Chicago. Dad favored the *Chicago Tribune,* even though he despised the politics of the publisher.

I once asked him why he took the paper when the editorials made him so angry. "It gives me things to think about when I'm working in the fields," he said.

Whenever you couldn't find something you needed anywhere else, you could be sure they had it at Woolworth's. Name it and they had it— goldfish, gumdrops, hair ribbons and hand towels, school

WISHFUL THINKING. Gazing at window displays along Main Street gave kids something to dream about and save money for.

supplies and sewing thread, lipstick, lockets, canaries and kites.

Running the length of the right-hand wall was a *long* lunch counter with low stools that squeaked and the best chicken salad sandwiches anywhere. It was a favorite gathering place for morning coffee and noon lunches.

Most of the towns around us had a municipal band that played a concert every week during the summer. The Dixon band played on the courthouse lawn.

People either spread blankets on the grass, used the permanent benches or sat in their cars. Those in the cars honked their horns instead of applauding. Kids ran around along the edges of the crowd, playing tag or hide-and-go-seek.

Saturday night was the *big* night downtown. To enjoy it to the fullest, the trick was to find a prime parking place. That meant you had to eat supper early and get the dishes done fast.

In our town, the best parking area was on Locust Street, right in front of Sears & Roebuck. Sooner or later during the evening, everyone would stop in at the store.

We'd sit in our car and "people-watch" after our shopping was done. Usually we brought along a big bag of popcorn from home to munch, but the best nights were when we picked up fresh caramel corn from the little hole-in-the-wall shop next to the theater.

When friends walked by, you gave a discreet beep on the horn and they'd come over for a chat, the husband on Dad's side of the car and the wife on Mom's.

Later in the evening, after most of the stores had closed and families had gone home, the high school kids tumbled out of the basketball game or movie theater and took over the soda parlor. A half dollar bought you and your date a cherry Coke, french fries and a hamburger. The jukebox played *Chattanooga Choo Choo* or *Mairzy Doats* over and over again, and life was about as good as it could get.

What I remember most about "downtown" was that people seemed to smile a lot. They weren't in a hurry and seemed anxious to exchange pleasantries. I guess *people* were as much a reason for going downtown as was buying stuff.

Today, lots of downtowns are deserted. Plywood covers the store windows. And where are the people? "Out at the mall," where not many people are smiling and everyone is in a hurry.

"That's progress," people tell me. They say that the giant discount chains offer a bigger selection of merchandise at lower prices. They say the malls bring more business to town.

Well, the prices may be good, and I can tell by the clothing labels that mass marketing has created a lot of employment—in Taiwan and Haiti, anyhow.

And they do have masses of merchandise, certainly a lot more than that friendly menswear store I mentioned earlier. (It didn't have acres of clothing, but "my clerk" knew exactly what I liked and somehow had it in stock whenever I needed it.)

I'm far from convinced, however, that we can afford the high price of losing what "downtown" meant. The merchants supported the bowling teams and bought ads in the school play program. They cared about beautifying and improving the community, and they were always there to lead the hospital fund-raising drive.

I haven't yet seen a mall that can replace the downtown I once knew and remember so fondly.

Fourth of July Was The Highlight of Summer

SPARKLING MEMORIES of the Fourth recall Dad lighting fireworks as in this 1930s photo. Kids were mesmerized, but Mom was often terrified, warning *Don't burn down the house!*

How I looked forward to the good old Fourth of July when I was a kid! It was the major high point in an otherwise uneventful summer bracketed on either end by Memorial Day and Labor Day. From my point of view, the Fourth ranked second only to Christmas in the year's exciting events. No other holiday came close.

Shortly after school let out, I began accumulating capital for the Fourth in the same frantic way a squirrel saves acorns for winter. A substantial arsenal of the necessary explosives required plenty of money.

That meant negotiating odd jobs with Mom and Dad—tasks over and above my assigned and mandatory chores. Paint the chicken house? Sure. Spade and rake the garden? You betcha! If the price was right, I'd do just about anything.

In late June, I'd begin scouting the fireworks market. In those days, our town had none of the supermarket fireworks stands next to used car lots at the edge of town that you see today. But various merchants laid in alluring displays of stuff that went bang.

As far as I can recall, the best selection was at Hallett's, which for the other 50 weeks of the year was a stationery and bookstore. Counters and tables were cleared off to make way for fireworks of every description.

The first critical decision was which cap gun to purchase. The cheapest were single-shot models. You put one cap under the hammer, pulled the trigger and...*pop!* Then you shook out the scorched piece of red paper and inserted another cap. Or if you wanted more noise, you used two caps.

This definitely was not how the West was won.

Pricier models could be loaded with a whole roll of caps that fed up from inside the gun butt, like tape in an adding machine. You could squeeze off 50 shots without reloading. That was the theory, at least. Unfortunately the long strip of red paper with little dimples of gunpowder had a bad habit of jamming. Was this what you wanted when you had Bonnie and Clyde cornered? Not likely.

Another model was a six-shooter that looked convincingly like what Hoot Gibson or Tom Mix would carry. It used little paper cap disks and never jammed. Now *this* was more like it.

The real problem with any cap gun was that it didn't make a lot of noise. It was nowhere near as much fun as firecrackers, where "the bigger the better" was all you needed to know.

However, Mom was one of those prudent mothers who set strict limits on the size firecrackers I could tote home. She usually went along to Hallett's with my sister and me, hovering in the background to occasionally scowl and shake her head as I fondled firecrackers the size of dynamite sticks.

The tacit rule in those days was that you didn't shoot off fireworks of any kind until the dawn of the

Fourth. So I carefully hid my bag of fireworks so that sister Mary couldn't pilfer from it and impatiently waited for the big day.

At the first hint of sun in the east, we scrambled downstairs and out on the back steps to fire our first salvos. That was the signal for the dogs to dash for a dark spot under the porch, where they huddled in terror the rest of the day.

As the morning progressed and we tired of blazing away at each other with our cap guns, we naturally turned to experimenting with ways to get "more bang for the buck". One favorite was to slip a firecracker under an empty tin can to see how high we could launch it into the air. Throwing firecrackers into the horse tank also produced an interesting effect.

PARADE INTO THE PAST. This decorated view of Main Street in Delhi, New York shows folks staking out places for the Fourth of July parade—in the days when folks dressed up for the event. The variety store (far left) advertised National Fire Works For Sale.

But one experiment took an unexpected direction. I discovered a perfect firecracker-sized hole that long ago had been drilled through the white-painted cedar siding of our house. The hole opened into the basement.

Mom and Dad were taking an afternoon nap, which made it too tempting to resist. (I know, I know…but it made sense at the time.) I inserted one of our bigger firecrackers into the hole, lit the fuse and stood back.

BANG! To my horror, cedar splinters flew in all directions, leaving a blackened 2-foot crater on the side of the house.

The only prudent course would have been to leave home immediately and flee to the safety of Australia. But I had spent all my money on fireworks.

Or maybe…just maybe…Dad would remember his own youthful Fourth of July disaster. He sure enjoyed telling about it.

When Dad was about ten, he and his brother had come across an 8-foot length of 2-inch iron pipe. A solid cap had been screwed onto one end. Those were the days when almost every farmer had blasting powder around to blow stumps out of the ground.

Yes, Dad and his brother poured blasting powder into the pipe, inserted a length of fuse, stuffed the opening with rags, lit the fuse and moved off a distance to hear what they figured would be the Fourth of July blast to end 'em all.

Surprise! They had anticipated Wernher von Braun, the German rocket scientist, by 40 years. The pipe didn't blow up. Instead, an angry jet of flame burst out the end, propelling the pipe at a faster and faster pace toward the cowbarn. Ducks, geese and guinea hens flew in all directions. The pipe went clean through the barn, eventually coming to rest a half block away in the pasture.

Dad always chuckled when he told the story. Dare I hope that he would see the humor in my miscalculation?

Strangely enough, he was not amused.

Of course, there was more to the Fourth than just blowing away my hard-earned savings. Usually my mother's relatives showed up for the day. It was a major family reunion.

There were big platters of fried chicken, bowls of potato salad, fresh-picked green beans, Parker House rolls from the bakery, and the dreaded lime Jell-O salad with shredded carrots.

After the meal, Uncle John would stretch out on the front porch glider and favor us all with a virtuoso snoring concert, thereby eliminating the porch as a place to sit and chat.

Others of us took part in the traditional front lawn croquet tournament, even though the result was known ahead of time. Grampa Stevens was a ferocious, merciless and expert player. He *always* won. So the battle was really for second place.

On other Fourths, the tribe assembled at the local park for the day. Uncle John or Uncle Bill went there early in the morning to stake out a claim and protect picnic tables from poachers. If they didn't, we ended up sitting on blankets, warily watching for sprinting urchins who were likely to run right through the bowl of potato salad. Or, with luck, the Jell-O salad.

The municipal band always showed up to play a rousing concert of Sousa marches, finishing off with *The Star Spangled Banner*. You could also depend on a congressman to deliver a patriotic speech from the bandstand. After reminding everyone what the day was really about, he would wander through the crowd to shake hands and admire babies.

The day ended at home where a big tub of homemade raspberry or strawberry ice cream was waiting. Everyone would ladle out a heaping bowlful and then adjourn to the lawn or front porch to await the fireworks.

The best display was about 2 miles away at the town's only country club. By today's standards it wasn't a *great* display, but it certainly dazzled us back then. During lulls, Dad would set off *his* fireworks (while Mom fretted and nervously cautioned him to please not blow off his hand or burn down the house).

There were pinwheels he tacked to the telephone pole, little cone-shaped volcanoes that spewed out big, bright sparks and Roman candles that went *pffft, pffft, pffft* as they spit colored balls of fire into the night sky.

And just as today, the finale came when sparklers were distributed to all the kids.

Finally the relatives went home. Peace and quiet descended. The dogs came out from under the porch. It had been a memorable, fun-packed Fourth of July. Now then, how many days were there until Christmas?

ℋalloween...The Spooks And the Spooked

Well-intentioned citizens have been delivering passionate speeches about "what is wrong with this country" ever since Paul Revere clattered through sleeping towns on his midnight ride.

Everyone has their own theory. Mine is simple. If you want to know one thing that's wrong, just take a look at what has happened to Halloween!

Nowadays, kids are herded like little flocks of costumed geese from house to house by apprehensive parents. Mom or Dad lurk just beyond where the porch light shines, firmly reminding the little ones who forget a polite "thank-you" as they leave the door with their treasure.

Worse still, many communities have had to make Halloween a *daylight* event because of traffic and other perils.

It's a shame, because Halloween just isn't Halloween without the mystery of ominous darkness and who-knows-what terrors hiding in the deep shadows and shrubbery. Yet all these precautions are prudent and necessary—"and that's what's wrong with this country," he said, pounding the table.

Today's costumes are store-bought. Of course. A truly scary mask costs upwards of $25. Yes, it really does. The grandchildren took me to their Halloween store and proved it last year.

The treats we dole out are (*must be!*) store-bought. Try handing out a freshly baked doughnut from your kitchen and be prepared for a visit from the police. What a windfall for the junk-candy makers!

So, what we've ended up with is another commercialized, sanitized event for kids that's about as much fun as reading the Yellow Pages.

Think back to the Halloweens of a half century ago, and you can understand why people over 60 shake their heads and start talking about "the good old days".

Halloween used to be the one night of the year when a kid could indulge in a little creative devilment, and the community would tolerate it. Yet there were still limits which everyone understood.

The unwritten rule was that anything was OK as long as it could be fixed in a few minutes the next day. You could mess around, but don't be a destructive little hoodlum.

Tipping over outhouses was almost a cliché. My grandfather brooded over the problem for an entire year until he came up with a plan to foil the outhouse-tippers. He knew they always approached from the rear, slinking through the inky darkness at the back of the lot. So, Grampa moved his outhouse just a few feet toward his home, leaving the pit uncovered.

Maybe he was inspired by tales of tiger hunters who used pits to snare their quarry. Whatever, his plan was, let's say, a howling success.

The next year he took the easy way and simply sat inside the privy, his shotgun loaded with rock salt. Wouldn't you know, the little sneaks crept up and tipped the outhouse forward so the door was flat on the ground. Grampa was trapped! His angry roars alarmed people a block away and brought the family to his rescue.

The great Halloween challenge was to come up with a clever costume that didn't cost anything. Heedless of the need to be frugal, I usually started out with some grandiose, improbable idea that only a Hollywood special-effects expert could have pulled off.

For example, there was the year I had decided to go as Buck Rogers, complete with silver space suit and rocket gun.

"I think you'd better go as a hobo, instead," Mom counseled. Well, that was no big trick during the Depression. Raggedy clothes were in abundant supply.

I pawed through Mom's "rag bag" and salvaged a tattered pair of bib overalls and one of Dad's discarded work shirts with holes in the elbows. With a few rips here and a few snips there, I soon had an outfit that no self-respecting hobo would wear to a dogfight. A discarded felt hat for the head and a few smudges of Shinola shoe polish on my face completed that year's Halloween costume.

Today they call that "recycling", but we just called it "being poor".

The sad discovery, though, was that I was indistinguishable from several dozen other little "hoboes" on the street that night. Lots of cash-strapped mothers must have had the same brilliant idea.

Trick-or-treating in the country was clearly impractical, so Mom and Dad would drive sister Mary and me into town, where we'd rendezvous with some school pals at a family friend's home.

GIMME A TREAT! Years ago, witches and goblins weren't spooked when receiving homemade treats. But today, only store-bought candy is acceptable.

From there we'd set out in a noisy, boisterous pack, grocery sacks in hand.

Along the curbs, long piles of burning leaves cast eerie, flickering shadows on the trees while perfuming the autumn air with a smoky incense. (You still want to know what's wrong with this country? How about the fact that you can be fined for burning your leaves, but it's perfectly OK to burn the American flag on your front lawn!)

Each stop was special. At one house, the lady handed out homemade fudge. A few doors farther on there were plates of crunchy cookies

Don Condon

DELICIOUS FEAR. The anticipation of ghosts lurking in the dark made for the best trick-or-treating atmosphere.

or fresh donuts that were crispy on the outside and still moist and warm on the inside. The loot mounted—popcorn balls, caramel apples, slabs of homemade peanut brittle and still more cookies and fudge.

But we all knew that the ultimate test was still ahead—the dark, ominous house of The Mean Old Man. Eventually we had to face him. We'd have been branded as hopelessly chickenhearted had we not stopped there.

The biggest kid among us was delegated to lead the way up onto the porch and knock on the door. The rest of us huddled near the porch steps, poised for instant flight.

Slowly, slowly the door would open. A huge figure loomed, spookily backlit by the dim hallway bulb overhead so that his face was nearly invisible.

"What do you kids want?" he'd snarl.

"Trick or treat," we squeaked.

He'd glare at us, letting the suspense build, and then reach into his pocket to produce a handful of pennies, doling one out to each of us. Giddy with relief, we would flee down the steps, thrilled to have survived yet another year's confrontation with The Mean Old Man.

Truth to tell, The Mean Old Man played a key role in making Halloween successful, and I expect he knew he was performing a vital public service. Something or someone had to scare you just a little bit, or else it wasn't Halloween.

I've read that the thrill of riding roller coasters comes from what is called "secure insecurity". On one level, you're scared silly, but deep down you know you'll live through it. That was the essence of an old-fashioned Halloween.

You could soap a downtown store window, dreading the possibility of being caught. But you also knew that the worst you could expect was the indignity of scraping the window clean the next day while your pals taunted you from afar.

Finally we would return to our home where Mom and Dad were chatting with their friends and waiting for us. There was fresh cider to sip while we inventoried our "haul" in the grocery bags and relived the chilling encounter with The Mean Old Man.

On the way home, Mom would utter the famous warning *every* mother has uttered since the first trick-or-treat night: "Now don't eat everything at one time, or you'll be sick for sure!"

We'd promise not to…and then, of course, we did. And I don't recall ever being sick—any more than I ever got cramps when I went swimming sooner than an hour after eating.

It's too bad my grandchildren can't savor the excitement of running loose for one glorious night, spooked by the shadows and the imagined terrors that lurk nearby. But too often, these days, the terrors are all too real, and parents should impose caution.

Several years ago, I rigged up a 6-foot, sheet-clad dummy and hung it from a rope up in the branches of a large tree in the front yard. At night when you couldn't get a good look, it passed as a fairly authentic ghost.

The rope ran up through a pulley and down to where I was hiding in some bushes. Whenever a group of trick-or-treaters had collected their booty at our front door and started back for the street, I let the dummy swoop down toward the ground as I let out what I hoped was a fearsome moan.

The result was something like throwing a tomcat into a flock of pigeons. The little tykes fled, screaming down the sidewalk.

A few mothers complained the next day. I apologized. Obviously they didn't understand why the neighborhood needed a Mean Old Man to make Halloween complete.

$\mathcal{T}$hanksgiving Left a Feast of Memories

Back in grade school, I truly dreaded the month of November. Not because that's when the weather was likely to turn nasty. And not because major league baseball was over and the Chicago Cubs had finished up in the cellar again.

No, nothing like that. I dreaded November, the month that harbors Thanksgiving, because I couldn't draw turkeys. I couldn't even cut them out if someone else drew them on paper.

But, as we all know, drawing turkeys and Pilgrims was required of all grade-schoolers. Never mind that you still spelled it "turkie" and didn't have the faintest idea what Pilgrims were. No, sir. Draw 'em and cut 'em out!

Not until years later did I realize that this had nothing to do with developing our artistic talents. It was the cunning way ruthless teachers exploited child labor to decorate the classroom and impress the school board.

The most interesting thing about Pilgrims, as far as I was concerned, was that they dressed up in black clothes with white collars and cuffs. The men wore high-crowned hats with a buckle in the front. They always appeared to be dressed for church. Didn't they own any work clothes?

Students who possessed natural artistic ability got to draw Pilgrims and turkeys. The artistically challenged were condemned to cutting them out. Even so, my turkeys ended up looking like stumpy-legged ostriches. I was not adept with scissors. Girls, of course, were.

Deep down in my heart, I suspected that Pilgrims also served venison, squirrel and rabbit for their Thanksgiving dinner. Now, I could draw a pretty fair rabbit, but I never met a teacher who would listen to reason on the subject. It was turkey or nothing.

That's how it is with Thanksgiving. We recall the good old days, and things have to be a certain way. There are foods that simply *must* be on the table or else it isn't Thanksgiving.

Gramma Strock was a tiny woman of German stock, and her cooking was traditional Pennsylvania Dutch. She had grown up feeding hardworking farmers who ate more for breakfast than most of us now eat in an entire day.

On Thanksgiving, Gramma always prepared a goose. I didn't especially like goose, but was delighted that there was now one less honker on their farm to terrorize me.

She also prepared a guinea hen, a ham *and* a huge piece of roast beef. This, mind you, for fewer than 20 people, if the whole clan showed up.

Turkey was *not* on the menu because Gramma didn't raise turkeys. The main reason she raised geese was for their feathers, which she stuffed into pillows and feather ticks. Turkey feathers make bum pillows.

In addition, Gramma served mashed potatoes, sweet potatoes, squash, string beans, red beets and creamed corn in a casserole. There also was tangy cranberry sauce in a cut-glass bowl and two or three varieties of home-canned pickles.

And there was oyster stuffing, which my youthful taste buds rejected as unfit for human consumption. Oysters were an alien critter in northern Illinois, but not in Maryland where Gramma's family originated.

After the meal, when everyone declared they couldn't eat another bite, the men would go outside while the women cleared the table and did dishes. But this was only intermission. The grand finale was ahead.

In an hour or so we reassembled at the table and out came the desserts. Mince pie, pumpkin pie, sour cream apple pie, shoofly pie, chocolate cake, rice pudding and cookies.

Yes, it was a feeding frenzy and a nutritionist's nightmare. I doubt there was anything on the table (*not one thing!*) that today's health-conscious generation would consume without a week of deep remorse.

Nor did the family go out jogging afterwards. We couldn't, of course, because spandex jogging duds and $180 running shoes had not been invented yet. Besides, it was time to go home, feed the livestock, gather the eggs and milk the cows.

Thanksgiving has always been the day when homemakers stage their biggest culinary extravaganza of the year. But please, it's not the day for "creativity".

This is *not* the time to try out new recipes, no matter how good they are. Thanksgiving is all about family traditions. You may have 18 interesting new recipes filed away for stuffing. Fine. Try them out some Sunday. But not on Thanksgiving.

Every family has its firm idea when it comes to "proper" turkey stuffing. While Gramma Strock used oysters, it would have been sweet potato corn bread stuffing, had she been raised in the South.

She would have used cranberries in place of the sweet potatoes, however, had she been raised in Massachusetts. A Minnesota childhood would have dictated stuffing based on wild rice and almonds. In Washington or Idaho, she likely would have learned to fix potato stuffing. In the unlikely event she had been Hawaiian, Gramma might have presented a turkey plump with macadamia nut stuffing.

Whatever you grew up with, *that's* the right way and the only way to stuff a turkey.

This brings up the cause of unexpected domestic strife that no one warns you about before you approach the altar. It develops when a girl from a bread-and-celery stuffing family gets married to a boy from a sausage stuffing clan.

With only one turkey for the oven, someone has to give in. Okay, bread and celery. But next year, ask Mom and get the recipe for a proper sausage stuffing.

Not that you asked, but here's *my* idea of the perfect Thanksgiving dinner. The turkey, of course, is stuffed with bread and celery, lightly kissed with sage. Mashed potatoes, please, so I can drown them in that rich turkey gravy.

Candied yams are important, too. And jellied cranberries (I detest the stewed whole ones). Then there absolutely *must* be a generous helping of small white onions in a cream sauce. And please don't even bother to pass the rolls, carrot sticks or olives. That's everyday stuff.

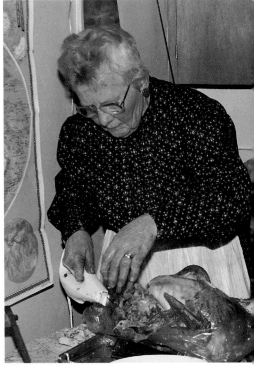

THE RIGHT STUFF. Family tradition and geographical location determine which type of stuffing one considers "proper", so possibilities for a squawk go up when cooks of differing opinions find themselves sharing a kitchen on Turkey Day.

Men are well-advised to stay out of the kitchen on Thanksgiving day. Even the gentlest woman, I have learned to my sorrow, gets snappish when she's preparing six different things at once and a man bumbles in, opens the refrigerator and asks where the salami sandwich meat is.

Women are the proper stars of the day. Men, pushed out of the spotlight, must settle for their one moment on stage—carving the turkey.

Watch the average man take apart a Thanksgiving turkey, and you gain a fresh appreciation of why good surgeons go through so many years of training and charge so much. (On the other hand,

Paul T. McMahon/Heartland Images

I would like just once to watch a surgeon carve *his* family turkey. I cherish the hope that he's as bad as the rest of us.)

You also learn a lot about people when it comes time to serve the turkey. There are the dark-meat people, the white-meat people and the "I'll have a little of both" people. By golly, they know what they want!

But then there are the "Oh, I don't care" folks. I've known a lot of them over the years, and not a single one ever amounted to much. (Never put such a person into a position of responsibility.)

So, the meal has been polished off. And there won't be leftover pumpkin pie for a midnight snack because once again, Uncle Leo and Aunt Gertrude asked for seconds.

Now here we come to the bad part. Every square inch of counter and table space in the kitchen is covered with dirty plates, glassware, silverware and serving dishes. The sink is jammed with pots and pans.

The rich and famous don't care, because they have a bunch of scullery maids and scullery lads to clean up the mess. How nice to walk away from the table guilt-free and flop on the sofa or take a nice leisurely walk.

Lucky them! Cleaning up after Thanksgiving dinner is like being asked to rewrap all the Christmas presents and put them back under the tree on Christmas morning.

Still, I'm glad the Pilgrims came up with Thanksgiving. I'm pleased that they invited the Indians, too. It was the neighborly thing to do and set a good example for the rest of us.

I just wish they would have served rabbit instead of turkey. I know how to draw a rabbit.

When Christmas Held Pure Enchantment

The autumn leaves are still on the trees, the local supermarket is selling Halloween candy and the weather is deliciously warm during the days and just crisp enough at night for a light blanket.

But wait…what's going on here? The department stores and such are featuring Christmas gift wrappings, tree ornaments and lights, and toys piled to the ceiling. Can Christmas really be close at hand?

Not really. December 25th is still three months away!

As best I can remember, there was a time when you celebrated Thanksgiving in November—and *then* you started to think about Christmas.

Each holiday was separate and special. They didn't all smoosh into each other. In places like New York and Philadelphia, the annual Thanksgiving Day Parade with bands and floats and Santa Claus was the official *opening* of the Christmas season. Nowadays, those same parades seem more like the halftime show.

When I was young, all of the anticipation and excitement of Christmas back then was packed into about five weeks. The magic began the day after Thanksgiving. That's when shop owners downtown unveiled their windows filled with Christmas merchandise, and we kids would spend the weekend pushing up close with our noses against the windows, straining to see every single item.

All around you, kids were shoving, pointing and chattering with excitement. Back then, none of us had already been preconditioned by a hundred television commercials pushing the season's new toys. This was brand-new stuff!

Girls *oohed* and *aahed* over Shirley Temple and Dionne quintuplet dolls. Boys exclaimed "Wow!" when they saw the miniature steam engine heated by an alcohol lamp, powering miniature saws and machines.

And everyone wanted the Giant Deluxe Tinkertoy set that came with enough pieces to make windmills and even a Ferris wheel! There were chemistry sets, new board games, doll buggies, cradles, miniature kitchen stoves and molds you could use to cast your own lead soldiers, cowboys and Indians.

One year, I was especially entranced by the new "Official Dick Tracy Detective Kit", complete with handcuffs and disguises. Our community wasn't infested with crooks, but it still seemed like a good idea to be able to slip into a disguise and help nab John Dillinger or Pretty Boy Floyd if they ever *did* come to town.

And snaking its way through this glorious display, puffing smoke and tooting its whistle, was the glorious American Flyer 12-car electric train that I absolutely *had* to have!

In our hometown, the two stores with the best Christmas windows were Wyne-Deavers and Sears & Roebuck. The smaller stores had window displays, too, so we kids prowled from store to store, mentally compiling our Christmas lists.

The local merchants went all out to transform our modest downtown area into a holiday wonderland. Christmas music played from loudspeakers and colored lights transformed Main Street into a dazzling canopy at least 4 blocks long.

The city fathers even made the ultimate sacrifice—they put red bags on the parking meters so that parking was free for nearly a month. We packed a lot of excitement into that brief period. The normally placid sidewalks were jammed with shoppers who would greet acquaintances asking, "How are you coming with your shopping?"

Ewing Galloway

Oftentimes a December snow would turn the streets slushy and the sidewalks slippery, but most everyone agreed there was nothing better than a white Christmas.

Now things have sure changed and, to my way of thinking, not for the better. The Christmas season comes along in dibs and dabs, starting with the mail-order catalogs that show up in September and October. Just as the leaves are doing their best to make autumn beautiful, you discover that Walgreens has moved out the garden hoses and bug sprays from the shelves and replaced them with wrapping paper and ribbons. Workmen are busy putting up a giant fake Christmas tree near the fountain in the mall.

Then you pick up the local newspaper in late October or early November to learn that the stores are having their Giant Pre-Christmas Sale Spectacular this weekend, with no payments due until April.

When you sigh and finally head out to do your early Christmas shopping, you rarely see those enchanting storefront window displays anymore, especially in the big malls.

Inside the stores, toys are securely sealed up in colorful cartons. There are piles of boxes everywhere and nary a clerk to answer questions. "Take it or leave it" seems to be the prevailing attitude.

Somewhere along the line we have managed to mess up my favorite holiday. Personally, I blame it on the invention of plastic Christmas trees. They don't smell like the real thing, they look much too perfect and they don't shed needles like the real thing.

And that's just the point—they aren't the real thing. They don't even fool the family cat, who refuses to climb up into the branches so he can topple the whole thing down onto the sofa.

I have dandy memories of the days when Christmas tree lots were full of *imperfect* real trees. The whole family got involved in choosing the one that would be just right for our living room.

First Dad held each tree erect while the rest of us circled, giving our critical judgment:

"There's a big bare space right here."

"We could put it against the wall where no one would notice."

"But then this long branch would poke into the sofa."

"Right. Let's look at some others."

Finally, we found what we deemed to be the best, yet affordable, tree in the lot and tied it on top of the car with twine. Once it stood in our living room, it seems like Dad always had to chop 9 inches off the trunk. (How do trees grow taller on the way home?)

He would put it into the tree stand and go to work with his

SEARCHING OUT the perfect tree was like looking for a pine needle in a haystack. *Reminisce* reader Leona Cullen of Melrose, Massachusetts shared this 1958 photo of her son Sean. She notes that when he finally found the *right* tree, he pulled it home on his sled.

saw, saying that only God could make a tree...but there was no reason why Oscar Strock couldn't offer a little help.

Surplus limbs were carefully removed; then holes were drilled in the trunk around bare areas. Into the holes went the severed limbs, and after half a dozen amputations and implants, even the scraggliest tree looked pretty decent.

Then everyone pitched in to do the decorating. The last item to go on the tree was a tall, spiky ornament Dad called the "Kaiser Wilhelm" because it looked like the spikes on the German helmets he'd seen in France during World War I.

When everything was finished and the lights were turned on, we all sat down to admire our work. Every year we reached the same conclusion, saying *this* year's tree was surely the prettiest ever!

All of us have our unique and cherished memories of Christmas. To my mother, it was the childhood delight on Christmas morning of finding an orange in the toe of her stocking. Imagine that—*a single orange.* This was a special treat for her generation, and she carried the warm memory with her for more than 90 years.

What lasting memory have I passed on to my children and grandchildren? Well, I go back to a Christmas from the bleak years of the Great Depression. Money was scarce, so most of our gifts were handmade. Mine was a plywood checkerboard Dad crafted for me. It wasn't a work of art because Dad was a farmer, not a carpenter.

Although bone-tired from long, hard days, he had stayed up late at night to make the best checkerboard he could. He also fashioned a miniature kitchen cabinet for my sister's doll pans and dishes using an orange crate the grocer had given him. To Mary, it was better than any kitchen cabinet she'd seen in the stores, and Dad had made it!

What we both remember is the love that went into those two gifts. If I could give my grandchildren the perfect gift this year, it would be a Christmas they will remember as fondly a half century from now as I remember so many of mine.

And I would hope they remember it because of the caring family surrounding them, rather than the dozens of gifts they will receive. Love does not come gift-wrapped from a store, and it stays with us long after the toys are forgotten.

Christmas Has Always Lighted Our Lives

Harold M. Lambert

Lights! Lights! Lights! As a youngster, lights and more lights are what made Christmas so thrilling to me.

Suddenly the most modest little homes and the dreariest downtowns turned into glorious peacocks. And our rather ordinary living room seemed to become the glittering drawing room of a French chalet.

The Fourth of July gave us fireworks in the sky for a few minutes, but Christmas lit up our whole world for weeks and weeks.

Just as in springtime, when every day brought the happy surprise of new things in blossom, December slowly bloomed with lights until they were everywhere.

These days, we have twinkling lights and blinking lights and lights that "chase" each other around the festooned eaves of homes. There are even lights commanded by a tiny computer chip which tells them to perform all sorts of nifty electronic tricks.

But the basic idea has never changed. My mom told of her childhood when Christmas trees were illuminated with real candles. That's hard to imagine in these safety-conscious times, but it was either that or hang kerosene lamps on your tree.

I'll certainly not argue that today's lights are technologically much better than the first ones I can remember. The strands of bulbs I grew up with had the life span of an ailing firefly, and when one perished, the whole string went out.

That meant facing the tedious, baffling and frustrating job of tracking down the offending bulb. You started at one end of the string and, bulb by bulb, tested each socket with a new one. Count on it every time—the bum bulb was at the opposite end of wherever you started.

Dad was our bad-bulb stalker. Sometimes he got lucky and found it on the third or fourth try. Other times he'd go through the whole string with no success, which left two possibilities. Either the test bulb was a lemon, too, or else more than one bulb had expired at the same instant.

Mom never came right out and said so, but you could tell by the set of her mouth that she figured Dad didn't know what he was doing, especially after the first try failed. (To be honest, his record for repairing electrical stuff wasn't all that good, so she had cause for her skepticism.)

Dad also had made things tougher than they should have been by splicing together four or five strings of lights with black friction tape. Instead of having just a dozen bulbs to test, he sometimes had to check 50 or 60 on his monster string.

The difficulty of the job was also compounded by the tinfoil reflectors attached to most of the bulbs. You slipped the bulb through a hole in the gaudy reflector then screwed it into the socket. Reflectors did create a more radiant tree, but they made twice as much work when looking for a dead bulb.

Invariably, Dad found the problem and the whole string would burst to life. Then he'd look at Mom with a sly smile, as though to say, "Ha! And you thought I couldn't fix it."

My favorite bulbs were shaped like tiny candles, four inches high. Inside was a liquid, and heat from the light made bubbles rise in a never-ending stream, seemingly coming from nowhere then going nowhere. (Perhaps they were a metaphor for our lives in those tough years of the Depression.)

We had a nice collection of store-bought ornaments, but they were as fragile as soap bubbles and shattered into a hundred pieces when they hit the floor.

Like every cat I've ever known, ours reveled in sitting up on his hind legs while batting ornaments back and forth in sort of a one-cat tennis match. They couldn't take a lot of that treatment, so we were careful to hang them just out of his reach.

Like most people, though, we made a lot of our tree decorations. My sister Mary and I strung cranberries and popcorn on strong thread from Mom's sewing basket. Popcorn went fairly fast, but cranberries were small and messy. From Mom's standpoint, that was just fine because it kept us busy for hours.

Then there was the paper-chain trick they taught us at school. You remember—cut out strips of red, green and white paper, mix up some flour-and-water paste and start making paper links. The paste, alas, got smeared all over the paper and the links were far from uniform, but Mom always praised our handiwork. Mothers know how to do that with a perfectly straight face.

One year we tried marshmallows for ornaments. Somehow, they slowly disappeared as the holiday went along. Mary and I loudly protested our innocence, and Dad offered the cat as a prime suspect. Maybe so...but we all knew Dad had a fondness for marshmallows.

We also created ornaments from walnut shells that we painted gold or silver, and from big pine cones with paint-frosted edges. People living near southern Atlantic beaches collected sand dollars and, with a little paint, turned them into elegant ornaments, each with a delicate star created by nature.

By the way, does anyone know what happened to those old-fashioned tinfoil icicles that you draped from the branches after the rest of the tree-trimming was done? Today's wispy plastic stuff doesn't have the *heft* to hang right and tends to slip off the tree every time someone walks near. And it's almost impossible to pick off and save for next year. Did someone decide the old-time stuff was a health hazard, or what?

A dusting of fake snow added a nice touch, too. Nowadays it's called flocking and comes from spray cans, but 50 years ago our snow came out of boxes of Lux or Ivory flakes. It was cheap, and we tossed it on by hand. Environmentalists would have approved.

This holiday season, we're sure to see a fresh crop of what I regard as bizarre tree ornaments. You know what I mean—Indy racing cars, the latest fad Disney characters, tiny locomotives with winking headlights or spaceships that give off weird noises.

I marvel at the ingenuity of the people who create them, but they just don't seem right for a Christmas tree. The Little Drummer Boy is fine, and so are tiny rocking horses and shiny little angels and wooden Santas. But I can't figure out how the Starship Enterprise earned a place on the tree—unless Donder and Blitzen have retired.

Like so many families, we have a nice collection of handmade ornaments that rate a special place on our tree. As we hang each one, so many warm memories of Christmases past and special people we love come flooding back.

For many years, my wife's Aunt Ella gave her a handmade ornament every Christmas. Each one is a unique work of art, made with hours of toil, care and love.

There's nothing we could buy in a store, no matter how rich we were, that could ever replace Aunt Ella's ornaments. And as Peg places them on our tree, her Aunt Ella again shares a Christmas with us.

Now as for *outdoor* decorations, they weren't all that common back in the '30s. In fact, they were an out-and-out luxury, so sometime during the holidays—ideally after a

COLORED LIGHTS formed a sparkling canopy over the peaceful, snow-covered downtown "Main Streets" in most cities during the good old days.

fresh snow—we'd bundle up and wrap lap robes around our legs for the drive along Locust Street. That's where all the well-to-do homes were clustered together.

Dad would slow down or sometimes stop at the really dazzling displays, speculating on how many strings of lights it must have taken to decorate that tall pine in the front yard.

Locust Street took us to the "main drag" of downtown Sterling, where we'd drive the length of the business area, right through a

H. Armstrong Roberts

tunnel of lights and greenery that arched overhead from curb to curb.

Yes, Christmas is our festival of lights. Indoor lights. Outdoor lights. Electric candles in the windows. Or real candles burning throughout the house, scenting the air with bayberry or cinnamon.

The beauty of those lights provide hundreds of flickering reminders in every home, and tens of thousands of reminders in every town, of the One Light that lit the way to the manger nearly 2,000 years ago.

May all your Christmases be full of light and love.

New Year's Eve Was a Glittering Event

Archive Photos

Somehow the older I get, the more New Year's Eve seems to be a non-event. Usually, Peg and I manage to stay awake until the magic hour and exchange kisses. But not always.

The major significance of the new year now is that we'll most likely date our checks wrong for at least a month.

It certainly wasn't that way when I was a kid, though. Wow, a New Year! A new start. A new birthday on the horizon. New promises to yourself that you'd turn into a model citizen and try to put your laundry in the hamper instead of hoping Mom picked it up.

The best part was that we made New Year's Eve a family event. It was the one night of the year when my sister and I were encouraged to stay up *really* late. What a thrill to gather around the radio with Mom and Dad, munching popcorn and fudge as the excitement built.

The climax was when the NBC Blue Network went live to New York City, where Guy Lombardo and his Royal Canadians were playing at the Starlight Roof of the Waldorf or some other glittering ballroom.

There we sat in our living room, with threadbare carpet and slip-covered furniture—staring at the light on the radio dial and trying to imagine what "Royal Canadians" looked like as beautiful ladies in evening gowns and tall, trim men in tuxedos danced to their music.

Then the orchestra swung into *Auld Lang Syne*, and the crowd counted down: "Four...three...two...one...HAPPY NEW YEAR!"

At home we hugged and kissed each other, took the empty popcorn bowls out to the kitchen and went to bed, each with our own thoughts about what fine things this New Year might bring.

Next morning, of course, was New Year's Day. The first order after breakfast and chores was to take down the Christmas tree, which by then had dropped a solid carpet of needles on the floor. We wrapped all the decorations in tissue, and Dad lugged the box up to the attic.

And now what to do? Maybe some people were busy writing down resolutions and planning the year to come, but somber reality smacked us kids right in the face.

The holidays were over. The new toys and games had lost their novelty. There was nothing in the immediate future but a dark, grim tunnel of school, school and more school!

The only glimmer of hope left for those of us who lived north of the Mason-Dixon line was the prospect of a good old-fashioned serious blizzard.

I don't know what sustained the spirits of kids in the South or on the West Coast. Maybe the possibility of a rousing flood. But for us, the very real possibility of a blizzard or two gave us hope. Ideally it should start on Sunday night and, if possible, just before you faced a major test in arithmetic.

A blizzard meant being snowed in—and if you were snowed in, the schools would be closed.

In the '30s, a really good storm kept you snowbound for *days*. It wasn't that storms were more severe or snow was deeper (despite what I tell my grandchildren today). The simple reason was that snow-removal equipment wasn't anything to shout about in those days.

Our county road department had only horse-drawn road-graders which were helpless in deep snow. A real blizzard meant the county paying a dollar a day to anyone who would show up with a shovel. It was bone-chilling toil, but men arrived by the dozens.

The best possible blizzard was a screamer that dumped at least a foot of snow, followed by a night of subzero temperatures. When one of those perfect ones came along, you'd find towering snow drifts topped with a thick, frozen crust so solid that you could walk on them. In fact, I recall once when Dad actually got to town by driving on top of the drifts in our Willys auto.

My sister and I would bundle up, find a couple of Dad's shovels and begin tunneling into the drifts. One year, we excavated a series of enormous snow caves interconnected by a maze of tunnels.

Then we chopped out hunks of snow the shape and size of a concrete block and fashioned a domed entrance just like the one we'd seen on Eskimo igloos in *National Geographic*. Those Eskimos knew their business: The design kept cold winds from reaching inside our caverns. Everything was cozy, surprisingly warm and very quiet.

After hours of digging and hauling snow out of the caves, we came back to the house soaked, tired and hungry, pausing outside the door while Mom brushed the snow from our clothes with a broom.

Inside, we brought the feeling back into our frozen legs by sitting down on a toasty steam radiator. Meanwhile, Mom was fixing hot cocoa with a fat marshmallow melting on top of each cup. Hard work had its just rewards!

One year, Mary and I decided to build a snow hill. The part of Illinois where we lived was unrelentingly flat, so there were no nearby slopes for sledding. Okay, we'd build our own.

We spent most of a day packing bushel baskets full of snow which we then hauled and dumped at the site of our proposed Strock Mountain. It took forever and yielded a ramp no more than five feet high at its top.

Then we carried water from the stock tank to dump on the snow

IT'S A NEW YEAR, BABY! *Reminisce* reader Bruce Thompson of Waukesha, Wisconsin shared this family favorite of his son, Steve. It was photographed on New Year's Day in 1953.

pile, hoping things would freeze solid overnight.

Sure, you know what happened. We had a major thaw the next day.

Being snowbound had other nice benefits, though. For one thing, it meant that dad, a farmer, spent more time in the house. That was great, because he was an enthusiastic game player. Before long we'd all be gathered around the dining room table and the Monopoly board.

Monopoly is one of those rare games that is as popular today as it was a half century ago. But I'm not sure if today's players get the same giddy thrill from it that we did during the Depression.

Talk about the ultimate escape from reality! Why, with just a few lucky tosses of the dice, you had enough cash in front of you to join the crowd that had danced to Guy Lombardo and his Royal Canadians high above Manhattan.

You could own railroads. The electric company. Houses. Hotels. And get out of jail free. Maybe.

Or you went bankrupt. Well, that's what had happened to all the Wall Street high rollers in 1929, so you were in good company.

There were other games we played, and some of the best were the ones my sister and I invented. We dreamed up our own battlefield game. The best part was that there were absolutely *no* rules to argue over.

We'd stretch a sheet over two dining room chairs, divide up my army of lead soldiers and take up positions on opposite sides of the sheet. Shielded from the other's view, we'd craftily arrange our troops on the carpet.

Mary and I were each armed with a knotted-up washcloth. On

the command *Fire!*, we'd each heave our missile over the sheet, hoping to fell as many enemy troops as possible. The last player to have a soldier standing was declared the winner.

Tiring of games, we would turn to solitary pursuits—paper dolls and jacks for Mary and "newspaper publishing" for me.

Yes, I was the unheralded 9-year-old editing genius of Whiteside County, Illinois. Circulation was limited to our family and advertising revenue was nil. (Thanks to my loving mother, a few copies still exist. I really wish they didn't.)

My newspapering venture was fostered by "The Home Printing Set" I'd received for Christmas. It consisted of hundreds of tiny pieces of rubber type that you patiently wedged into a wooden block, inked with a pad and then pressed onto a piece of paper.

The result was a short paragraph of typeset copy. Putting together a 1-page newspaper took hours and hours...put type in the wooden block, stamp the page, put the type back and start another paragraph.

The spelling was hit-or-miss, both because I was never destined to win a spelling bee and also because the rubber letters had to be set backwards. Years later when I was hired to work as a cub in a newspaper print shop, the old hands were amazed at how well I could read type upside down and backwards. Little did they know what a seasoned veteran they had hired.

The Strock Family Times was a newspaper only a mother could love. Typical headlines on a given day might read: *Baby Chicks Arrive in Good Condition, says Oscar Strock.* Or, if I had on my investigative reporter hat: *Mary Strock Skips Another Day of Violin Practice.*

Ah, the pure joy of a good blizzard! The luxury of lying snug and warm under layers of blankets, with no demands that you get up this minute or you'll be late for school! No need to muster the courage to spring from bed and dress near the warmth of the cast-iron cookstove. No neglected homework to feel guilty about.

Those great, howling, swirling, sky-blocking winter blizzards were the one best hope on the horizon on the day after New Year's. The thought of them lifted us out of the doldrums that signaled the end of another happy holiday season. Just as they do today for my grandchildren.

Let's Bring Back Common Courtesy!

Fred Presler/Unicorn Stock Photos

With a warm sparkle in her eye and a genuine smile, the 60-something lady at the cash register handed me my package. "Thanks for giving us your business," she said. "Y'all come back!"

I was stunned. A clerk actually *thanked* me for coming in. She made it sound like she'd be thrilled if I came back!

These days, graciousness and courtesy—even to complete strangers—seem to be in woefully short supply. I regret the passing of what used to be called "good manners," and so does my wife, Peg, who misses being treated like a lady.

She enjoyed the days when men stood up as a woman entered the room and rather liked having doors opened for her (not that she couldn't open them herself). She felt it was nice to

FILLED WITH FRIENDLINESS. The now-extinct gas station attendant of yesteryear was eager to "fill 'er up" *plus* clean windows and
check the oil. You can bet his customers saw service with a smile!

be treated special and wasn't at all offended when a man
walked on the curbside of the sidewalk—even if she didn't need
to be protected from runaway horses.

Some of those social courtesies seem a little quaint nowadays.
It's no longer fashionable for women to have the "vapors", and I
can't recall the last time I saw a woman swoon. Dueling is generally out, too, no matter how much a man thinks his honor has
been offended.

But there's a lot to be said for the good manners and social
decorum that were so prevalent in the good old days. It made
the world a nicer place for all of us.

There was a time when ladies didn't use gamy language, and gentlemen didn't cuss in their presence. It wasn't so much a matter of prudishness as a matter of mutual respect.

When company came, children were expected to greet the guests, shake hands...and then vanish. It taught them manners, and it also made them aware how adults rated their own special time, too.

I'll admit that as a kid, I didn't especially care for the "children are to be seen, not heard" rule. But I also understood that when adults were wrapped up in serious conversation, I wasn't to interrupt. And any public display of childish temper carried such a high price that it was simply unthinkable.

"Respect your elders" was the rule. Kids didn't call their parents by their first names, and they didn't sass their Uncle Charlie, even if he was as goofy as a waltzing mouse.

When I behaved out of line, Dad didn't say a word. He simply nailed me with his special death-ray glare, which was strong enough to disable airplanes high in the sky and evaporate Lake Michigan. I *knew* what it meant: My manners were seriously lacking, and not one more peep would be tolerated.

Those were the days when people got up to give their seat on the bus or train to someone elderly, pregnant or disabled. Boy Scouts actually did good deeds, such as helping old folks across the street and carrying their packages home.

I guess they were the "kinder, gentler" days President Bush wanted to see again. Maybe the essence of good manners is as simple as being kind and respecting one another.

A college-professor friend of mine was recently asked by a student why he always wore a coat and tie when teaching class. "I do it out of respect for the school, out of respect for myself and out of respect for you," the professor replied. (He knew respect is a two-way street—give it, and you receive it.)

Not too long ago, a high school pal I hadn't heard from in 50 years wrote me a letter full of reminiscences. In it he mentioned a teacher we had both admired. "Have you heard anything from Mr. Twardock?" he asked.

Not "Twardock"...not "Art"...no, it was *Mister* Twardock, even after more than half a century. Mr. Twardock had been tough and demanding, but he also made it clear that he cared about us. The respect for him we had as 16-year-olds lasts to this day.

Back when I *was* 16, men wore hats (always doffed when talking with a lady), and ladies wore hats and gloves when they went "downtown" on shopping excursions. It was considered the proper thing to do. Take a look at the garb you see in the malls today. How times change!

If there's one place where good manners still prevail, though, it's in the South. A particular virtue of most Southerners has always been that they aren't in such an all-fired hurry that they can't take time to be pleasant to each other.

I had my first taste of it when the Army moved me to the South during World War II. I was impressed with how Southerners asked how Aunt Millie's lumbago was and mentioned they had some extra okra in the garden if you wanted to stop by and get some. Eventually they got around to business, but only after the niceties had been covered. It wasn't phony or nosy either—they were genuinely interested.

Southern children answered "Yes, sir" and "No, ma'am". Younger men automatically addressed older men as "Mister", even if they knew them pretty well. The spinster lady down the block was politely titled "Miz Margaret".

At first I thought the whole South was acting out something scripted by William Faulkner, but I soon realized Southern manners and courtesy were not to be scoffed at. There's nothing wrong with taking the time to be interested in one another, and nothing's wrong with some simple courtesy.

It sure beats the automatic, bored "Have a nice day" that's supposed to represent courtesy these days. On a recent trip to the shopping mall, eight people wished me a nice day, and I'm reasonably sure that not one of them cared much one way or the other.

Instead of commanding people to have a nice day, all those little courtesies of yesteryear *made* it a nice day. When you were hobbling on a bum foot and a young lady gave you her seat on the trolley, that made it a nice day. When the butcher tossed in a soup bone for your dog, that made it a nice day...for you and your dog.

When the friendly neighborhood baker added an extra Parkerhouse roll to the dozen you'd just purchased, he didn't need to bid you a nice day. He had already done his part toward it.

Do you suppose there's a chance we could restore some of those welcome courtesies before they become forever extinct? Is there a chance we could slow down enough to care about one another again?

I suspect it's people like us—the ones who read (and write) *Reminisce*—who still remember how nice the world was when we took the time to be kind to each other. We've seen outbreaks of war and violence and other kinds of human misery; now maybe it's time for an outbreak of courtesy and kindness.

And who better to get it rolling than those of us who so clearly remember the days when such virtues were more common? No matter how out of place these courtesies may seem, I'll bet they work as well today as they did generations ago.

NO BONES ABOUT IT. The jovial butcher really did his part to "make it a nice day" as he cut orders to the customer's liking then threw in a tasty bone for Rover. Maybe the respectable dress of shoppers helped earn such courteous treatment.

*E*lection Year Nastiness
Is Nothing New

GRABBING MORE VOTES
meant plastering on smiles, but yesteryear politicians weren't above some mud-slinging, either. In spite of using wit, Adlai Stevenson (shown left) couldn't beat the incumbent, Dwight Eisenhower (above) back in 1956.

These days, whenever a big presidential campaign comes around, mud starts being slung, names are called and each party accuses the other of dirty tricks...and worse.

As bad as this seems, it's far from new. My dad, for instance, liked to tell about a campaign in our hometown during his younger days.

One of the candidates for sheriff was well known for being overly fond of the grape. Early on election day, he was lured into a local saloon, where generous strangers plied him with booze. Eventually, he fell into a sodden slumber at the bar. He was then carried to the nearby polling place and laid out on a bench near the door where voters entered, giving them a close-up view of the snoring candidate. He lost by a landslide.

Yes, dirty tricks in politics are as American as apple pie. Indeed, the only man who ever ran for President of the U.S. without being smeared by the opposition was George Washington. That's because he had no opposition and was elected by acclamation.

Thomas Jefferson had the dubious pleasure of running in the first true contest. The opposition labeled him a coward, drunkard and atheist. Worst of all, they called him a "philosopher", which in those times was today's equivalent of "egghead".

My first memory of a political campaign goes back to 1928 when Al Smith was running against Herbert Hoover. Smith, a raspy, swaggering New Yorker, was also a Catholic, and the opposition had worked to turn his religion into an issue.

One afternoon, Dad and a neighbor were leaning against the fence in the barnyard, talking politics. "If Al Smith is elected, the Pope will run our country," warned the neighbor.

I had no idea who or what a pope was...but it sounded ominous and made a lasting impression. I was only 4 years old.

The first President I recall with any clarity was Franklin Delano Roosevelt. As a campaigner, the man was without equal. He used humor and sarcasm like stilettos, and lots of Americans loved it.

He was first elected in 1932, and during that term in office, three Republican congressmen opposed him at every turn. In the 1936 campaign, FDR made them a symbol for everything that stood in the way of progress. "And who fought against creating more jobs?" he'd ask. "Martin, Barton and Fish!"

Soon all FDR had to do was pose such a question, and his adoring audience would chant back the answer—*Martin, Barton and Fish!*

One time, a false rumor was spread that during a visit to Alaska, he had accidentally left behind his beloved Scottie dog, "Fala". FDR was accused of sending a navy vessel back to get the dog, costing the taxpayers millions.

Did Roosevelt get riled at the charge? Not at all. Instead, he turned it into what has been called "the greatest example of invective in political history".

Roosevelt told his audience he didn't mind attacks on himself, his wife or his sons—that just came with the territory.

But, he said, the opposition was out of line attacking Fala. FDR pointed out that the dog, of Scotch descent, was furious that anyone thought he'd be the cause of wasting taxpayer money. My dad roared with laughter as our family listened to that speech on the radio.

Next on the American scene came Harry Truman. He moved into the White House following the man who had given us hope when things were hopeless—the man who had confidently joined us for "fireside chats"—had died.

It was a tough act to follow, but Harry turned out to be a peppery, no-nonsense President. Nevertheless, he was given little chance when he ran for election against Thomas Dewey.

Truman was denounced as a "failed haberdasher" and a key member of Kansas City's corrupt Pendergast machine. Dewey was the successful crime fighter from New York.

The most telling blow against Dewey came not from Truman, however, but from a famous woman columnist, who snippily asked who could possibly vote for a man who looked like "the little bridegroom atop a wedding cake". It was one of those unforgettable, delicious lines people couldn't wait to repeat to their friends. I still think it did more to defeat Dewey than any campaign speeches against him.

The man from Independence, so different from FDR, turned out to be a winner. I was thoroughly awestruck after I was invited—along with 47 other college students—to meet feisty Harry in the Oval Office.

He assuredly moved down the line, asking each of us where we came from. "What a fine town!" he'd say. "I think your Lawrence Park is one of the prettiest in the country." Truman never failed to include a personal note in the conversation. What a politician!

Then came Ike Eisenhower, who was nearly every soldier's personal hero. He was accused of being a political chameleon, having no history of standing with either the Republicans or Democrats.

His opponents made frequent mention that Grant, another military hero, hadn't been much of a president. But still, it was hard to slash away at the man who had crafted the biggest military victory ever.

Later, Ike was condemned for spending too much time on the golf course and delivering baffling ad-libs that never really answered anything. He wasn't a favorite of the press.

For sheer nastiness, Ike's 1956 run for re-election against Adlai Stevenson stands out in my mind. Stevenson was a thoughtful, eloquent man. He was fond of telling Lincoln-like down-home anecdotes and proved to be another candidate who was adept at using humor to make his point.

One line of Stevenson's that I recall came during his attack on the way Republicans were fighting against the expensive defense build-up in progress. "They remind me," Stevenson said, "of the man who refused to put water on his burning house, saying his water bill was too high already."

During that campaign, Eisenhower was criticized as a do-nothing President, reviving Will Rogers' line about Coolidge: "He did nothing while in office, but he did it better than anyone else."

Ike's successor, Jack Kennedy, was another who understood the power of wit over nasty invective. When he ran against Richard Nixon (decidedly not a great American humorist), Kennedy had the perfect target.

During the 1960 campaign, Nixon had to be hospitalized. Kennedy immediately announced he would not attack Nixon while he was ill.

A couple of weeks later, the press asked Kennedy when the truce would end. Said Kennedy: "I promised I would not mention him while he was hospitalized unless I could say something good about him. So far, I have not mentioned his name."

To Nixon's credit, he strictly forbade anyone in his party to introduce "the religious issue" by bringing Kennedy's Catholicism into the campaign. Rather, the Republicans settled for spreading rumors about Kennedy's health and his father's dubious sources of wealth.

Using a candidate's religion as an issue did rear its ugly head in '64 when Barry Goldwater ran for President. He deftly defused the issue with a personal anecdote, explaining he had once applied for membership in a country club, only to be turned down because of his religion. "But I'm only half Jewish," Goldwater had protested. "Can't I just play nine holes?"

Goldwater was also portrayed by his opposition as a trigger-happy, war-mongering zealot who would plunge us into nuclear holocaust. Who can forget the television commercial that still ranks at the top (or bottom, more accurately) of the vicious political advertising list?

It showed a sweet little girl plucking the petals from a daisy in a beautiful field. Suddenly the picture is overpowered by the blinding light from a nuclear explosion.

"This will be the consequence if you vote for Goldwater" was the clear, if unspoken, message. Widespread public outrage resulted in the commercial running just once, but we still remember it over 30 years later.

And in case you think raising fears about Social Security is a new ploy, that 1964 campaign also featured a commercial from the Democrats showing a Social Security card being torn in half. That's what will happen if Goldwater is elected, the commercial warned. The Social Security system will be destroyed.

Ronald Reagan restored humor again as a winning tactic. Remember his smiling, baffled "There you go again!" during a televised debate with the strident Jimmy Carter? It was just four words and a grin, but Reagan won the debate hands down.

Realizing that his age was an issue in some minds, Reagan countered again with a smile, promising "not to make my opponent's youth a campaign issue".

These days, humor in politics seems a lost art. Both parties promise to run high-minded, issues-based campaigns...but as election day draws nigh, the nastiness builds. Too often, it leaves us feeling we must choose between scoundrels.

Will Rogers put things in perspective long ago. "If we didn't have two parties in this country, we'd elect the best man and things would run just fine. But as it is, we nominate the worst ones and then fight over them."

He also said, "The short memories of American voters is what keeps politicians in office."

But my favorite Will Rogers anecdote is this one: "I said to the President that I wanted to tell him the latest political jokes. He replied, 'I already know 'em. I appointed most of them.'"

Will Rogers, why can't you come back? It would make election years a lot more fun for us all.

$\mathscr{M}$odern-Day 'Survivors' Should've Seen the '30s

Brown Brothers

H. Armstrong Roberts

SURVIVING was tough in the Depression. Relief projects provided work, like this WPA program repairing Park Avenue near Grand Central Station; carpenters (inset) used their skills on another Federal Works Project.

Few things ruffle my feathers more than hearing a present-day celebrity sigh and say, "Yes, I've always been a survivor."

I have to wonder just how tough "surviving" can be in a multi-million-dollar home with a swimming pool and a platoon of servants. Hey, pal, I remember when surviving was a decidedly grim business, and even strong people fell by the wayside. It was during the 1930s.

Surviving meant standing on a street corner, feet like blocks of ice, trying to sell apples or pencils to people as hard up as you were. It meant begging for food at back doors or waiting in long, slow lines at outdoor soup kitchens.

Desperate people tried everything and anything to make a buck. Among the most miserable schemes of all were the dance marathons that seemed to occur everywhere during the Depression. The idea was that the last couple left standing won a modest cash prize.

The music played on and on...and on. For days and even weeks at a time, bone-weary, hallucinating men and women staggered around the dance floor, with only the briefest of breaks for food and new bandages to cover the blisters on their feet.

Meanwhile, the curious bought tickets to watch and speculated on who would be next to crumple unconscious to the floor.

These days it's not necessary for people to survive on their own—there are myriad "safety nets" and government-sponsored welfare programs for the needy. But back then, surviving was, indeed, up to the individual.

Those in need turned to family for help. Grampa and Gramma Stevens lived in a fair-sized five-bedroom house, and at various times during the '30s, it was filled to overflowing with unemployed children and their children, plus an unmarried daughter still living at home.

Years later, I asked Gramma how she endured so much stress and racket. She thought about it and smiled. "Well...it sure taught me patience."

We had our share of temporary boarders at our house, too. There was Dad's sister, one of Mom's brothers and her sister with husband and baby. Some were with us a few weeks, others many months at a time.

Was it an inconvenience? Sure. But it was what you did in those days—your door was always open to family members in need.

Not long after Franklin Roosevelt became President, 30% of all workers were jobless. A bunch of innovative programs were launched to help desperate people without hope. One of the best was the Civilian Conservation Corps. This program set up work camps that were run by Army officers throughout the U.S.

More than a quarter million men were taken off the breadlines and given food, shelter, clothing and medical attention plus $1 a day in wages. For that, they cleared brush, planted trees, fixed roads and developed state and national parks.

Roosevelt predicted, "This enterprise will pay dividends to present and future generations." How right he was ...and what a good idea it would be to revive in the '90s!

One direct relief program was less than successful, for a reason that underlines the character of people in that era. Few signed up for its benefits because being on relief was shameful.

Then the program was changed to "work relief". A person receiving, say, $10 a week in grocery or rent vouchers was asked to work on public projects for enough hours to earn the $10.

A government official explained: "Fine people who would not come to us for direct relief would come for work relief because it was like a job."

A smattering of towns and counties did manage to rig up welfare programs of their own. Often, a list of recipients and how much they'd been given was posted outside city hall. Names weren't removed until the money had been repaid in full.

Meanwhile, *Popular Mechanics* and other magazines carried ads promising quick riches. My particular favorite was headlined "Raise Giant Frogs!"

This instantly raised two questions in my mind—just how big was a giant frog anyway...and how would Mom feel about having several in the house?

An uncle of mine was taken in by an advertisement that promised he'd harvest riches growing mushrooms in his basement. It was damp and dark enough, for sure...but it turned out that Sterling, Illinois wasn't a promising market for mushrooms. He soon abandoned the enterprise.

Others were attracted to raising foxes for the fur market. (Remember those little wraps made up of tiny foxes, head and all, that well-to-do ladies wore back then?) The market for fox furs eventually collapsed, and most fox-raisers were...well, skinned!

A more beguiling path to wealth, one that involved practically no work and very little capital, was the chain letter. Soon every mailman's bag was bulging with chain letters.

H. Armstrong Roberts

"Just make three copies with your name at the bottom and send a dollar bill to the name on top of this letter," you were urged. "In a month or less, you will receive as much as $2,000." Who could resist?

Many a captain of industry went almost overnight from riches to rags and moved from the penthouse to the park bench or joined the long lines standing outside factories, waiting for jobs.

Other people took matters into their own hands. My mother, a fine seamstress, found part-time work doing alterations at a local dress-shop. Some of her friends took orphans into their homes because the county paid $10 a month room and board for each child.

Others advertised "Tourist Rooms" for a dollar or two a night or took in full-time "roomers".

Kids were expected to find jobs, too. I worked when I could for a neighboring farmer, who paid me $1 a day plus a scrumptious lunch prepared by his wife. They more than lived up to their family name, which was Good.

Other kids sold magazines door-to-door, worked as Western Union messengers, delivered groceries, shined shoes—anything that would produce a few dollars. Arriving home at night, they emptied their pockets on the kitchen table, and Mom added their earnings to her household money.

Even the frugal and prudent found themselves penniless when banks closed. Until they re-opened and could pay off their depositors, people had to learn to survive in a world without money.

Some towns issued "scrip"—temporary unofficial money that could later be redeemed for real cash (it was hoped).

In short, people did whatever it took. They lived on wit, ingenuity and sheer grit. Welfare was an option only when all other possibilities had been exhausted, because being "on the county" destroyed a person's pride and reputation in the neighborhood.

So you see why I get riled when someone with a safe deposit box full of pricey jewelry and Renoirs on the wall asks for my admiration because they are a "survivor". In their own eyes, I'm sure they truly believe it. Everything is relative.

But it's tough to swallow if you can still remember the days when surviving was a matter of searching the house for five pennies that would buy the loaf of bread a family of four needed to stay alive another day.

I know...I was there. 🚕

THE EXHAUSTIVE search for money in the '30s found this brother/sister team in a dance marathon. The last couple "standing" earned a cash prize.

$\mathcal{R}$emember Those Crazy Fads of Yesteryear?

H. Armstrong Roberts

If there's anything that moves faster than a supersonic airplane, it's the speed with which we Americans embrace goofy fads. A new one turns up in California on Tuesday, and by Friday it's the hot topic in Bangor, Maine.

Fads are a benign form of national insanity that can afflict people of all ages. But they've always burned brightest in the hearts and minds of teenagers.

Remember a few decades back when 30 million youngsters decided they simply *had* to have a hula hoop? (Don't blush—I'll

ALL THE CRAZE. Coonskin caps, poodle skirts and body-stuffed Buicks were just a few fads of the past young people embraced with a vengeance.

bet you had one, too.) Hula hoops sold for $1.98 and you saw them everywhere during the '50s. With a little coaxing, even Mom and Dad tried their skill, too. Plump hips were shimmying from coast to coast.

The first fad that captured me was during the '30s and involved bottle caps from soda pop bottles. Inside the bottle cap was a cork disk. With a jackknife and a little patience, you could pry the cork out of the bottle cap. Then you put the cap on the outside of your hat or jacket and pressed the cork back into place from the inside.

I have no idea why we boys wanted to go around festooned with bottle caps, but we did. (With the benefit of hindsight, you realize that fads never make a lot of sense.) The kid with the greatest number and variety of bottle caps was the one everyone envied, of course.

Soda pop in those years was a luxury item seldom seen in our house. So I haunted filling stations and parks, searching for bottle caps that didn't duplicate the Nehi, Orange Crush and Hires Root Beer caps that I already had.

Boys old enough to have cars competed on another level. A foxtail flying from the radio antenna was essential. So was a "spinner" knob that clamped onto your steering wheel. Spinners allowed you to drive one-handed and freed up your right arm to snuggle with your best girl. Or so you hoped. If only you *had* a girl.

Those also were the days when spare tires were mounted on the rear of the car. Some canny marketer came up with spare tire covers made from heavy oilcloth. Most of them carried advertising, but the really neat ones were reflectorized and were works of art.

Or you could customize one to be uniquely yours. Come to think about it, they must have been the forerunner to today's bumper stickers that let you make statements to the world—"I Support the Right to Arm Bears," for example. Or brag about how your kid is an honor student. Tire covers have made a half-hearted comeback on the spares of vans and motor homes, but usually they're just an ad for the van manufacturer.

Young men attending eastern universities developed an unexplainable taste for swallowing live goldfish. They gulped them down by the score, which may account for my lifelong uneasiness around graduates of Ivy League schools.

During World War II, there wasn't much time to pursue fads, although there was a brief period when "zoot suits" and lengthy key chains that dangled down to the ankles scandalized sensible folks.

While technically it wasn't a fad, the wartime scarcity of silk stockings led to something new called "leg makeup". Some women even enlisted a friend's help in drawing a straight dark line down the back of each leg to simulate stocking seams. The result looked a lot like real stockings—unless it rained.

At war's end, Americans were ripe for some new fads. Women tottered about on clunky platform shoes and wore stick-on "beauty patches" and the so-called "New Look" in women's dresses.

Enter the decade of the '50s. Besides the hula hoop, there was a mini-boom in coonskin caps, fueled by the *Davy Crockett* television program. It was a bad time to be a raccoon.

Girls rushed to the hairdressers for "poodle haircuts" to go with their "poodle skirts" made of felt and festooned with sewn-on teddy bears, kittens or daisies. High school boys came home from the barber's with ducktail haircuts.

College students were caught up in "stuffing"—a bizarre fad that consisted of seeing how many bodies could be packed into a small space. Phone booths were popular (22 stuffees seems to have been the record) and so were Volkswagens (40 bodies, believe it or not).

Nor were we adults fad-proof in that decade. A new card game called canasta seemed to appear from nowhere. Never mind pinochle or hearts or bridge. You could find canasta tournaments all around town on a Saturday night.

Then along came something called chlorophyll, touted as a wonder deodorant. Otherwise-sensible people hurried to buy products laced with this chemical which is found in every green thing, including the grass in your lawn. You could buy chlorophyll pills, toothpaste, soap and even chlorophyll-treated socks.

What brought this madness to an abrupt end was a letter to the editor of *The Saturday Evening Post*. It was a poem which for some perverse reason has stuck in my mind to this day:

> *Why reeks the goat on yonder hill,*
> *Who feeds all day on chlorophyll?*

They were just 13 words, but I credit them with killing the craze in a hurry.

The fad-fertile '50s also brought us the first flying saucer sightings, plus a national fascination with Bridey Murphy, a Colorado housewife who claimed to have vivid recollections of a prior life as a 19th-century Irish lass.

Suddenly all sorts of people were trying to get in touch with their "former selves", convinced they once had been Queen Isabella or Genghis Khan or John Alden. I can't recall any of them who reported having been a convicted pickpocket or a Chinese coolie in an earlier life.

In Detroit—"Motor City"—kids barely old enough to drive began to customize their cars, although more for speed than appearance. The most prized were Fords in which the original engine was replaced by a Cadillac motor. The police soon begged for better cars of their own so they'd have some sort of chance to catch the speeders.

Health fads aren't a new invention, either. There were water diets and grapefruit diets, as well as copper bracelets worn in the hope they would ward off arthritis. We balanced on Bongo Boards, strained on rowing machines and pedaled to nowhere on stationary bicycles.

An achievement-oriented boss of mine bought a treadmill and a *music rack!* While he paced and paced on the treadmill from 5 to 6 a.m. every day, he read office correspondence that he had piled on the music rack.

I suggested to him that only hamsters, endlessly spinning the little wheel in their cages, could possibly empathize. He was only mildly amused.

While adults were preoccupied with health, their children were picking up on the latest grooming and fashion fads. I was less than pleased when my teenage sons insisted on letting their hair grow to shoulder length and beyond during the '60s. (Rather than deliver lengthy tirades about it, I tried not to notice. My silence bothered them more than anything else I could have done.)

As you recall, those were the days when young people were protesting almost everything—except having free room and board at home. It was the era of granny dresses, round wire spectacles and semiannual bathing. I never did figure out why you had to be filthy and smelly to be a serious protester.

The big adult fad of the '70s was CB radios. It went up faster and disappeared faster than any fad I can remember. For a brief time, no car was complete without its CB, and no driver was without his cutesy-poo "handle". "Lead-foot Mama" and "Peoria Adonis" and "Laredo Cowboy" spoke knowingly of County Mounties (police) and Smokey in a Plain Wrapper (unmarked state patrol car).

But boredom with the new toy set in fast. How long can you listen to truck drivers swap smutty jokes?

Today, those same rebellious kids, including my sons and daughter, dress for work in "power suits", carry cellular phones and pagers in their pockets and lug laptop computers wherever they go. Who am I to suggest that they've just swapped one set of fads for another?

Well, there's no sense in getting all riled up about fads. They vanish almost as fast as they appear. Yesterday's fad is tomorrow's ho-hum. Today it's white sidewall haircuts for boys and Army boots for girls. Plus earrings for boys, gold nose rings for both sexes and tattoos in the darnedest places.

Tomorrow, who knows?

I'm sure it won't be the return of those jazzy "spinners" on steering wheels, because they're illegal now. Nor will we see jackets and hats studded with bottle caps. They just don't make bottle caps like they used to.

$\mathcal{I}$ Wish I Never Threw It Away!

RIDING a wave of nostalgia, Clancy Strock's father (above) couldn't bear to part with the buggy he used in courting days. Also pictured is blind horse, Barney, who faithfully found the way home at night, allowing his trusting passenger to take a snooze.

When mom and dad were married, they moved into a newly-built, square two-story farmhouse with a big porch across the front. You've seen identical ones throughout the Midwest, I'm sure.

Nearly 50 years later, they built Mom's "dream house" nearby. Like most people when they get up in years, the new house was considerably smaller than "the old home place".

So, when the time to move drew near, they had one whale of a problem. Half a century's accumulation of "stuff" filled the attic, basement, closets, garage, and several farm buildings.

Dad, like most farmers, wasn't much on throwing things away. "You never know when it might come in handy," was his motto.

So, there were horse collars and old harness hanging on pegs in the stable, even though horses had been replaced by tractors 30 years earlier. There also were spare parts for assorted makes and models of tractors, long gone to tractor heaven.

In the garage was the buggy Dad had used to court Mom before he entered the Army during World War I. Except for a patina of dust, it was nearly in mint condition. Mom and Dad told how the buggy had been pulled by a blind horse.

After dropping Mom at her home after a date, Dad would tell the horse to "giddyup" and then curl up on the buggy seat for a snooze during the half-hour trip to his home. Somehow the horse knew the way. When the horse stopped walking, Dad put him in the stable and went to bed.

Dad never could bring himself to part with that buggy, despite some tempting offers. I'm sure it was because of all the good memories it evoked.

Meanwhile, every nook and cranny in the house was crammed, too. Especially the attic. What to do with it all?

The solution was the same one everyone must finally face. Mom and Dad kept a few special family heirlooms and moved them to the new home. Others were eagerly accepted by my sister and me. More were offered to the grandchildren.

A few pieces of furniture and a lot of clothing went to a local charity, and an antique collector paid big money for the buggy.

Even so, this was but the tip of the iceberg...or junk pile, to be more precise. So we carted several loads to the dump and used still more of it to fill in an eroded gully before it deepened into another Grand Canyon.

But now (too late!) I realize that all that "junk" we hauled to the dump or buried in the gully would today be worth enough to make a down payment on a nice waterfront condo in Florida.

If you think I exaggerate, spend an hour browsing through an antique shop or flea market. You'll find that an old horse collar in fair shape fetches more than it did when new. In fact, more than the horse itself cost in those days.

Rusty milk cans (we threw away a dozen) are prized by artsy ladies who clean them up and lovingly paint them with flowers and twiny vines.

The old kerosene lamp that once lit Dad's way to the barn on dark nights now carries a price tag that makes you shake your head in amazement. It sure gets you to thinking about all the stuff you've thrown away over the years…*stuff you should have kept!*

I remember begging for weeks before Mom caved in and let me send off for a cereal bowl with "Skippy" molded into the bottom. (And for you trivia fans out there, this was the very first household item to be made from a mysterious new substance called "plastic.")

The last I knew, even General Mills, the company that distributed the bowl, didn't have one in its archives. The few still around are priceless collectibles.

I also recall the Tom Mix trinkets you could get from Ralston Purina for two boxtops and 25 cents "to cover postage and handling". I had the ring made from a horseshoe nail, allegedly just like the ones used to shoe Tony, The Wonder Horse. I also had a wooden model of Tom's famous six-shooter and a replica of his red bandanna handkerchief. They all disappeared somewhere between childhood and my first mortgage.

And how about you? What happened to your Shirley Temple doll? Where is that original 1959 Barbie that's now worth more than your first little house? And where is the Mr. Peanut figure where you once stored your spare change? Hey, it's worth *big* change now!

There's hardly a man today who didn't once have a baseball card collection. As boys, we chewed bubble gum until our jaws ached to get those cards. Lots of times we just kept the card and threw away the gum.

It grieves me more than a little to know that practically *any* baseball card for *any* player before 1941 is worth a small fortune today. I didn't save a one.

Nor did I save the "Alf Landon for President" button mounted on a yellow felt sunflower (in honor of Kansas, the Sunflower State.) Who would hang on to a button promoting such a loser?

Not I. But recently I saw one at a collector's gathering. (Believe

Dianne Dietrich Leis

Eileen Marie

IF ONLY WE'D KNOWN! Baby dolls and baseball cards could've been big bucks had we not gone on a cleaning binge and decided to get rid of those "useless" childhood relics.

me, Landon wasn't the only loser.)

And does anyone know what happened to my 10-volume collection of Tom Swift books, along with all those Hardy Boy mysteries?

They now sell for $10 and up. That's quite a lusty appreciation from their original price of 99 cents.

A special passion of mine was collecting matchbooks. Back in the '30s a surprising amount of creativity went into making them. Every restaurant, hotel, bar, bowling alley and filling station had its own custom-designed matchbooks.

One masterpiece I recall was from the local bowling alley. The matches inside were shaped like bowling pins. I had hundreds of matchbooks from faraway places like Peoria and Chicago. The entire back of my bedroom door was covered with rows of them, hanging from strings.

They disappeared when I went away to school. Mom viewed them as a definite fire hazard. But I'll bet, somewhere, there are people who'd pay a tidy sum for several hundred matchbooks from the 1930s. You just don't find such spiffy ones these days.

But I can't blame Mom for trashing my collection of 78 rpm records. That was my idea. LPs were the wave of the future, so out went Harry James playing *Ciribiribin* and *Carnival of Venice* and dozens of other favorites.

Those regrets don't go 'round and 'round too long, though—not when I think of other "useless" odds and ends I tossed.

For example, Dad had nailed all his old license plates to a wall inside the garage. They dated back to 1924, when he had purchased a new Willys-Knight sedan. There were even a couple from the World War II years that were made from heavy fiberboard because steel was needed for armaments. I took all of them down and stored them in a cloth Pioneer Seed Corn bag when the folks moved into their new home.

I hung onto those plates for years, but finally disposed of them all. Bad move! Today even the old cloth seed corn bag would be worth something.

After I was married and the kids were born, we bought a complete set of what were supposed to be kid-proof dishes called Fiesta ware. Ours were a vivid slime-green color (just what you want to make food look appetizing).

They also were far from kid-proof, so it was a happy day when we finally dumped them into the garbage can and could afford something prettier. Who could suspect that 40 years later, Fiesta dishes would become a hot collectible?

You name it, and you shouldn't have thrown it away. You should have treasured those old tools, kitchen utensils, ugly lamps, fern stands, cream separators, floppy hats, wooden-shafted golf clubs, autographed movie star photos, Philco radios and framed tintypes of unknown ancestors.

If you don't believe me, just ask Jackie Kennedy's children.

There's even a lively market for old movie posters. Theater owners pitched them out along with the empty popcorn boxes and Tootsie Roll wrappers. Why not? I'll tell you why not. Recently a 1931 *Dracula* poster sold for $70,000.

The moral to the story is that today's trash is likely to turn into tomorrow's treasure. Even that horrid CD of *Hootie and the Blowfish.*

Photographic Design

GATHERING DUST but also gathering value, some of today's pricey collectibles include buttons, license plates, campaign buttons, 78 records, butter stamps and ice picks.

Getting On with Life Was Postwar Pleasure

Millions of lives were put on "hold" during the World War II years, and not just for those in service. Folks on the home front had to suspend their normal lives, too.

Women went to work in defense plants. Children found themselves temporarily without daddies. Rationing and scarcities of everything forced people into new ways of living...just when there seemed to be light at the end of the long dark tunnel called the Depression.

Then the war was over and some 12 million men and women came home from military service, all with a lot of catching up to do. I remember feeling acutely that my own 4 years in the military had put me behind the pack. There I was, 22 years old, trying to stay even with 18-year-olds just getting out of high school.

I'd married just a month before going overseas, so I came home to a wife who was practically a stranger. Some of my buddies came back to children they'd never seen.

It was tough on the kids, too. Who was this stranger in the house called "Daddy"? Things had been just fine until he showed up.

Employment was scarce, too. Vets who'd been promised that their old jobs would be waiting for them found out it didn't always turn out that way. In desperation, many of us joined the "52-20 club". I went to a government office and signed up for employment. Uncle Sam would pay me $20 a week for 52 weeks to tide me over, but I had to go to work if a job turned up and I was qualified.

I was sent to interview with a weekly newspaper, located in shabby offices above a dry goods store. Things went well until the editor noticed the wedding ring on my finger. "You're married?" he gasped, as though I had leprosy.

"Yes, sir," I replied. "Is that a problem?"

"Of course it is. I can't possibly pay you enough to support two people."

Well, fine. What I really wanted to do was return to college on the GI Bill, which at the time paid $40 a month plus books and tuition for single students ($10 a month more if you were married). It wouldn't support a lavish life-style, but with my discharge pay and quite a bit of part-time work, it looked like we could make it. So my wife and I returned to Iowa State, where I had 3 years to complete and she had a year remaining.

That's where we ran smack-dab into the other big problem faced by returning vets—housing. There wasn't any.

Iowa State had an enrollment of 5,600 students before the war. In 1947, it ballooned to 12,000—in a town with a population of 10,000.

RETURNING VETS welcomed the opportunity for a college degree through the GI Bill, which paid tuition, books and $40 a month.

Eventually we found an elderly couple willing to rent us

a bedroom with an enormous walk-in closet. The closet became our kitchen, family room and study nook. We washed our dishes in the bathtub down the hall.

Nearby, one notorious landlord had converted a large two-story house into what he grandly called "apartments" for married students.

The place was locally known as "Termite Towers". There were 11 couples living in it, plus three single men who shared attic quarters reached by climbing a rope ladder through a small scuttle in the ceiling.

The university scrambled to erect "temporary veteran's housing" adjacent to campus. The first units were flimsy mobile homes imported from Oak Ridge, Tennessee, where they'd housed workers in the secret A-bomb project.

It soon became obvious that these mobile homes weren't designed for frigid Iowa winters. The sole source of warmth was a tiny fuel oil heater, hopelessly overmatched against subzero temperatures.

The galley consisted of a stove that used pressurized white gas and an icebox that barely held a 50-pound block of ice and two quarts of milk.

Near the kitchen was a foldout studio couch recycled from the Spanish Inquisition, and there were no bathroom facilities. Each encampment of trailers shared a Spartan central facility, which also had a few coin-operated washing machines.

Close by was a small village of Quonset huts which seemed quite posh from the standpoint of the trailer residents. Meantime, across the railroad tracks in what was named Pammel Court, the ultimate in student housing was rapidly taking shape.

The units, a gift from the military and known as "tropical barracks", were slab-mounted duplexes made of corrugated tin. Each had a small living room, a kitchen with a kerosene stove and icebox, a bath with a metal shower enclosure, two small bedrooms and a fair-sized storage closet.

My wife and I moved from our lodgings with the elderly couple into a house trailer just in time for a particularly miserable winter.

Many nights, with the oil heater giving out barely more heat than a candle, we piled our winter coats on top of the blankets and went to bed all bundled up, wearing woolen socks and stocking caps.

Later, after constant whining and pleading with the Director of Student Housing, we made the leap to the tropical barracks...and a whole new set of problems.

The tracks for the main line of the Chicago & Northwestern Railroad were not more than 100 feet from our unit. Every morning at 4:30, a long freight train cannonballed past, tooting its whistle and rattling dishes out of the open kitchen cupboards.

Every university in the country faced the same overcrowding problem. But it wasn't unique to schools—veterans who opted to go back into the workforce had just as much trouble finding a place to live.

The government promised 2.7 million houses by 1948 to shelter these newly formed families. Meantime, in North Dakota, a group of veterans turned surplus grain bins into apartments.

It was a heady time for the home-building industry. One Detroit builder purchased an immense tract of land and used bulldozers to scoop out eight-block-long trenches. He poured footings 8 feet apart, put up concrete block foundations, filled the narrow spaces between foundations and slapped up little two- and three-bedroom look-alike houses. In the building trade, they were called "GI Specials", and thanks to GI home loans, the houses sold faster than they could be built.

In New York, contractor Ted Levitt turned home-building into an assembly-line process much like that used by the auto industry, except the houses didn't move along the line, the workers did.

First came the concrete men, then the carpenters, then the electricians and plumbers, followed by the plasterers. Soon an entire block of nice, extremely affordable houses was finished.

Levitt produced more than 17,000 homes in about 4 years for the house-hungry market. Even though we didn't recognize it at the time, Levittown—a planned community with schools, churches, parks and shopping centers—was the beginning of a major American revolution called "suburbia".

Automobiles were another postwar scarcity—none had been built for 4 years. Henry Kaiser, whose factories had churned out Victory and Liberty ships during the war, decided to turn his talents to car-building. His Kaisers and Frazers got lots of publicity but, alas, were a flop when they finally appeared on the market. The

Detroit automakers knew how to build what Americans really wanted.

The new car shortage brought out the worst possible side of car dealers. The whole process of dickering was turned upside down—instead of the buyer trying to get the lowest possible price, dealers doled out cars to the highest bidders.

I remember Dad's rage when he went to buy a new Oldsmobile. He'd saved for 4 years and could pay cash for a car for the first time in his life. The dealer started with the basic car and began adding on every optional extra in the GM inventory, telling Dad he just couldn't stand to see him buy a car without a radio…seat covers… white sidewalls and more.

When there were no add-ons left, Dad proudly began to write a check for the car. The dealer was aghast—after all, he made his money on financing. He told Dad he would have to finance the car.

That did it. Dad put away his checkbook, stood up and wished the dealer well with his car. Sort of. There was a long pause, and then the dealer decided that cash would be OK…but strictly as a favor to a longtime customer.

Eventually I was able to buy a car, and later we purchased our first home, a modest place cheek-by-jowl with the neighbors on either side. Every male in the subdivision was a vet with a young wife, and every little house was filled with kids under the age of 8.

Nearly all of us fenced in our backyards to keep the little ones from straying. One day my folks came to visit. Dad and I went for a walk around the neighborhood and came to a spot where the view of fenced backyards stretched as far as the eye could see.

Dad rubbed his chin. "Looks just like the pens at the Chicago Stockyards," he observed. He was right.

But as chaotic as those first postwar years were, I nevertheless look back on them with great fondness.

We had lived through the war…and we were still young, ambitious and full of hope. America was on a roll, and we were part of the excitement and opportunity. It seemed like there was never a better time to be alive.

The Hours Flew When We Traveled by Train!

Nowadays, long-distance travel is an easy proposition—just jump in the car or board an airplane, and in nearly no time, you can be in another state or clear across the country.

Things were different before World War II. Air travel was almost nonexistent, and as late as 1950, 41% of American families didn't even own a car, much less the two or three common today.

So how did we travel before the days of "frequent flier miles"? We boarded the train. And what a grand experience that could be!

The first half of this century was the heyday of train travel, and I'm glad I got to experience it. Whether visiting relatives in Cleveland or Birmingham or taking a short "interurban" trek between nearby cities, the train was the way to go.

Every trip started at the local depot. ("Depot" is a word we swiped from the French, who took it from the Latin language, and I like it a whole lot better than "terminal".)

The depot was always an exciting place to be. In small towns, the man who sold tickets doubled as the telegrapher, so you'd often have to wait while he mysteriously *clackety-clacked* away on his telegraph key.

My Grandfather Stevens was once a railroad telegrapher. During slack periods, he'd play chess by telegraph, often having four or five simultaneous games in progress with men he'd never met in towns he'd never visited.

At the end of every depot was the Railway Express Office, which was a beehive of activity—especially as "train time" approached. There was outgoing mail on baggage carts, cream and eggs headed for the big city, and parcels and packages of all shapes and sizes.

As the clock ticked toward arrival time, you could hear the train whistle somewhere off in the distance, and people began crowding onto the brick station platform. Some had come to meet people, and others were ready to depart.

Soon the great locomotive would rumble into the station, slowly grinding to a stop. The conductor would have the passenger car door open so he could stand on the bottom step and put his metal stool on the platform the instant the train stopped rolling.

Another thing I remember about train travel is how people dressed up for their trips—hats and gloves for the ladies, ties and suits for the men. (By contrast, many airline passengers today seem to dress down!)

The well-dressed men and women all climbed onto the train, and soon everyone was aboard, except for pairs of sweethearts stealing last-minute smooches.

Then the conductor would yell, "BOARD!" and the engineer would give a toot or two on his whistle. Up ahead you could hear the locomotive grunting *Chuff!...Chuff!...Chuff!* as the train rolled slowly away from the platform.

Inside, the passengers waved from their windows and blew kisses to folks still on the platform, who waved back and called, "Don't forget to write!"

Once the train was under way, you became a ward of the conductor. After each stop he walked through the cars calling out, "Tickets, please! Tickets, please!"

If you didn't have a ticket, he'd be more than glad to sell you one—or else evict you at the next stop. Hiding out in the restroom didn't help, either...somehow he always seemed to know you were in there.

Conductors generally came in two varieties—genial, smiling ones who took time to admire babies and flirt with elderly ladies and grumpy ones who seemed to look upon travelers as an intrusion on their lives.

No matter—whether you were traveling 30 miles or clear across the continent, train travel was a grand adventure indeed as a panorama of America reeled past your window.

You might pass through the forests of Minnesota...the endless cornfields of Illinois...the eerie Oklahoma night sky lit by burning gas from oil wells...or cotton fields in the red soil of Texas.

Crossing the Great Plains, you could watch farmers in their fields, herds of cattle and occasionally a few antelope. Passing through countless little towns, you observed people from all walks of life going about their business.

Plains travel was scenic, but nothing could match a trip through the soaring Rocky Mountains. Best of all was the Burlington Railroad's trip through the matchless beauty of the Feather River Canyon.

Detached observation was usually enjoyable, but I remember one Christmas Eve during World War II, when I was on a night train from Chicago to Detroit, that it wasn't.

We passed through many tiny towns whose Main Streets were bright with Christmas lights...and occasionally I caught a fleeting glimpse into homes where families were gathered near the Christmas tree, smiling and opening presents. I've never felt lonelier or less connected to the real world in my life.

A COMFY TRIP. Traveling by train provided passengers with a relaxing ride, plush, comfortable seats and an unbeatable view of the countryside that you could feast your eyes on.

Troop trains and passenger trains, though, were a different experience altogether—especially when it came to food. For working-class folks like my own family, the dining car offered a glimpse into the world that we envisioned wealthy people inhabited all the time. The tables were covered with heavy linen tablecloths, all starched and white. Upon them stood glass goblets, silver coffee urns, sturdy tableware and fresh flowers.

The dining car steward was invariably cheerful and polite and treated you with a deference normally reserved for the Rockefellers and Astors. I'd happily trade a single relaxed dining-car meal for a hundred airline meals, during which dreadful food must be eaten under impossibly cramped conditions.

And nothing could top the pleasure of lingering over your third cup of coffee as the Broadway Limited rolled along the Hudson River, while up ahead the sunrise highlighted the New York City skyline. It was pure magic, because for a half hour or so, you really felt like "somebody".

When you finally arrived at your destination, be it Marshalltown, Chicago, Albuquerque or Minneapolis, you got off the train smack in the middle of town. (You didn't have to hike a mile or more through an endless airline terminal and then take a harrowing 45-minute cab ride!)

Grand Central in New York, Union Depot in Chicago, the awesome St. Louis Depot and a score of others always seemed to me like great palaces with an undercurrent of excitement and mystery.

From overhead would come the voice of the train announcer: "Now leaving on Track 14, the Super Chief for..." followed by a string of towns and cities, their names hopelessly garbled as they echoed off the marble walls and high ceilings.

Meanwhile, redcaps scurried through the throngs, a bag under each arm and one clutched in each hand.

Newspaper photographers would occasionally cluster around platforms, holding enormous Speed Graphic press cameras at the ready. That was a sure sign that a movie star or some other celebrity was about to appear.

Important people didn't mingle with the common herd, of course. VIPs traveled in snug private compartments or in the luxurious chair car at the end of the train. They didn't have to wait for a place in the dining car, either—food and drink was delivered to them.

Still, even for us "common folks", train travel was satisfying. So what if it took you 36 hours to get from Minneapolis to Houston? You had a chance to relax, enjoy good meals and strike up some new friendships in the club car.

I'm glad my children had a chance to experience train travel when it was still a thrill. They vividly remember a wonderful trip with their grandparents from Chicago to San Francisco, then down the Pacific Coast to Los Angeles, with a stop at the Grand Canyon on the way home. (A hint for grandparents: It's still possible today.)

One of my most special memories is of a train trip I took with two of my sons from Minneapolis to Chicago. Not more than 6 or 7 years old, both of the little guys had decided to travel in their cowboy getups.

There was scarcely a passenger walking through our car who didn't stop to visit with them as the scenic Mississippi River rolled by alongside our train. It was a glorious, memory-making trip for all three of us.

Early Airline Travel
Was 'Plane Going'

Back in the '30s and early '40s, two things especially scared the dickens out of people.

One was the arrival of a telegram. In those days, they almost always meant bad news because no one went to the expense of a telegram to say, "Hey, I thought you'd like to know we're all feeling dandy."

But even scarier was the prospect of flying. Fortunately, this wasn't a major worry for ordinary folks, because flying as a means of travel was something done mostly by rich or important people like movie stars.

The early commercial flights were made aboard Ford Trimotors

—the legendary and near-indestructible "Tin Goose" introduced in 1926. A few of those sturdy, deafening 10-passenger planes were still in service well into the '60s, ferrying vacationers out to islands in Lake Erie. And not just because they were quaint antiques. A Trimotor could land on a dime and give back 4 cents' change—just the ticket when you had to land on a tiny island.

The appeal of flying was not helped one bit by the deaths of Carole Lombard, Knute Rockne and Glenn Miller, all killed in crashes. And Jane Froman barely survived a splashdown in the Atlantic off the coast of Portugal.

Still, by the end of World War II, a lot more Americans had personal experience with air travel, thanks to service in the military.

The workhorse commercial plane introduced in 1936 was the DC model. It was slow, noisy and uncomfortable, but it always got there. The twin-engine plane earned its reputation for reliability during World War II, ferrying troops and cargo over the "Hump" in the China-Burma-India theater of operations.

A slightly wider version of the same aircraft, introduced just before the war, was made up into a sleeper, with upper and lower berths for a dozen passengers. Imagine dozing all comfy and snug in your bed as you flew through the night! But you had to pay for the privilege—a whole $15 extra.

Only a few years ago, my wife and I flew on a DC-3 during a vacation in Honduras. Rain leaked in through the ceiling light fixtures onto the floor of unpainted plywood. There were lots of ominous creaks and squeaks and rattles, too, but we didn't worry. Not a lot, anyhow.

Safe as the DC-3 was, the idea of leaving the ground simply unnerved people. And not without good reason. Those were the days before radar and reliable weather information.

Pilots didn't fly around bad storms; they flew *into and through* them. Lightning bolts would flash just off the wing tips, thunder would rock the plane as it violently bounced up and down, and sometimes ice coated the entire aircraft.

Today's sophisticated navigational electronics hadn't been invented, so landings in fog, rain or snow took every bit of the crew's skill. Often two or three attempts were made before the landing was accomplished. Passengers with white knuckles hud-

dled in their seats and vowed, "Never again!"

Of course, after surviving the terrors, those same people couldn't wait to tell about the trip, just possibly embellishing the perils a teensy bit to nail down their status as bold pioneers of the Air Age.

A popular movie of the era, *The High and the Mighty*, was not a source of comfort, either. In it, John Wayne barely manages to avert disaster during a flight in which *everything* goes wrong.

If The Duke had that tough a time, what kind of chance did you stand with just any ordinary pilot?

Confronted with the need to fly, it wasn't un-common to check your

FLYING WAS A BIG COMFORT in this American Air-lines giant four-engine DC-6 Flagship. Meals were served on individual tables which fit snugly into the arms of the seats. And just look at all that leg room!

will and give your spouse and children especially affectionate good-bye kisses and squeezes. After all, you never knew....

Meanwhile, airline companies tried to calm travelers' fears by creating an atmosphere of determined cheerfulness. Everyone smiled and chirped, no matter what.

Stewardesses were comely graduates of nursing school who were trained to handle every possible emergency. They were even sent to charm school and learned to walk with a book balanced atop their head, among other social niceties.

Stewardesses knew how to soothe the frightened, tend the (fre-quently) airsick, call each passenger by name and pretend that every child truly was adorable.

The early passenger planes weren't pressurized, so your ears tended to hurt a lot as the plane returned to earth. You always knew when you were about to land because the stewardess handed out gum. Chewing automatically helped relieve the pressure buildup inside your aching eardrums.

Today your "flight attendant" is confronted with short flight times and anywhere from 120 to 350 passengers. Too often, she (or *he*) doesn't have a chance to be much more than a flying waitress. But in the early days, when a flight from Minneapolis to New York took 4 hours, a stewardess had time to stop at your seat for a friendly chat.

Stewardesses were flying ambassadors of good will. They helped spread the popularity of air travel as much as any other single factor I can think of. And more than one stewardess wound up marrying someone she first met as a passenger. And why not? Young and single men who traveled by air were probably rising businessmen and good prospects for marriage.

Not long after World War II, Northwest Airlines introduced the flying public to something they called a "Stratocruiser". It was a 4-engine behemoth with big, roomy seats and aisles wide enough for a wedding procession.

But the most interesting innovation was a downstairs lounge. A short spiral staircase led down to this cozy area where you could play cards or just chat with newfound friends. What a great idea—an airplane with a basement rec room!

The Stratocruiser wasn't going to set any speed records, but for its day, it was the ultimate in comfort.

The popularity of air travel grew rapidly after World War II. So rapidly, in fact, that airports were caught by surprise. The places where you checked in (hasn't anyone ever considered that the word *terminal* is not something to associate with flying?) were woefully small, uncomfortable and inadequate.

Willow Run outside Detroit was cavernous, but only because it was a converted hangar that had been used to assemble bombers during World War II. It obviously had been changed over in haste and was not a desirable place to spend a few hours waiting for a delayed flight.

Midway in Chicago appeared to be a series of prefabricated

247

buildings connected by one endless, narrow corridor. And Atlanta's airport terminal had one cavernous room with row after row of what looked like recycled oak church pews, but were even less comfortable. And those terminals served the *big* cities.

Being progressive-minded, bigger-is-better Americans, however, we soon corrected things, building larger and larger and still larger terminals. Now it takes longer to walk from the plane to your car than it did to fly in from Des Moines. (Somewhere wandering the endless corridors of the Atlanta airport is, I'm positive, a white-haired old gentleman who entered the place as a jaunty young man and has been hopelessly lost ever since.)

Perhaps no one better typifies the story of commercial air travel than my mother. She was positive that if God had meant her to fly, He would have given her wings. No way was she ever going to set foot off the ground in one of those contraptions!

Then, when she was well into her 70s, Mom found herself in a situation where an airplane flight was absolutely unavoidable. It was either fly or spend the rest of her days alone in Cheyenne, Wyoming. Cheyenne was fine, but it wasn't home.

So, she boarded a plane. She knew she wouldn't survive, but figured that she had enjoyed a good, long life and sat down in her seat, resigned to her fate.

She arrived safely, of course, and to the eventual dismay of family and friends, she became a walking, talking, non-stop advertisement for the joys of flying.

Even so, her favorite mode of travel was the Greyhound bus. It was a lot slower, but she discovered that everyone was nice to little 80-year-old ladies and loved to tell her their life stories. They would even bring her back ice cream cones after the bus made a rest stop. "You just can't believe all the interesting people I meet," she'd enthuse.

Plane travel is no big deal today, even though every year you discover they've given you less leg room and narrower aisles than the year before. But thousands of times a day, those bewildering huge aircraft take off and land, safely bringing husbands and wives and parents and grandchildren to us.

They are the magic carpets that in a few hours whisk us to Switzerland or Hawaii, Springfield or Helena. How easily we've taken to growing wings in the last half century!

The Late '40s Made Us Suburban Pioneers

Ewing Galloway

"And right there is our very first house," I pointed out to my grown-up children.

"But it's so little!"

"Yes, but it seemed like a palace at the time."

"Did we *all* live there?"

"Actually, we sold three of you to gypsies when you were very young. Later, the gypsies paid us to take you back."

"*Da-a-aad!*"

"Of course we all lived there. It had three little bedrooms, one bathroom and even a fireplace. When you live in Minnesota, a fireplace is a necessity."

"Just *one* bathroom?"

"You girls were real young. It's not until girls become teenagers that you need five or six bathrooms."

"*Da-a-aad!*"

"It was a very nice house. I think it cost about $14,000."

"But the houses are so close together!"

"Well, that made it easy to borrow a cup of sugar. You just reached out the window and…"

Soon after World War II was over, several million new families were looking for places to call home. As I remember, the pickin's were mighty slim.

For one thing, there'd been precious little house building during the war years because just about everything needed to build a home had been declared critical to the war effort. Never before in history had so many people needed homes when so few were available.

In bigger cities where demand was greatest, the answer was to go out where land was cheap and build whole new communities—"subdivisions".

Among other things, subdivisions were "sub" in terms of amenities. Bulldozers flattened everything, scraped off the topsoil, knocked down the trees and turned perfectly nice land into bare terrain.

Usually there were no sewers, sidewalks or municipal water. New owners quickly learned about the joys of septic tanks and pump maintenance.

That little "GI special" home I took my kids back to see was the one we'd been in for just 2 days when the floor drains in the basement began to back up.

Frantic, we called the builder. He knew we had four small children and surmised one of them had probably flushed a teddy bear down the toilet. He warned that digging up frozen ground in February required a jackhammer, which would cost us $50 an hour if the trouble was our fault.

I called from work every hour for progress reports. Six hours went by—$300! My monthly paycheck was $400—before deductions…financial ruin loomed.

Eventually, the problem was located. Oops! Someone had forgotten to install sewer pipe before the bulldozers backfilled. The children wouldn't have to be put up for adoption after all.

The creation of subdivisions was a watershed event in the sociology of America. For the first time, we had entire communities that were "mono-cultures".

Every family in the neighborhood was about the same age and income level and had a similar background. And all of them seemed to have 2.4 small children and a dog named "Trixie".

It was quite a change from older, established neighborhoods with their blend of old and young, poor and not-so-poor. Many of these families had lived in the same house for generations.

I learned about that in the Army. When Bostonian met Bostonian, each knew everything he needed to know about the other by asking one simple question: "Where'd you go to school?"

"St. Agnes," one would say. "I went to Holy Trinity," the other would respond. Such answers did a lot more than identify a school—they described a neighborhood and the people who lived there.

Every old-fashioned neighborhood had a rich and diverse cast of characters. For example, there was always a nosy old lady who peered out from behind her lace curtains to watch the comings and goings of people on her street.

My grandmother and her sister were full-time street-watchers. "I wonder why Mr. Martin left his house so early this morning," one would say. "Do you suppose he and his wife had an argument?"

"I don't know," observed the other, "but their son was out until nearly 11 last night."

The cast of characters had to include a grumpy old man who was rumored by kids to have terrible secrets buried in his basement. His house was a test of everyone's courage on Halloween.

Then there was the nice grandmother who sat on her porch and offered fresh-baked cookies to youngsters walking by.

Just down the block lived the promising young man who had gone away to college and come back to the neighborhood to open a law office.

And, of course, there was the lazy son-in-law who hadn't looked for work in 6 months. He was decried by the street-watchers for "not contributing a penny toward the groceries!"

Old neighborhoods had their own "ma and pa" grocery stores where you could run a tab until the next payday. There was usually a bakery, a corner drugstore and a variety of churches within walking distance. A doctor or two had offices in their homes.

Back in the 1930s, the neighborhood was really a big extended family. Like most families, there were occasional feuds and fallings-out, but mostly people got along pretty well with a live-and-let-live attitude.

You didn't see any "Neighborhood Watch" signs back then—they weren't necessary. When a kid stepped out of line, a friendly neighbor made sure his parents knew about it. When a stranger appeared on the street, everyone took notice. There was also the local beat cop, who knew everything about everyone.

The new suburbs of the late '40s and 1950s were nothing at all like the old neighborhoods. Suburbs were "car cultures" because there was no public transportation, and stores, churches and even schools were miles away.

Mom became the family chauffeur for everything from Cub Scout meetings to the movies to visits to the orthodontist.

I remember the excitement when, after 2 years, a tiny strip mall opened within walking distance of our subdivision. It held a grocery store, dry cleaners and hardware store. Civilization had arrived!

People would ask, "Why do you want to live way out there?" The answer was that we didn't want to live "way out there"…it was the only housing we could afford.

One geographical oddity was true nearly everywhere: The "new lands" were invariably west of the central city. Of course, that was understandable in cities like Milwaukee, Chicago and New York, where east of those cities was decidedly damp real estate.

But it also seemed typical in places that weren't built beside lakes or oceans. The result was that you could spot suburban dwellers by the squint lines around their eyes, caused by driving into the sunrise in the morning and the sunset at night.

Newlyweds in the 1950s were lucky to have one car, much less two, so car pooling became essential.

All of us who experienced the dubious pleasures of car pooling have a special affinity for Dagwood Bumstead, because every car pool had its Dagwood, chronically late, to the annoyance of everyone else in the car.

Each car pool also had the husband who regularly asked to stop for "just a minute" at the supermarket to pick up a couple things needed at home. Twenty minutes later, he'd stagger out clutching four large bags of groceries.

Meanwhile, young mothers were housebound most of the time. A neighbor perfectly summed up her life in suburbia: "I spend my life keeping Joe's precious grass wet and his precious children dry," she sighed.

Ah, yes, suburban lawns! There was unspoken competition among the men to see who could produce the greenest, most lush lawn from the patch of bare clay left by the builder. The best possible housewarming present was money for sod. Most of us, alas, had to do the best we could with seed.

Because the houses were small, most of us eventually "finished off" our basements to create "rec rooms" where the kids could play without messing up the whole house.

The extra space was great for neighborhood parties, too. For a dozen years, I celebrated New Year's Eve in subterranean surroundings. Later, it was quite a surprise to discover that most of the world still celebrated the event above ground.

Looking back, I realize suburbia, for all its problems, wasn't all that bad. The best part was we all came together as strangers, looking for friends. There were plenty of kids of similar ages, so they had an easy time finding pals, too.

None of us were affluent. We didn't worry about "keeping up with the Joneses" because the Joneses were as deeply in debt as we were.

We found ways to have fun together without spending a lot of money. An evening of bridge with a bowl of popcorn and a pitcher of lemonade certainly didn't disturb the budget…nor did a backyard barbecue to which everyone brought their own meat and a dish of potato salad or beans to pass.

We celebrated promotions, birthdays, anniversaries and holidays together, played croquet in the backyard or table tennis in the rec room. Neighbors minded neighbors' kids when no baby-sitter was available.

Of course, we eventually all moved on…to new cities, bigger homes, better jobs. Things were never quite the same again.

I've revisited some of those early suburbs and marveled at how plain and cramped they look. I have a hard time matching up my good memories with those austere little neighborhoods.

I realize now that they were really a jumping-off point for our dreams. I expect the people who started out from Missouri on their long trek across the Oregon Trail to the West must have looked back in later life on their journeys much the way we pioneer suburbanites do today.

If Only These Walls Could Talk

THE WALLS of this old farmhouse where Clancy Strock grew up would have plenty to tell. Standing by his snowman, young Clancy was probably eager to get back inside those cozy walls and sit by the wood-burning stove.

If only these walls could talk! How often that old saying has popped into my head over the years.

Here's an example: One time I paused while taking a stroll along the streets of Haddonfield, New Jersey, where we had lived for a few years. Across the street was an immaculately preserved residence, with "1768" displayed in wrought-iron letters above the door.

I stood there and wondered who had built that home in this little town, just across the Delaware River from Philadelphia. What turbulent, uncertain times those were. I could just imagine the conversation between a husband and wife:

She: *If we're going to start a family, we need a home of our own. We can't stay with Mom and Dad forever.*

He: *Yes, I know. But maybe this is a bad time. Ben Franklin and some of his friends over in Philadelphia are talking about revolting against the king.*

She: *Dear, you know that will never happen. Revolt against the king?*

He: *Probably not, but things are getting serious.*

She: *But how much longer can we wait?*

He: *You're right, dear. Let me talk with a carpenter.*

Or, maybe that's not how it went. If only those old walls could talk! How many families have they sheltered in the more than 2 centuries since they were put up?

Our own place in Haddonfield started as a tiny, two-story cube with three little bedrooms in the '20s. Rolls of blueprints I found in the attic when we were living there showed that each time the house changed hands, the new owners made improvements.

One had added a sun porch across the back and doubled the size of the kitchen. Another put in a laundry room and a downstairs guest bath. Yet another owner expanded a bedroom by adding a second floor above the one-car garage. The attached garage later became a dining room, and a new garage was built.

Then we came along and made several changes of our own, and so did the newlyweds who bought the place from us.

Imagine all the voices and fragments of lives in those walls! The various owners inhabited this house through the Depression years and World War II. They brought new babies home from the hospital, worried through the great polio epidemic and probably had a few wedding receptions, too.

Big chapters of seven families' lives were written in that house. If only those walls could talk!

The same kind of feelings hit me when I discover an abandoned old farmhouse on a country road. Who lived there? Were they happy? Did the children have a rope swing made from an old rubber tire tied to a branch of that old oak tree? Why did they leave? Where did they go?

Recently I drove past the farmhouse in which I was raised. It's now elegantly remodeled and part of a nice subdivision. The small Colorado blue spruce Dad planted so he could have a lighted Christmas tree outside is now a towering giant. The front porch where I lolled away so many summer hours is no longer there.

I wonder if the walls remember Mom and Dad's first tiff as newlyweds.

Dad, raised in a family where lunch ("dinner") was the *big* meal, came in from the fields. Mom (raised in a family where the noon meal was more akin to today's lunches) proudly served him a big bowl of homemade vegetable soup.

Dad devoured the soup, pushed back the bowl and said, "Now what's for lunch?"

Somehow, the marriage survived for another 50-odd years, but Mom always mentioned the story whenever she served vegetable soup.

Those same walls are permeated with my baby squalls, the horrible skreeks and toots of my sister learning to play the violin and me the trumpet and the laughter of the four of us listening to the clatter as Fibber McGee opened his closet on every weekly radio show...all the stuff of family life.

I also stopped in Dixon to look at the square, stern two-story house where my mother's two aunts once lived. I wondered if the walls remembered the third resident—a raucous parrot.

As you stepped inside the door, it greeted you with, "Hello, Pat! Hello, Pat!" (No one in the family had ever been named Pat, but the ancient bird was a hand-me-down, so there was no telling who Pat may have been.) Within three minutes, the crusty old creature would start up a new chant: "Good-bye, Pat! Good-bye, Pat!" (I guess hospitality wasn't his long suit.)

During the summer, the bird's cage was moved to the front porch where the two elderly aunts sat in rocking chairs, trying to cool themselves down with cardboard fans from the local mortuary. You didn't need to check the thermometer to know the temperature: the hotter it was, the faster they fanned.

Meanwhile, the parrot periodically sang out, *"Tramp, tramp, tramp, the boys are march-ING!"* You could hear him blocks away on quiet afternoons. In addition, every passerby was greeted with a "Hello, Pat!" as soon as the bird spotted them, followed up with a quick "Goodbye, Pat!" as they walked past.

Do the walls remember?

The first house I ever owned was in a suburb of Minneapolis. Well, okay, I owned a little of it and the bank claimed the rest. We were the first to live there, so the walls contained no old memories. It was all of 1,200 square feet—not exactly sumptuous for a couple with four small children.

I'm certain the walls remember the night I awoke at 3 a.m. to the unmistakable sounds of a burglar in the kitchen. Chairs were being moved around and drawers squeaked open and shut.

Well, folks, I'm not Wyatt Earp or Agent 007. The idea of confronting thieves did not thrill me, but my wife had pulled the covers over her head, so the Man of the House had to do his duty.

Approaching the kitchen, I could hear whispers as I reached for the light switch, determined to defend my family to the bitter end.

Imagine my surprise when up on the kitchen counter stood my sons, ages 2 and 3, in their Dr. Denton feet pajamas. They were busily digging into a box of Cheerios! (It may have been coincidence, but the next morning I discovered my first gray hairs.)

I once worked in a building that was supposedly built on a Quaker cemetery dating back to Revolutionary War days. Those walls didn't talk, but they supposedly housed a genuine *ghost*! Not that anyone saw or shook hands with the ghost, but it made its presence known in many ways.

One night watchman who claimed to have had many encounters finally quit. He said that down in the basement storeroom, a door would mysteriously swing open. Then the resident cat would arch his back, following an invisible *something* with his eyes until a door at the other end of the room slowly opened and closed.

To my way of thinking, we Americans have been too obsessed with "newer and better". We tear down grand old buildings and homes, and the dump trucks haul away all those walls full of memories.

The traditionalists in Beverly Hills, California are properly upset as landmark mansions are pulled down and replaced with monuments to the egos of the newly rich. There's even a term for some of those old places when they come on the market—they're called "tear downs".

Imagine it! A wrecking ball demolished the longtime home of Bing Crosby and took away those walls saturated with Bing's voice and all the songs he sang. And his place was only one of many that have met the same fate.

Lots of those mansions were the same ones pointed out by

the friendly guide as you took the "See the Homes of the Stars" bus tour many years ago. Now they're gone, and it's a shame.

Fortunately, we've finally taken an interest in preserving some of our history-filled treasures by putting them on the National Register of Historic Places. Without this safeguard, I suspect, Independence Hall, the Old North Church, the Chicago Water Tower and many of Frank Lloyd Wright's masterpieces would someday have fallen prey to the insatiable greed of the developers, backed up by civic boosters crying out for progress.

Over the years, I have made the unsettling discovery that I rarely lived in my own house. Instead, I lived in "the old Smithers place" or "the old Widow Chesterton's place".

"Where do you live?" someone would ask.

"At 201 Sherman Avenue."

"Oh, the old Wilson place," they'd correct.

You see, not until *I* moved on would it become "the old Strock place".

How many times have you stopped for instructions and listened to a lifelong local resident tell you to go ahead 2 miles and then turn right, just past "the old Johnson place"? Well, sure—who doesn't know where the old Johnson place is?

And what better proof do we need that the walls which shelter us are full of lasting memories? I know...I was there.